PERSHORE
Where D'Ye Think?

Margaret Bramford

MALCHIK
MEDIA

A Malchik Media & richardlynttonbooks Publication

Published by
Malchik Media & richardlynttonbooks

Copyright © 2024 Richard C.G. Lyntton

ISBNs:
978-1-959755-16-6 (Paperback)
978-1-959755-17-3 (Hardback)
978-1-959755-15-9 (eBook)

Library of Congress Control Number: 2024912197

Cover and interior repackaging by
Gary A. Rosenberg ~ www.thebookcouple.com

Thank you in advance for reading
Pershore—Where D'Ye Think?
Worcestershire & Malvern History Series Book 4

● ●

You might also enjoy

*From Cottage to Palace ~ Worcestershire &
Malvern History Series • BOOK 1*
www.amazon.com/dp/B09WB2LQHM

Listen now on Audible at: www.audible.com/
pd/From-Cottage-to-Palace-Audiobook/
B0B3PQTSGZ

Enjoy your FREE *From Cottage to Palace
BONUS book:* dl.bookfunnel.com/rfawyptxt4

*This Was Our Malverne, Vol. 1 ~ Worcestershire
& Malvern History Series • BOOK 2*
www.amazon.com/gp/product/B0B1JHQSJH

Listen now on Audible at: www.audible.com/
pd/This-Was-Our-Malvern-Audiobook/
B0BM55D4lY

 *Upton-Upon-Severn Recollections ~ Worcestershire & Malvern History Series* • **BOOK 3**
www.amazon.com/gp/product/B0B1QX1BZ8

 Listen now on Audible at: www.audible.com/ pd/Upton-Upon-Severn-Recollections -Audiobook/B0BGYH9XGV

For more information about the Worcestershire & Malvern History Series by Margaret Bramford, or to sign up for our FREE richardlynttonbooks (fiction and nonfiction) newsletter, VISIT this richardlynttonbooks website link:

richardlynttonbooks.com/contact/

We would be most grateful if you could please leave a review on Amazon if you enjoy the series. If you would like copies for your library or school, please contact us via richardlynttonbooks.com

Thank you and best wishes
Richard Lyntton • Philadelphia, June 2024

(Margaret Bramford's nephew, and author of THE DECEPTION SERIES)

ACKNOWLEDGEMENTS

This is a light-hearted Social History of a country town in Worcestershire. These are the memories of sixty-four Pershore and district people, recorded in recent years. They reflect Pershore life in the 1920's and 1930's for the most part.

The author and her family lived in Pershore for 50 years – between 1931 and 1981. She dedicates this book, with gratitude, to those Pershore people who readily shared their memories with her. She has preserved here their own vigorous descriptions, their crisp, individual, buoyant speech and their cheerful attitude to life.

Contributors in alphabetical orders:

John Annis M.B.E.
Ella Patricia Ardern (née Swann)
Elsie Barnes
Ruth Baster
Roy Beard
Avril Bramford
Ruth Brant
Nora Bristow (née Collins)
John Bristow
Leslie Brookes
Edith Brown
Sid Champken
George 'Nobby' Clark
Charles Clemens
Laurence Coggins
Les Conn
Lucy Conn
Edward Crowther
Walter Davies
Blanche Dufty
Jim Dowler
Eve Elliott
Ernest Fuller
Marjorie Godfrey (née Twigg)
Rene Giles (née Parker)
Albert Haines
Bob Haines
Kitty Haines (née Barber)
Barbara Hartley (née Fagg)
Jack Heeks
Edwin Hill
Betty Hughes

Freda Hutley-Reade (née Bickerstaff)
Marion Knight
Rosie Long
Peggy Maple (née Roberts)
Esther Marshall
Malcolm Meikle
Nigel Montandon
Fanny Newick
Effie Palfrey
Walter Palfrey
Mabel Phipps
Marjorie Revers
Mary Revers
Bet Rhodes
Doug Rhodes
Ethel Rock
Bill Scarrott
Cyril Smith
John Smith
Mary Stubbs (née Howes)
Margaret Taylor
Betty Tuffin (née Overd)
Stan Tuffin
Esme Westcott (née Champken)
Donald Westcott
Lyn Westcott
Joan Wicks
Ellen Willis
Elwyn Wilson
Alec Witts
Alice Young (née Need)
Lois Young

ACKNOWLEDGEMENT OF PHOTOS AND QUOTATIONS

I acknowledge the generous loan of photos in this book from:

John Annis M.B.E.
Carol Domingo
Sheila Smith
Patricia Welford
Esme Westcott
Lois Young
Ted Edwards
Betty Tuffin

I thank Mr. W.D.E. Vizard of Down Hatherley, Gloucestershire, for permission to quote the poems about Pershore, composed by his grandfather, W.D. Vizard.

I thank Annie Jones of Putley, Herefordshire, for permission to quote from Dave Jones' book 'The Roots of Welsh Border Morris'.

I thank Liz Foxen and Sue Barsch for permission to quote from material which they researched for an Exhibition about Pershore Pubs, in the Heritage Centre, Bridge Street, Pershore.

PORTRAIT OF PERSHORE

The grey-green Avon nurses, cherishes, the town,
Caressing the ancient bridge,
Russet and mellow as the pears
Which gave Pershore its name.
Veiled memories of Cavaliers clashing with Cromwell's men
Linger among the dreaming willows.
The hill of Bredon broods, a friendly presence,
Emanating domesticity from its green pastures and golden villages.
Bridge Street begins abruptly by the aged mill.
Tall houses, their glowing red brick faces
Of Georgian symmetry, outlined in white,
Eye each other, with dignity and elegance.
Broad Street recalls loud fairs and market stalls,
Of centuries gone by. The bustling atmosphere
Of commerce, now less strident, still remains,
Reminding the visitor of post houses, post horns,
And long-departed coaches on their way to London.
Iron balconies, plane trees, yield a continental air
To the fleeting stranger.
Dominating all, the Abbey's majestic tower
Presides in a timeless zone of green peace,
Implanted by the monastery of old:
Symbol of serenity, inspiring music and the arts
In this, our present age.
SPRING: the frothing sea of white blossom,
Plum and damson, laps the town; creamy may
Adorns the hedges, whilst the cuckoo sings.
SUMMER'S sweet smell of plums pervades the gardens;
The lulling drone of distant harvesters is heard.
AUTUMN'S bonfires fade into WINTER'S chill,
And there is snow on Bredon Hill.

MARGARET BRAMFORD
1975

IN PRAISE OF PERSHORE PAST

"I like Pershore. I've been born and bred here and never been out of it," said Ethel Rock to me. "I was born in Head Street in the early 1900's. My father couldn't a-bear to go to Worcester. My oldest sister and me – we took father to Worcester one day, on the bus. He kept saying in Worcester, 'How much longer have we got to stay here until we gets back?' As soon as we got back to the top of Bomford's (Allesborough Hill) he said, 'Thank God for that – there's the Pershore Abbey!'

He used to like Pershore. We couldn't get him to go anywhere. No! Not on an outing. Only as far as the bridges for a walk. It was different, long ago in Pershore. People used to stop and converse with anyone. You knew almost everyone then. If you were not well, in those days, people would knock the door and say, 'Are you all right? Is there anything I can do for you?' Yes, I've had a good life."

Alice Young told me: "In the 1920's, Pershore was a much smaller place only about 3,000 people. There were plenty of fields to play in, or we children could play in the streets, then."

"Pershore was like a big family, in the 1930's," recalls Marjorie Godfrey. "Every day you could find something to do. Sunday School, and church three times on Sundays. Girls' Friendly Society, Brownies, Guides. And young people wanted to join. Youth Fellowship was twice a week, in the old school rooms, with Table Tennis. You knew everyone. If you saw a stranger in the town, you would soon know who it was! People would help you. Your old friendships never end, after all these years."

In 1925, William D. Vizard, from Cheltenham, wrote a delightful guidebook, in poetry, about some Cotswold and Bredon Hill villages and towns, which he had visited. He composed these two poems, inspired by two very old Pershore sayings. They expressed the feelings of fruit growers when plum harvests were GOOD – or BAD!

PERSHORE, WHERE D'YE THINK?

You ask me where and whence I come,
From Pershore, where d'ye think?
Where do we grow the yellow plum?
Why, Pershore, where d'ye think?

Where do the trees hang down with gold?
And where produce a hundredfold?
Where do the church bells peal in tune?
Where brightest shines the harvest moon?
At Pershore, where d'ye think?

BUT

After a poor crop of plums, on which their livelihood depended:

PERSHORE, GOD HELP US!

You ask me where and whence I come?
Pershore, God help us.
Don't ask about the crops at home,
God help us!
Last April, every spring and spray
Was deck'd with pearly blossoms gay,
Last August, every branch and bough
Was bent with yellow plums, but now,
God help us!

Where is it Jill hath pawned her dress?
Pershore, God help us.
And Jack's as bad as Bill or Bess
God help us!
For every mortal in the place
Doth seem to wear a fiddle face.
Here's Giles the gardener in arrears,
And Black and Brown are both in tears.
And many more will come to pot.
Good Lord! the court will see the lot.
God help us!

Who last year loudly thank'd the Lord?
Pershore, God help us.
And now we scarcely raise a word.
God help us!
We know we still owe thanks, but then,
We cannot sing, nor say amen.
But when to church we do repair,
We breathe this little humble prayer
God help us!

ix

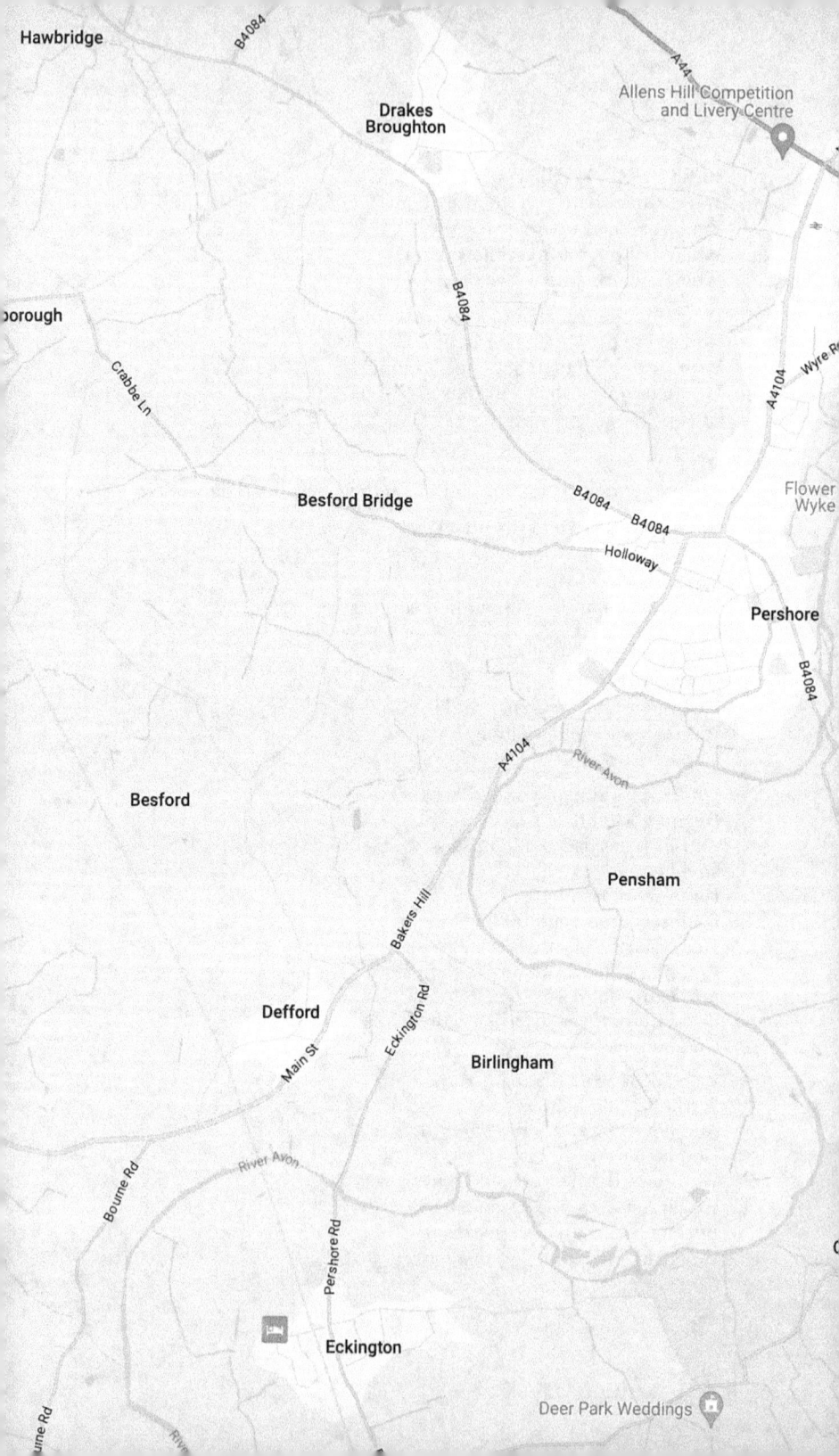

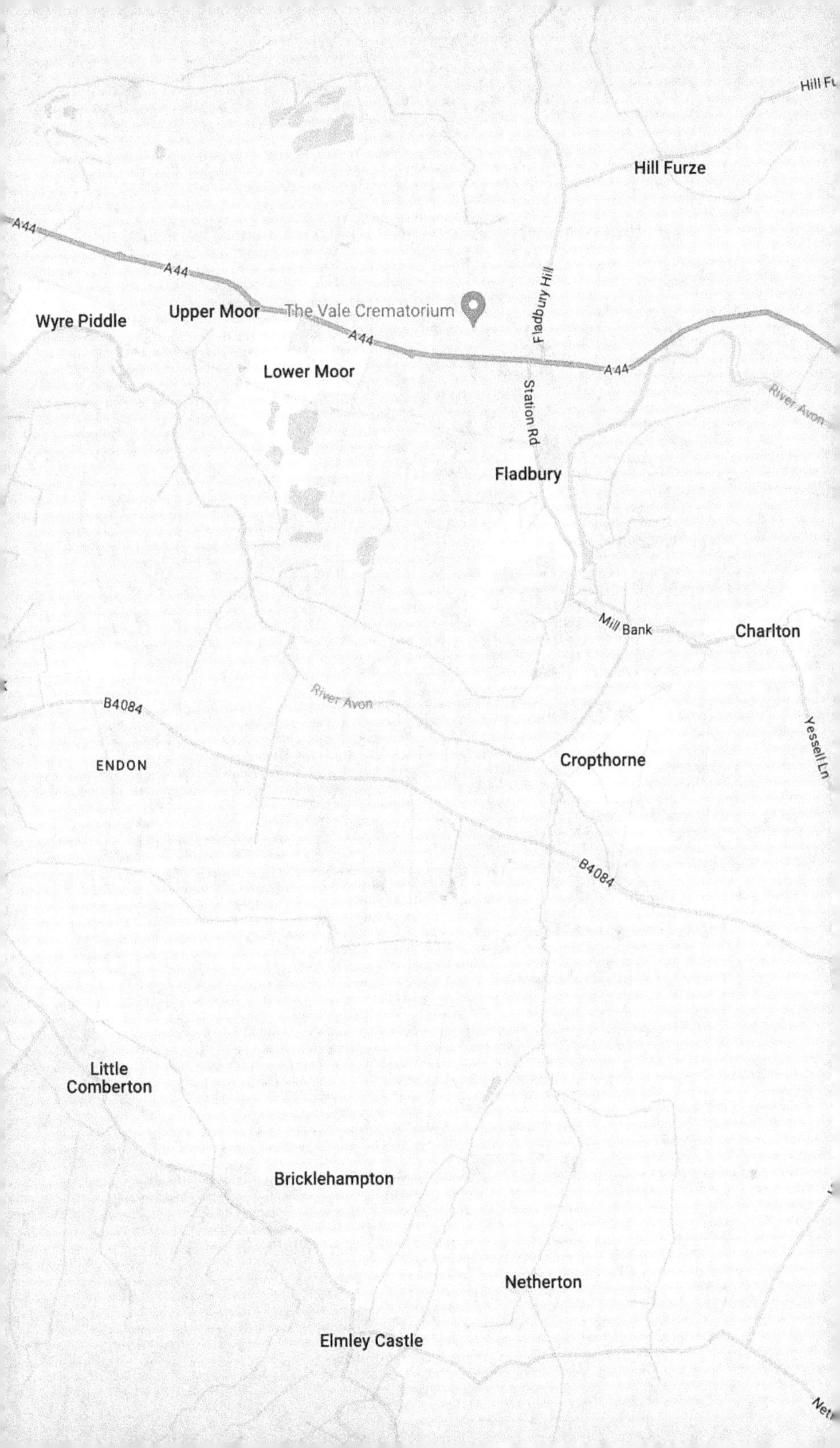

Hill Fu
Hill Furze
A44
A44
Wyre Piddle
Upper Moor
The Vale Crematorium
A44
Fladbury Hill
Lower Moor
A44
Station Rd
River Avon
Fladbury
Mill Bank
Charlton
River Avon
B4084
Cropthorne
Yessell Ln
ENDON
B4084
Little
Comberton
Bricklehampton
Netherton
Elmley Castle
Net

PERSHORE

Plan showing some old landmarks (not to scale)

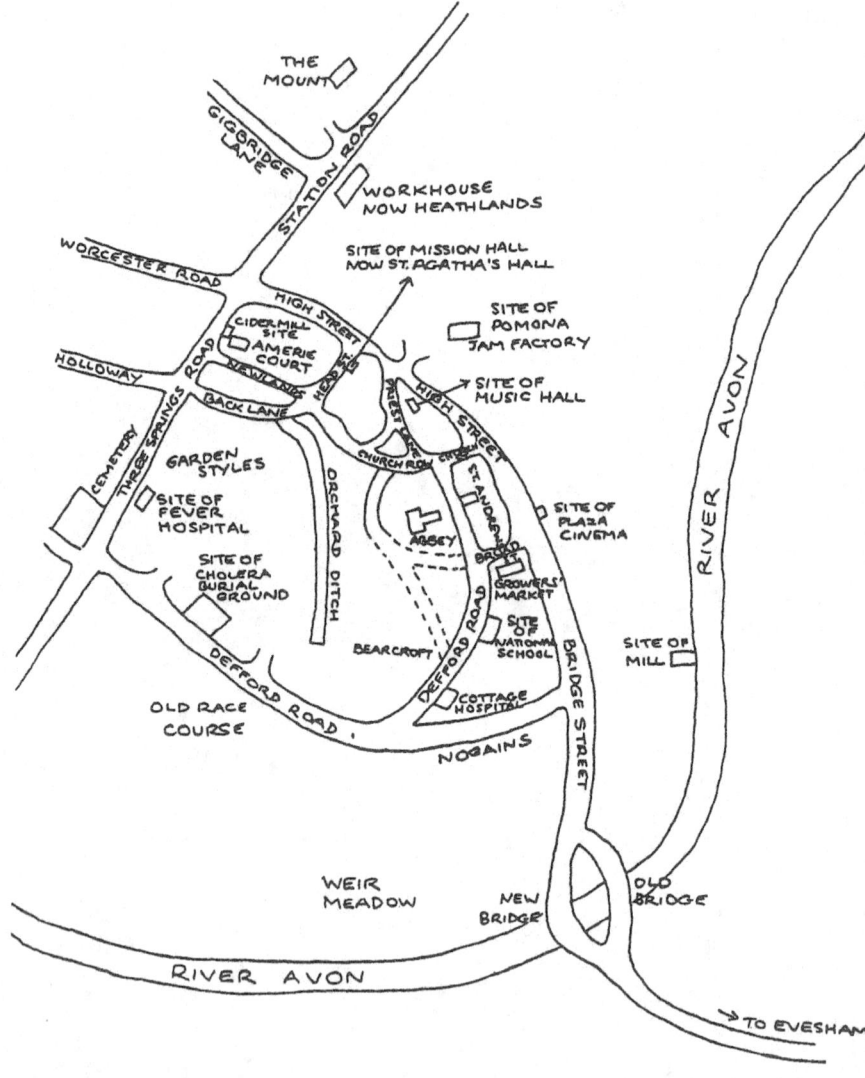

Map by Margaret Bramford

CHAPTERS

A NOTE FROM THE PUBLISHER

Philadelphia, USA, May 2024

This fourth book in the WORCESTERSHIRE & MALVERN HISTORY SERIES is close to my heart. As a boy in the 1970s, I recall visiting my grandmother Mabel (Meg) Bramford at 71 Station Road, Pershore. My grandmother cooked endless cakes, biscuits, and good old-fashioned Sunday roasts. We ate Pershore plums, gooseberries, blackberries (my favorite), and pears from the garden.

In those days no one in my family had a car, and we used to walk nearly a mile to the Pershore shops and Pershore Abbey. I remember having tea at "Number Twenty" (the posh café on the High Street), running down the long garden of the Angel Hotel to the river, and having lunch there on special occasions. Another fond memory is walking to Pershore Abbey (in our Sunday best), followed by 'refreshments' at St. Andrew's across the road.

This series is local history at its best. When she was in her seventies and eighties, Margaret Bramford spent several years whizzing around Worcestershire on her moped recording several hundred ordinary locals (rich and poor, happy and grumpy) as she began to create and compile this series. She created an authentic, first-hand historical document of the people, life, and times of the area over the last century.

Please note that the grammar, syntax and punctuation (as well as the occasional typo) remain as in the original first publication for interest and archival value.

Chapter one

OLD DAYS, OLD WAYS

Within the space of a century, there have been enormous changes in attitudes towards family life, housing, educating, crime and punishment and the social classes. Pershore has reflected these changes.

FAMILY LIFE

"There were ten of us in family – six boys and four girls," said Blanche Dufty. "I was born in Newlands in 1892. When I first got married, I lived at No.4 – two doors away from here. So I haven't moved very far. I'm still in Newlands at the age of 101! (Blanche died in 1996, two days before her 104th birthday). I was a Bell. Edmund Bell's tombstone is in St. Andrew's churchyard. He lived at Bell's Castle, Kemerton, and he collected contraband from the Bristol Channel. My father was Head Gardener at The Mount (Pershore Hall) with the Humphries family. I was named Blanche after the Humphries' daughter."

"I had six sisters," said Charles Clemens. "I was born in 1894 and I was the youngest in the family. But having all these sisters, I didn't want for anything. Patricia was mother's help. Mother sent her to classes on cookery, in Pershore. Mabel was a nursery governess. Florrie died when she was nineteen. She was moving furniture and injured her back. Gertie was a schoolteacher, strict, like my Quaker mother. Elsie was a dairymaid at Bricklehampton Hall and learnt butter making. May was with the Woodwards and went off to India as a nursery governess. My father was always in great demand as a tenor soloist."

"There were nine of us," said Esme Westcott. "Most of us had red hair. We all got on well. We were not allowed to quarrel for long. We had to sit down and settle it, or else my mother would never let us go to bed."

1

Alice Young described her mother. "She was very quiet, but very strict and methodical. All our boys had good hidings, but I never did. I was the youngest and the favourite."

Elsie Barnes told me: "The day I left school, and reached home in Newlands, me little hat cum off. Mother said, 'Now you've left school, you must give your mind to work, and God'll give you strength.' My mother was a very good, religious woman and brought us all up the same."

"We were a pretty poor family – seven of us," Sid Champken told me. "Things were handed down to us. Bicycles for instance, were cleaned up and re-painted and that was a Christmas present for the next one in family - the same old bike. For Christmas we just got an orange, an apple and some sweets."

Blanche Dufty said: "My father, William Bell, couldn't read or write. But my mother went to a private school in the front street (High Street) in Pershore. My mother was a Cosnett – a good old Pershore name! A very proud family they were!

My father was left an orphan at 8-years old. One aunt would take him, then another aunt. My mother was sorry for him. She had a rich man who wanted to marry her. He used to take her out in a pony trap. She liked him, but the orphan was always in her mind. And that's the one she married in the finish. She used to say to me. 'See, look what I've missed! You wouldn't have wanted for anything.' Her sisters married pretty well. One went to Australia and she never saw her again."

Kitty Haines said: "The James family were poor. They had seven boys. They lost the little girl. Dr. Browning advised them to go to Canada, under the emigration scheme. So they went. Their home in the passage in Bridge Street only had one up, one down for all those children. One of the boys came into Miss Salmon's shop and said, 'We're going to Canada'. There were tears in Miss Salmon's eyes. Some of the boys came back here in the Second World War – in the services. Their grandfather had lived in a caravan and sold pegs and baskets, made from osiers."

"My husband, John Andrew Dufty, was a very, very smart man, although I say it," said Blanche Dufty. "He wanted me to go

2

out to India to get married there. He was in the Royal Artillery – a signals' instructor. But I wouldn't go. I wouldn't leave my mother. So he came back to England as the First World War finished. When he first arrived back, he was standing outside the Working Men's Club. Mrs. Wood at the butcher's shop opposite said, 'Who is that fellow over there?' 'Oh, it's Miss Bell's young man.' 'Well, he's the smartest man that ever came to Pershore,' replied Mrs. Wood. People called us a handsome couple. I always thinks of that!"

"Hurst Park was built in 1921, before Cornmore," Rene Giles told me. "They were originally Council houses – very small, semi-detached and built in pairs. I've lived here since these houses were built – on the site of the old donkey races. We helped each other in the old days. We knew everyone. No mums with children under school age went out to work. There were no cars here. The fields behind were always full of cowslips and, later, blackberries. You could see the boats on the river.

When Hurst Park was first built, they were the best houses going, apart from the town houses. People here had maids in the 1920's. A bank manager, Mr. Halliday, lived here. The Reverend Fourdrinier was here. The people who owned the Atlas Works lived here. Quite some notabilities then!"

Kitty Haines told me: "I was a Barber – a very old Pershore family. The Barber girls were always parlour maids at the Vicarage. The boys and men were bell-ringers. For a long time, the whole team of Abbey bell-ringers were Barbers."

Bob Haines said: "The mediaeval bank, to stop flooding from the Avon, was built before the Abbey was built. Vestiges of it can be seen in a rounding of the ground, in places, on the allotments behind Nogains. Also, notice where High Street rises from Broad Street, up to the Post Office, and the slope in Church Walk, approaching the Abbey and St. Andrew's."

STREET NAMES

They were different a hundred years ago. High Street was

sometimes known as 'the front street'. Head Street was Yud Street. From the Plough Inn to the corner of Station Road was Worcester Street. Church Street was Lych Street, leading to the Abbey's Lych Gate. Priest Lane was Plough lane for its top half. Bearcroft, off Defford Road, had a big paddock by the side, where horse sales were held. "You never got no profit from the land called Nogains, 'cos it was liable to flooding from the river." The Bottoms is now the cricket field. Pershore, like Tewkesbury, had lots of passages leading to terraced houses which had no back doors. Bull Entry was off Newlands, Batchelors Entry off Bridge Street, Nash's Passage off Broad Street – where the telephone yard was.

Esther Marshall told me: "Ganderton's Row, off Broad Street, had 17 houses and, at one time, 32 children. A bit of real Pershore disappeared when those houses were demolished in 1938. They were well-built houses and had a large garden. At one time people called it Jessamine Terrace, because most houses had that shrub round their doorways."

There were two jails. One was the debtors' prison, near the Millers Arms in Bridge Street. The other, in Newlands, next to a butcher's, was for sheep stealers.

"The old lock-up in Newlands?" said Blanche Dufty, "Mrs. Bick, the butcher, used to keep her meat in there – next door to her shop. It was as good as a 'fridge. My mother remembers someone being put in that cell. It was a little tiny place with thick walls. They would put drunks in there, just for the night. They had to sleep on the floor and had a tiny bench to sit on. Mrs. Bick used the hooks in the ceiling to hang her meat on."

TWO ANCIENT HOUSES

Gladys Harris' shop at no. 14 Broad Street was being renovated in 1987, after she had left the premises. It had been her General Stores for very many years. I noticed that the old beams were exposed. They were pieces of carved wood from sailing ships on the Avon, and there were still the wattle and daub walls. Plaster was painted, in a grey-blue pattern, like a frieze. I was told that a room in the roof had been sealed up, long ago – yet the walls of this room were plastered and papered. An old undertaker's hat, with ribbons, had been found in the room behind the shop. Packing cases of very old corned beef had also been found.

Peggy Maple still owns no. 10 High Street. It is where her family lived and had their greengrocer's shop. Rent was ten shillings a week in the 1930's. Underneath the Georgian exterior, there is a mediaeval building. Wattle and daub on the outside and, on the inside, the walls are filled with pebbles. When they moved there, they found the floor upstairs, made of huge planks, was papered over with wallpaper and there was wallpaper over the attic door. They had to knock on the walls and listen for an empty sound, to find the attic door. No-one had been up there for 20 or 30 years. One oak tree beam still had bark on it.

Lois Young told me: "The Tollgate House at the bottom of Bridge Street took tolls to pay for the new bridge, before it was built in 1926. Next door is Wisteria Lodge. I remember the little 'duck path' raised above that part of the road to the old bridge. When the river flooded, I would walk along that path, wheeling my cycle, as I had to get home to Avonbank, where I lived then."

THE GENTRY

In the early 1930's, the ladies of Pershore were still very conscious of their social position," said Alice Young. "My son and all – they had to raise their caps to the gentry. Mrs. Rusher, the wife of Dr. Rusher, stopped me one day and said, 'I passed your son, Ken, this morning and he didn't raise his cap.' How different today!"

Blanche Dufty said: "There was quite a parade of the gentry on their way to church in the old days – the Cartlands, the Gandertons, the Holland-Andrews ... all the Myttons from Pensham walked to the Abbey on Sundays."

Chapter two

<u>CHARACTERS</u>

Like any small market town, Pershore has had its share of unique
individuals:

"BUSSY" COLDICOTT

He was a legendary character and very well known. "Bussy" was
a stout little red-faced man. In the 1920's, he had a horse-drawn
'fly' from Mr. Trapp's funeral outfit, to go up to Pershore railway
station, taking people there and back. He stabled it at the back
of The Angel Hotel. "You were quite a long time on that journey
– in all winds and weathers – in this open trap. You paid about
threepence. "Bussy" also fetched parcels from the trains. One
day, his poor, slow old horse was very tired. "Bussy" got level with
a man carrying his case. "Do ye wan' a lif' up to the station, sir?"
asked "Bussy". "No thanks," replied the man, "I'm in a 'urry."

"SIR" PETER HANSON

He was a tubby little man, like Pickwick, white whiskered, a
proper character, in Edwardian clothes. He lived at Bedford
House in Bridge Street, opposite the draper's shop, which he
owned; (Edwards in the '30's, now Seals). People called him
"The Mayor". His friends from Birmingham called him "The
Lord Mayor". He would walk jerkily about the streets, with a tape
measure around his neck.

"He was always a jolly man, you know," said Blanche Dufty.
"My mother used to have a Mothers' Meeting card for bedclothes.
She would go to his shop to spend it."

"Sir" Peter Hanson always wore a top hat and grey waistcoat.
When a sale was on in his shop, children would say, "Peter's
trousers are down again." He was the first Pershore person to

6

go up in Sir Alan Cobham's aeroplane, which had landed on Pershore's old racecourse. He was also a character in a coach in a film, based on Wick House. The title was "The King's Highway".

Peter was quite fond of a drink. He came home one night and couldn't unlock his door. His housekeeper came on to the veranda and said, "What's the matter, Peter? Have you forgotten your keys?" "No," he replied, "throw me down a bunch of keyholes!"

Peggy Maple remembers Peter as an old man. "He was shuffling up Bridge Street with a stick, wearing a cap and bedroom slippers. He had been very good at organising the August Bank Holiday annual Flower Show."

MERCY GREEN

Ethel Rock told me: "There used to be a half-timbered, thatched cottage where High Street turns into Station Road, on the right. Mercy Green lived there. She always wore a shawl. She used to make homemade sweets. Me and my sister went up there every Sunday to fetch Dad a newspaper. We bought toffees there – smashing sweets!"

"BLIND WILLIE" (WILLIAM CHARLWOOD)

He was the organ-blower and bell-ringer at Pershore Abbey for 57 years. Charles Clemens said: "He was a nice old chap. He blew the bellows of the organ in the Abbey. They needed a blower all the time in those days. He charged sixpence an hour. Some of those stops and pedals used to take a lot of wind – pumping like the Devil he was, when the organ was played. He was fond of the Needs – the verger's family. They had the key to the Abbey. When I called at the Needs' on my way to play the organ, William would always be there and he would accompany me to the Abbey."

Alice Young speaks: "Blind William used to help my father, William Need, in the Abbey. When I was young, we had a curfew at 8 o'clock at night. It was an old tradition. If my father could not go to ring this on the Abbey Bell, Blind William did this and I used to go with him. 'Come on, Dolly,' he would say. 'I haven't got a candle yet, Mr. Charlwood,' I used to say. He would reply, 'You won't want a candle, Dolly. Catch hold of my coat. I knows my way.'

But I used to dread going up those steps to the lantern tower, for fear I should slip through. Dad used to keep the stubs of the altar candles on that Hazlewood tomb, in between the stone figure's legs. And always there was a box of matches left there, so that you could go up the tower in the dark, holding a lighted candle stub."

JOSEPH SPIERS

"They said Joseph Spiers had read the Bible all through and knew it by heart," said Jack Heeks. "He had the right voice for it, because he was a Baptist lay preacher."

Fanny Newick told me: "Joseph Spiers was the basket-maker for the Growers' Market. He made 40 lb. Pot hampers, 12 lb. Chip baskets, some round punnets to hold strawberries and raspberries, and 'peck' (7 or 8 lbs.) baskets for picking fruit into. The baskets were made from willow canes cut from osier beds by the river. The canes were brought back to the bottom of his garden (he lived at no. 31 Bridge Street) in a flat-bottomed punt. They soaked the canes in a trough of water and the sodden bark peeled off, so you had white cane beneath. His men sat in a circle, making baskets."

JIMMY FORD

Roy Beard told me: "Jimmy Ford worked at the Atlas Works. He used to walk to work. During his lunch hour, he would rest for twenty minutes; eat his lunch for twenty minutes and rest for twenty minutes afterwards. That's why he lived to such a great age – to 101, I think. He lived with his daughter, towards the end. When he retired, he had an allotment. He used to sell his flowers from his barrow, or from his pram. His favourite flower was pinks."

Margaret Taylor said: "Jimmy Ford had a long white beard and looked like Old Father Time. The sight of him prompted little Betty Overd to cry out, 'I've just seen Santa Claus.' He lived in the almshouses in Defford Road. His housekeeper was Miss Wrench, who had bow legs. It was said of her, 'She wouldn't stop a pig in a passage!'" In Miss Matthews' 'Living Pictures,' Jimmy Ford and Miss Wrench dressed up as 'Darby and Joan'. The author recalls that these two brought their costumes in a case, which she saw behind the stage. It was labelled 'Mr. and Mrs. Ford'.

FANNY STEVENS

"She was like a little bird – very good at singing – opera mostly. She was conductor of Pershore Choral Society in 1919. They gave concerts in The Three Tuns Hotel ballroom."

Margaret Taylor knew her well: "We did some early 'Living Pictures' in the 1920's. I was 'The English Rose' in a long white dress, with my hair in long curls. I held a red rose. Meanwhile, Fanny recited an appropriate poem. She would do monologues for various charities.

Fanny was very well known and was very musical. She really was the musical person of Pershore in the 1920's. She taught in Worcester and came home to Bridge Street at weekends. Fanny produced operettas. I was The Queen in Goldilocks and The Three Bears. Tom Pettifer was the big bear; John Pettifer was the little bear. Marjorie Pettifer, my cousin, was a fairy in the chorus."

THE CARTLAND FAMILY AND BARBARA CARTLAND

Esme Westcott told me: "My mother, Mrs. Champken, was nanny to the Cartland family. When they lost all their money, Barbara Cartland (later to be famous as a romantic novelist) was 4-years old. Then Ronald was born and Anthony two years later.

They had lived in Birmingham. The grandfather, Colonel Scobell, let them have Bowbrook House, in Peopleton, but they had to look for something smaller. Lord Coventry offered them Amerie Court at a very cheap rate. They went through a very bad time in Pershore. They were extremely poor, by their standards, But Pershore people thought them very rich!"

Captain Cartland had been killed in the First World War. Colonel Scobell educated the boys at Charterhouse. Barbara was sent to school too. They eventually moved to one of his houses in Tewkesbury. "Mrs. Cartland always claimed to be my godmother," said Esme Westcott. "She sent me a little card and present each Christmas."

Cyril Smith said: "Many a time I have seen Barbara Cartland, as a girl, sat by the side of her dad in a horse and trap, coming from Amerie Court into Three Springs Road. Her mother was a lovely lady. She always brought me a Christmas present. She thought a lot of my Dad and Mum, when we lived at the cemetery."

Blanche Dufty remembers Barbara's mother, Mrs. Cartland, walking down Newlands, on her way to the Abbey on Sundays. "As she came past, I could hear every word she spoke. She had a lovely voice – absolutely clear. I told her daughter about it in the letter I wrote to her recently. She wrote me a nice reply."

THE MISSES MATTHEWS

There were three of them and they lived in Bridge Street – Nancy, Maude and Nell. Nancy was Head of Drakes Broughton School. We called them by their hats – red, purple and black. We would say, "Red hat was in church today!"

Nancy Matthews was well known for producing several series of 'Living Pictures'. Fifty or more people took part each time. You chose the picture you would dress up to represent. A large gold frame was erected on the stage of the Women's Institute Hall, with a black velvet background. Each tableau was shown three times, while the performers remained 'as motionless as a picture'. Miss Matthews rang a little bell to signal the drawing to and fro of the curtains. Subjects ranged from the classical to the humorous. Mr. Bligh from Benedicts, Tyddesley Wood, gave suitable commentaries on each picture.

THE LAWSONS

"Canon Lawson and his three daughters lived in Southern House, Broad Street, next door to Dr. Wilson, Senior. Miss Grace died at the age of 101. Miss Ruth joined one of the nunneries and became Sister Penelope. The youngest sister married and went to live in India. She got killed on horseback."

MISS MARY ISMAY

Esther Marshall said: "Miss Ismay was much loved and respected." Miss Ismay was 'Governess' or 'Head of the Girls' Department' in the old Defford Road School, with Mr. Chapman as Headmaster. She taught Needlework and Religious Knowledge. She cycled to her work at the 'senior' School, in Station Road. In later years she had a little car. With her friend, Grace Lawson, she organised the Girls' Friendly Society at Southern House.

THE MISSES WOODWARD

Fanny Newick told me: "The Woodwards; Miss Marion, Miss Laura and Miss Edith, lived in Western House and came into their aunt's property, HOUGRIJAN in Defford Road, on condition they lived in it. When they left Western House, Dr. Kennedy took it over." Charles Clemens contributed: "My sister May was with the Woodwards. They had a large share in the tea gardens at Assam in India. They asked May if she would like to go as nursery governess to their brother's son in Assam. He was a boy of eight. So off May went to Assam for four or five years and she learnt Hindu while she was there. I think the Woodwards gave their share in the tea plantation over to the Abbey in Pershore eventually. The name of their house – HOUGRIJAN, was a puzzle to everyone. But my family knew! Because it was the name of their tea gardens in Assam."

THE DOWTYS

Cyril Smith remembers: "The seven Dowty boys were all born in the house behind their father's chemist's shop in High Street (later Swann, then Elliott). I can remember seeing them playing out in the street. It was just rough stones then – not tarmac, in the early 1900's. The Dowtys were a very talented family. George became Sir George. William became the well-known local photographer.

MRS. MAY KNIGHT

"The mother of Fred and Jack Knight, was very stern – a matriarch," said Marion Knight, Fred's wife. "Mrs. Roberts of the fish shop used to say, 'She was the only one I was afraid of.' Mrs. Knight was one of her customers who regularly bought fresh fish. May's son, Fred, was put off fish for life. He loathed the smell of cod, which his mother used to have cooked in paper, and steamed.

Mrs. Knight used to watch out for "Bussy" Coldicott, from her window, at the house called The Vineyard, at the top of High Street. She knew he would be bringing fresh fish from the station, in his trap. Fish arrived by train then. Immediately she saw "Bussy" pass her house, she would go quickly to Mrs. Roberts' shop to be sure of buying her fish fresh!"

JOE GLOVER

A notable character, whom a dozen folk were ready to describe. He was thick-set, with a little moustache which curled at the ends – a 'close' man. "Dukey" Glover he was called, because his people had kept the Duke of York pub in High Street (now disappeared). That is where he lived before coming to Bridge Street.

When he first came to Bridge Street, he had nothing. They reckon he soon found the hidey-hole of his predecessor in that house – where this man had hoarded his money. After that, Joe blossomed out into all kinds of ventures. Outside his shop and 'garage' he would sell cans of petrol. In his shop window were all sorts of electrical gadgets and trinkets.

"Juicy" became his nickname (from "Dukey") and he used to charge all the accumulators for wirelesses. He was the first man in Pershore to have the wireless. During the General Strike of 1930, Joe had a platform over his door and he stood the loudspeaker on that, for people to hear the news, because there were no newspapers then, owing to the strike.

As you entered Joe Glover's shop, a bell rang. There was a 'button' under the floor, and he could tell, from bells ringing, just which part of the shop you were in.

Photography was his main interest. He took photos of all the weddings. He photographed Comberton maypole and Comberton lace-makers in the 1920's. He had an old Humber car in which he used to take paying passengers to Cheltenham.

There's a lot of doubt about Joe Glover's first wife. She just disappeared overnight and no-one knew what had happened. There were a lot of rumours. Mrs. Tillman and Miss Chick, who lived on the other side of Bridge Street, were great friends of the first Mrs. Glover. She was expected at a bridge party, but she never turned up. Some people thought Joe's first wife was buried under the floorboards. We still don't know. It was in the early '20's. Nobody investigated.

There was a man who lived by the Star Inn, named Jack Dolphin, and a man who was a brickie, who lived in Little Comberton. It seems that Jack called across the road to the brickie who had been working at the back of Joe Glover's house: "He buried her in the back and you've been and concreted her in now!" Of course, it was all rumours. Then Joe married his housekeeper.

If Joe came into the Library, when it was in Bridge Street, he used to ask the Librarian to find him a book which would make him laugh. He had the first T.V. in the town, apart from Mr.

Clemens. Joe would invite people into his house to watch it.

Let Cyril Smith, Curator of Pershore Cemetery, have the last word on Joe. "In 1949 we got short of burial ground, so I found room at the bottom of the cemetery for 30 more burials. The Cemetery Committee came up to see what I had done and were pleased. Joe Glover was one of them. He stayed behind and said to me, 'Has anyone bought the first one next to the gates?' I said, 'No'. He said, 'I am going to buy that one.' 'Why?' I replied. He answered, 'When the gates open, I can be the first one out!'" And there he is indeed, with his second wife, and quite an imposing gravestone. His epitaph should be: "Enterprising to the End".

JINNY SALMON

"She was hardly higher than the counter of her shop in Bridge Street. Cold meats were her speciality. She used to carve up the brawn and say, 'This is lovely brawn!' Then she picked it up in her fingers, put it on the scales and wrapped it up for you. I think she used to make a lot of it herself. 'Try my lovely polony,' she would say. And black puddings she made too and faggots."

Kitty Haines said: "My aunt, Miss Salmon, came to Pershore from Stratford-on-Avon. But first, she had been a very good cook in Comberton. To begin with, she had a shop in High Street where the Post Office is now. But it was a compulsory purchase by the Government, so she went to Bridge Street.

She used to sell boiled hams in a big dish and 'Beef à la mode'. She got it from Bristol. A lot of things came from Defford Station by horse and dray in those days. No vans then. But Collins from Evesham delivered pork pies every day, except Monday. In 1941 my aunt said, 'I can't cope with the rationing. Come and help me.' So that's why we returned to Pershore and lived in the shop for a long time and dealt with all the coupons for her.

My aunt was an old-fashioned character. You always had to go to church with her. You could always have time off to go to church, but not to go to dances. She was the original one in Pershore to have the Cyclists' Touring Club sign, round and yellow, on her outside wall. She used to put people up from this Club. They would write to her and book up in advance – very few 'phones then. She had the Avon Restaurant as well.

It was mostly in summer she had visitors to stay. When the new bridge was built in 1926, a lot of people came then, from Gloucester and Bristol. Some of them were the deep-sea divers who put in the foundations for the bridge, and they stayed with her a long time. Quite a lot of fishermen came from Birmingham. Some families came regularly to board."

Pershore children remember Miss Salmon, in her later years, as grumpy and wearing a man's cap. She is said to have cut a mouse in half as it ran across her counter and then she carried on carving the ham in front of her!

THE FEEKS

"I worked for Mrs. Feek as housemaid," said Freda Hutley-Reade. "She was the mother of Mr. Percy Feek. She used to frighten me when I was in her house at the bottom of Broad Street. Mrs. Feek used to wear a little white skullcap and long skirts. We didn't have flush toilets at home, but the Feeks did. The first time I heard their toilet flush it startled me. I used to hide behind the cooker when that happened!"

Esme Westcott lived next door to the Feeks. She said: "My sister used to help Mrs. Feek in the house – run errands and so on. She was a very nice old lady, who always wore a little lace cap and long dresses down to the ground, in a mauve or plum colour. She lived to be about 95. Mrs. Feek wasn't pleased if we stole her overhanging mulberries. But our boys were pretty good."

Her son, Percy, a very knowledgeable man, had been a Director of Education for Derbyshire. "He collected clocks," said Esme, "and also repaired them. We used to call it 'The House of Clocks'. Every time he got a new one, he used to say, 'Esme, would you like to come in and see my new clock?' One day, he said, 'Esme, what do you think of this?' It was an ancient contraption made of iron. I said, 'It looks like it would trap something.' He replied, 'Yes, it's a <u>man</u> trap.' He showed me how it worked and caught men's ankles, if they were poaching. It was a very vicious thing. He was going to take it to Worcester Museum."

WILLIAM NEED

Alice Young, his daughter, speaks: "My father was verger and parish clerk at Pershore Abbey for 46 years. He was under ten vicars. My earliest memory, at the age of three, is having to go in the Abbey and dust the pews with my parents. The Abbey was always a pleasant and happy place. Dad told me if I hadn't dusted under a book. He was very strict like that. When I'd started school, I used to often pop into the Abbey to see Dad. I was his favourite, being the youngest of six. He used to call me 'the scrapings of the pot' because I was so small.

It was hard work for Dad. He had to stoke up the stoke-hole to keep the heat in the Abbey. He had to go up the tower steps every day to wind the clock. And he had all the mowing of the churchyard and St. Andrews. He only got paid once in three months. So my mother had to pay the bread and the meat once in three months – for us six children.

My father used to patch up with wire, the different parts of the Abbey clock to keep it going. After Dad died, people said to me, 'He took his secret with him,' because the clock has never gone properly since. The glass doors at the West end of the Abbey were Dad's memorial. He always used to say, 'They need a pair of doors there, against the draught, instead of just a pair of old plush curtains."

An old man stopped me the other day and said, 'I wish old Billy Need was here today. He used to buy me an ounce of tobacco every week.' And my father was like that."

GILKIE ROSS

"He was an important clerk at Pershore Growers' Market. He could run his four fingers up four columns of figures and add them up – four columns at a time. He used to do it as a party trick!"

YOKKER COWLEY AND HARRY NEWMAN

"Yokker Cowley lived in Reddings yard. He was a drover. He drove cattle to market to be sold. He was very small – like a jockey, and always wore his cap on back to front. One avoided him if one could! That sort of drover would go into Wales and drive sheep or cattle up to Hereford market. Quite a distance – and all on foot."

"Yokker Cowley and Harry Newman were two right characters. Yokker led bulls up to the station, to go on the train. These two were odd-job men who used to go around with the threshing box. They worked for Tom Bomford mainly. They used to live up Station Road in Fred Colwall's barn, and in the barn where Bomford's pigs were. Yokker Cowley never had a home for years. A Mr. Wells of Stone Bow, Peopleton, found Yokker 'popped off' one morning, in his old Anderson air-raid shelter."

JULIA AND EMILY DAY

Miss Julia Day was a bustling, sharp, authoritative little lady, who lived at The Elms, Station Road. Her sister, Emily Day, was much quieter and rarely spoke. They had been brought up on a farm in Martley. Julia Day adored 'The Dream of Gerontius', by Sir Edward Elgar, whom she had seen at Three Choirs Festivals in Worcester Cathedral.

Their companion, Hilda Storm, was kind, but had a speech impediment. It was Hilda who was sent upstairs, by Julia, on their return home at night, to 'look under the beds' for intruders.

As children, we were regularly invited, with our parents, to tea with the Days, especially at Christmas. Their paintings of their Victorian ancestors and their prize bulls, looked stiffly down upon us from the walls. We always played card games after tea. I can still see the blue linen cloth on the card table. At each corner, was crocheted, in cream silk, either a large heart or a diamond, a spade or a club.

When "Day Storm", as we called them privately, came to <u>our</u> house to tea, in war-time blackout, Hilda Storm lit their way with an ancient storm lantern.

ARTHUR CHARLES SMITH, CHEMIST
(See also the chapter entitled 'We earned our living').

"He always had an anecdote for his customers," Roy Beard said. "He was a proper gentleman. He would talk to us children in a grown-up sort of way. He had a cure for most things. His rheumatism powders were well known all over the place. Even a lady from Colwall wanted some."

Rene Giles recalls: "He made all his own shampoos and all his own perfumes – verbena, violet, rose. I remember his 'Blackberry Cough Mixture' and 'Cremolia' for the hands. He had a lot of concoctions – very old recipes like Fullers Earth and sulphur ointment. The 'Vicar's Throat Pastilles' were very good for sore throats."

"Mr. Smith's father was a vet and he also pulled teeth out without an anaesthetic. He always had a man to hold you down and he gave you a tot of whisky to swill your mouth out!"

Arthur Charles Smith had a foul-smelling pipe. His wife didn't mix with anyone. She used to walk for miles round Bredon Hill. Her husband owned a hydrofoil boat and two islands in the river at Great Comberton. On the island was a summerhouse and plum trees, which disappeared when the Avon was opened up. Mr. Smith was interested in the archaeology of Bredon Hill and often used to walk on the hill."

HARVEY MARSHALL

"He was a 'pillar' of the Baptist Church in Broad Street, where he also lived." Esther Marshall speaks: "My brother Harvey, my father Reuben and my grandfather, Emanuel Jones, were all District and parish Councillors. And they all travelled many miles, as lay preachers, to take services in village chapels. My grandfather <u>walked</u> to Ashton-under-Hill and Bishampton to preach. It was said of all three, that they did not take off their Christianity with their Sunday suit. The Baptist Sunday School here, was started in 1804. The children were taught to read and write and were also clothed. I was a Sunday school teacher here for thirty-five years."

Blanche Dufty remembers Harvey Marshall cycling round the villages, selling Distilled Peppermint in bottles. This was a cure for all. He also sold homemade sweets and herbal remedies.

ISABEL GREAVES

"She was in charge of Fearnsides shop in Bridge Street – the newsagents and stationers, which also had a library at the back of the shop," said Walter Palfrey. "Miss Greaves was a 'Headmistress' type. She wore a long black skirt, a long-sleeved white blouse with a high neck and a black apron." The author found Miss Greaves very conscientious, but she had a good sense of humour, too.

Nora Bristow told me, "Miss Greaves worked at Fearnsides for 40 years. Any newspapers not sold, she took home to her house in Bridge Street. Her house was full of newspapers and old church magazines. How she didn't get <u>mice</u> I'll never know!"

JIMMY DANIELS

Jack Heeks speaks: "He was a chimney sweep. They used to call him 'Six Foot' because he was so short. He was also a lay preacher at the Baptist Chapel. He used to preach in the Masonic Hall at the back of The Angel Hotel, with Joseph Spiers, the basket maker."

As a child, living in Peopleton, Betty Hughes recalls: "Mr. Daniels, the chimney sweep, used to vanish up our old-fashioned fireplace. We had to go outside and watch for the brush going through the chimney. One day, some boys in the village took his bicycle and hid it. He was very upset, as he carried all his brushes fastened along the crossbar.

That was 'Little Sixpence. He used to go round the villages. We had to write a letter and book him up. He did several chimneys in each village on one day." His diminutive daughter, Nellie, was an elder at the Baptist Chapel in Broad Street, Pershore. She was known as 'Nellie the Hat' because she was a skilful milliner.

LADDIE BALLINGER

Cyril Smith recalls: "Laddie was my old pal. We used to go hunting and fishing together around Tyddesley Wood. Laddie used to work for 'Bruiser' Woods, who owned the old racecourse. Laddie cut the grass on five meadows, with the horse and old-fashioned machine.

One day, I saw Laddie coming along the road, pushing a motor-bike. He said, 'Will thee learn me to drive, Cyl?' I said, 'All right.' So I got him along one of the long paths. I said, 'When you get to the corner, shut her down to go round.' Instead of shutting her down, he opened her up! Up in the air went Laddie! He was lucky he did not hurt himself. He sold his bike after that.

All the members of the Croome Hunt knew Laddie. Mr. John Bomford of Allesborough Hill Farm had a racehorse named after him – 'Laddie Ballinger'. One day, Laddie went to London, along with the hounds, and they paraded up Piccadilly. Yes, Laddie sat next to lords and ladies on that day."

BILL PUGH

"He was a jolly, rotund bank manager at Lloyds Bank, in Broad Street. He was once in the carnival as the Carnival Queen, wearing a long blonde wig. This was a take-off, as there was also a proper Carnival Queen. He played tennis at the Tennis Club. If people got too serious about the game, Bill would start knocking balls all over the place, to make it funnier! He didn't like you to be serious. He took the part of a jolly monk in a pageant in the

Abbey."

Margaret Taylor said: "During the war, Mr. Pugh was on duty with my husband, Arthur, sometimes. Bill Pugh was noted for his loud snore.' The policeman on duty at night, could stand right at the corner of the market in Defford Road, and hear Bill Pugh snoring in bed at Bank House in Broad Street. My husband once dreamed that Bill had blown all the tiles off the roof with his loud snoring! Bill was a great sport and took it all in his stride."

RAYMOND LONG

Edwin Hill speaks: "Raymond was a marvellous mathematician. His Headmaster had been Mr. Chapman. Raymond didn't respect anyone. On the building sites, while we were having lunch, he would write maths equations and problems on the new plaster on the walls. He was a first-class carpenter, joiner and bricklayer. He used to have a piece of ground at Stocking, on the way out of Pershore towards Besford. He had some wonderful fruit trees there. This was his hobby and his means for keeping his family, because the building trade was not very well paid. Raymond played his cornet in a little band at the Mission Hall."

CYRIL CROOKE

"His was a very old Pershore family," said Edwin Hill. "He was an excellent carpenter in oak. He worked for Pettifers. The work he did, particularly for the Masonic Hall at The Angel, was remarkable. He did a lot of work in the Abbey too. He was a chorister and a bell-ringer."

ALICE BOUCHER

"She was one of the ladies of the Abbey who was always there," recalls Ruth Brant. "She used to attend all the services and do a lot of cleaning. When we were confirmed, she always helped us get ready and put our veils on. She would give advice on what to do and how to behave. She taught in the Abbey Sunday School for very many years."

Her relatives, John and Charles Boucher, lived at Pinvin, where they had a funeral business. On their van was printed the slogan 'Distance No Object'. For light relief, these two brothers took part in amateur dramatics in Pinvin.

JACK HEMMING

Kitty Haines told me: "He had a tailor's shop, under the name of Summerton. He used to do all the tailoring for the Earl of Coventry. One day he said to me, 'I'm going cycling over to Croome Court to fit Lord Deerhurst (the eldest son of the Earl). I cycled with him and, on arrival, I went into the kitchen and stayed there. The housekeeper showed me all the house bells. Each bell was named according to its room."

Walter Palfrey said: "Jack Hemming lived with his sister. During the Second World War, they called his house 'The League of Nations', because he entertained the troops of all nationalities. In his tailor's shop, he and his staff would sit in the window and you could see what work they were doing. They were bespoke tailors."

Roy Beard said: "In the war, the Red Cross in London would send down to Jack Hemming, Air Force men on leave – Canadians, Americans ..... his house was packed. The Hemmings would put them up."

GERTRUDE FAGG

Ruth Brant said: "Mrs. Fagg had a sweet shop. She was a lovely lady – plump and jolly with blonde hair. Her husband, Archie, used to drive a taxi."

MAURICE BANBURY

Many people were grateful for the kind and thoughtful manner of this gentlemanly dentist. His patients would return to him, even after moving many miles away from Pershore. Mabel Phipps of Wyre told me: "My son, Barry, kept on having nearly all his teeth out, because Mr. Banbury was so good. If I meet Mr. Banbury now, he always kisses me. He is a marvellous man.

Maurice Banbury's favourite catchwords, in his surgery, were: 'My whistling jet!'; 'Nice mix, Nurse!'; and 'Spit into the duck pond!' And he always said 'Goodbye' three times to his patients."

NICKNAMES OF SOME PERSHORE CHARACTERS

Nicknames were often handed down from father to son.

"Monkey" Miller, the draper;

"Bruiser" Wood, the butcher;

"Napper" Turvey of the "Napper Joe's" Morris dancers;

"Neighbour" Heeks;

"Wagger" Coombe;

"Yorkie" Waite;

"Packie" Rose;

"Chalkie" White;

"Vinegar" Annis;

"Very Bad" Cosnett - (when asked how he was, he would always say 'very bad');

"Straight Tip" Annis - (he was short and carried an army cane);

"Stanley" Baldwin, landlord of The Angel Hotel (after the current Prime Minister);

"Ping Pong" Crooke, the newspaper reporter of Bridge Street.

TWO EXTRA-SPECIAL PEOPLE (FOR ME) – MY PARENTS

"You had good parents, Margaret," said Elsie Barnes to me.
"Your parents were always very friendly," said Nora Bristow.
"Your mother was always sociable. She would talk to you," said
Alice Young to me.

GEORGE BRAMFORD

He was headmaster of Pershore Junior School 1931 to 1951.
His old pupils speak:

"He was a very kind, just, man; much respected," said
Barbara Hartley. "He was so nice, we felt we must do no wrong;
we must not displease him. We would say, 'We're going to Mr.
Bramford's lessons today.' Or, when we walked up Station
Road, we would say, 'That's where Mr. Bramford lives!'"

Ruth Brant said: "You felt that you had to do your very best
for him. We must not let him down."

"We lovingly called him 'Daddy Bramford'," recalls Edwin
Hill. "His birthday was on May 17th, which happens to be
mine. Being a very religious man, he taught Religious Studies.
It was a very happy school. I joined the Abbey choir and your
father was there too!' He liked music. He was a very versatile
man."

Marjorie Godfrey (née Twigg) remembered my father's
tweed jacket. She said: "If he opened the classroom door,
everyone immediately sat up a few more inches. He was very
popular – a very fair man. Pupils respected him."

Esme Westcott relates: "On the first day Mr. Bramford came
to the school, he said, at Assembly: 'This is going to be the
motto of the school: 'If a thing is worth doing, it is worth
doing well'.' And I've remembered that school motto."

Ernest Fuller recalled: "I used to think of your father as a
lover of nature. He would recite to us:

> "'He who does his duty' is a question
> Too complex to be resolved by me.

But he, I venture the suggestion
Does part of it, who plants a tree."

He used to quote that often to us lads, when we had to write an essay on nature for the Bird and Tree Competition." *(See Appendix – School Log Book for Pershore Junior School, entry for July, 1932).*

Nigel Montandon said: "He was a caring Headmaster. He used to give me extra homework, if I was weak in a subject. Once, I was playing marbles in the playground of the new Junior School at Abbey Park. There were classroom windows all around. My biggest marble flew up, as it hit a metal bar. Mr. Bramford happened to see this. He came up to me and said, 'Montandon, I think I'll take that one!'"

Charles Clemens said: "George Bramford was the ideal man for the Abbey choir. His voice, his behaviour and what he expected of the boys, helped the organist more that he knew."

Leslie Brookes recalled: "Your father brought a great deal of fresh air and common sense to Pershore. He had a delicious sense of humour and mischief. He had a twinkle in his eye and often made jokes with the Male Voice Choir of Pershore, of which he was a member."

Mabel Phipps of Wyre said: "I have a vivid memory of your parents singing a duet together. I really loved your father. He helped me to organise concert parties. He knew people who could sing and entertain."

Jim Dowler told me: "Your father loved his garden. He brought us some Michaelmas daisies for our new garden."

Blanche Dufty said: "Your father would often come and see Mrs. Badger at The Mount and talk about roses. He was interested in roses and The Mount garden had some unusual roses. They were very, very dark red ones – almost black."

Charles Clemens recalled: "Your father used to say to me: 'I like a village. I lived in Overbury for nine years and I loved it.' I liked your Dad. He'd get on with everybody."

MABEL (MEG) BRAMFORD

"She was one of the best – a cheery smile, a cup of tea and the Women's Institute!" was Roy Beard's spontaneous summary of her.

"Your mother?," said Ethel Rock. "I think she was a smashing lady! If you met your mother, she always spoke. She used to say, 'How are you?'"

Kitty Haines remembered Mrs. Bramford helping with the Girls' Friendly Society, of which Kitty was a member, in Miss Lawson's house, Broad Street. "Your mother was always smiling," recalled Kitty.

Barbara Hartley (née Fagg) said: "Your mother was a very sweet person. As she walked down the High Street, past our shop, she would wave to us."

Elsie Barnes told me: "I remember your mother taking you to church. She was a great member of the Abbey and she did a lot of work there."

Esme Wescott said: "I remember Mrs. Bramford singing with the Women's Institute choir, which I joined when I was 17. I used to try and stand by your mother, because she could read the music well. Whereas, I learn music by ear – but I can pick up more from a good singer."

Ruth Brant got to know my mother because of the Abbey Embroidery Guild. "She was always busy. And she always looked so neat and tidy – always smartly dressed; and she wore such nice hats!"

"I admired your mother. She was always so active," said Rene Giles. "I was very fond of her. She once said of my son: 'Never mind his not being given a place at Prince Henry's, Evesham. He has the brains, so he'll get on.' And he did!"

"She was a wonderful experience to most of us," recalls Edwin Hill. "She attended all the social functions in Pershore in those days. Wherever you went, Mrs. Bramford seemed to be involved – especially in the Women's Institute. She seemed to get on well with children. She had a way with us, in Cubs and Scouts. We did several plays with Mrs. Bramford. The most famous one was GREAT AUNT BARBARA. That was my part!"

Marion Knight remembered my mother as an excellent Secretary of the Ladies' Conservative Association, "Because she knew all the dates of other events in Pershore. She was active in so many other societies."

My mother spent her last four years in Roland Rutter Court, Newlands. Edith Brown, a fellow resident at that time, related: "I miss your mother. She always had a joke when you met her. She really was a scream, playing cards. 'Come on Meg, we're waiting to play,' we would say. She would stop and talk to everyone she met and held us up! One day, she said, at whist, 'She'll have to go!' She meant her Queen card. We laughed. She liked social occasions. She was on the committee of the British Legion right up to the end."

Chapter three

SCHOOLDAYS

"As the twig is bent, so the tree will grow". For relevant dates of Pershore schools, and some interesting sidelights, see also: 'The School Log Books Speak' in the Appendix to this book.

"My father could not write, because he had never gone to school," said Blanche Dufty, then aged 101. "He was an orphan and his aunts never sent him to school. So I used to do the writing for him."

In the early 1900's, several young girls in Pershore were pupils at Taylor's School, a private school at 'Woodville', now the Gentlemen's Club, in High Street. Three lady-like sisters ran this excellent school, which also took boarders, and where the girls were taught Dancing and French.

The school gave concerts in the Music Hall, opposite the Working Men's Club, in High Street. Miss Emily Taylor was the Headmistress; Miss Maggie taught music. Their sister, Mrs. Morrison, did the housekeeping. Later, the Misses Taylor left Pershore and went down to Bristol to run a school there.

Pershore National School (now vanished) was in Defford Road, surrounded by the Co-operative Market. In the 1920's, Mr. W. T. Chapman was Headmaster. "He was a good man," said Sid Champken. "In those days, you sat in your desk and you didn't move."

Alec Witts recalled his schooldays at the Defford Road School in the 1920's. "You all fell into lines in the playground, according to your class, when they blew the whistle. They would have a look at your hands to see if they were clean – although there was nowhere to wash your hands. You marched into school, while one of the masters sat at the piano, playing some tune. The whole school had prayers and a hymn.

Mr. Chapman used to address the school. Once he said, 'Lads, always remember this: 'We will teach you the rules and you will educate yourselves when you leave us.' And he was right! Because school education and education for life are two different things. The one is taught, but the other one you learn by experience."

Walter Palfrey speaks: "'Pop' Chapman was a great character. The last week of the summer term, before I went to Prince Henry's, Evesham, he slipped the usual tuppence down my neck – for being his monitor. Then he went to his tall desk and pulled out a sheet of foolscap and said, 'Now, take this home to your father.' It was an essay my father had written. Mr. Chapman had kept it all those years. He had taught my father as well. He was Headmaster of that school for a long time." (Twenty-seven years, in fact).

"Mrs. Webb, my favourite teacher, used to come to school in a pony and trap, from Peopleton," said Rene Giles. "And she used to pick me up here, at Hurst Park, on her way."

Nora Bristow remembers Mrs. Webb for a different reason: "She was very strict. She would rap a ruler on your fingers for bad behaviour. She taught sewing and I hated sewing. Mrs. Webb would say. 'Take that seam out – it's crooked!'"

"I always remember Mr. Osborne, another great character," said Walter Palfrey. "He used to read Dickens' 'A Christmas Carol' to us. There was an iron guard around the open fire in the classroom. For Jacob Marley's chains, he used to rattle this ancient fire-guard!"

Another well-remembered teacher of the late-1920's at this school, was the much-loved Miss Ismay, who taught Needlework and Religious Knowledge, and was always on her bicycle. She was Head of the Girls' Department or 'Governess'. The children had come up to the 'Market School' from the Infants' School, in New Road, where Mrs. Hutton had been Headmistress since 1901. She was ably supported by teachers, such as Miss Harris, Miss Woodward and Mrs. Nicholas.

Alec Witts said: "Whatever the weather, we came to school. There was no such thing as Wellington boots in those days. You just wore hobnail boots and your ordinary clothes – no uniform.

We often got wet. Your clothes were heavier then. They seemed to stand up to the weather better. Broadcloth will stand more rain than this flimsy stuff we wear today.

I used to like Geography and History. You were taught to be patriots. England was the most important country in the world. There was no-one like an Englishman. You learnt about English history and the British Empire."

Leslie Brookes commented: "I found it rather backward in Pershore when I went to school. In my Worcester school, we had had pens and paper. Here, in Pershore, we only had the old slates. This was in 1924. I was treated as a foreigner at Pershore School. The kids used to take a delight in pounding me, to see how much foreigners would take. Then they just accepted me after a while."

Nora Bristow remembered: "We had one hour of Scripture every morning, after Prayers, because it was a Church of England school. We listened to Bible stories taught by Miss Ismay. We had to learn passages from The Bible and hymns. Once a week the Vicar would come in and teach us. That was Canon Gresford Jones then."

Esme Westcott recalled: "All the lessons were very interesting. I used to enjoy Nature Study and Botany. And I was very fond of English Literature. I'm still fond of poetry. I think it's something to do with the rhythm. We had a good English teacher."

"I was going to be a teacher," said Blanche Dufty. "My 'Governess' (Headmistress) was preparing me for the sums. I used to write on the blackboard. I used to be Monitor. I had to teach other children beside me to read and write, because they were dunces really. They didn't want to learn. I was very fond of writing. Every year I had a prize from my 'Governess' for writing.

In 1906, when I was 14, my father died. He had promised me I wouldn't have to go into service, like the other girls had to – my sisters. I wanted to be a teacher, but it didn't come off. I had to help my mother to get the living. So I went into service. My 'Governess' was very, very nice to me. She was very sad when I told her I couldn't be a teacher."

Blanche Dufty has preserved her school exercise book of sums. It dates back to 1904, in the Defford Road School, and is most beautifully written. It deals with items such as calico and candles. 'If 17 yards of silk cost £4.13.6d. what will be the cost of 102 yards?' 'A greengrocer bought 4,500 oranges at 4d. a score and sold them at 4d. each. What profit did he make?'

The Defford Road School had been built in 1840. Generations of children had played in the playground; dusty in summer, muddy in winter, and surrounded by the noise of horses and drays in the nearby market. Through the open windows of the classrooms, pupils could hear the bellowing voices of the auctioneers. There was an all-pervasive, pleasant, smell of plums in summer. But the stench of the outside bucket privies was a most underlined unpleasant odour. In the girls' playground, there was a big tree. The surface was all gravel. If you fell over, you cut your knee and it was very painful.

Alec Witts remembers: "The girls were in a separate school. There was a very tall wall dividing us. You were not allowed to talk with the girls. If you were caught, you had the cane."

"You didn't dare associate with the boys," said Rene Giles. "We were taught separately. If you were caught putting a note over the separating wall of the two playgrounds – that was disgraceful!"

Marjorie Godfrey remembered: "We used to shout terrible things to each other over the separating wall in the playground. A ball would come over and we wouldn't give it back to the boys."

"We used to play whip and top; tag; skipping," said Mary Stubbs. "We made the girls we didn't like to sit in that tall wire rubbish bin, in the playground. One girl from Nogains was very spiteful. We took great delight in getting hold of her and sitting her in the bin and leaving her! She couldn't get out!"

The games in that playground were handed down by tradition. I myself, recall long lines of big girls, holding hands, sweeping up and down, trying to catch little girls on the perimeter. That was called 'Fly-catching'. Certain ball games, like Sevenses, persisted.

Even the singing games, which had been sung there in Blanche Dufty's day, in 1906, were still being sung by the girls of the 1930's. Here are two which I remember:

'The big ship sails on the Alli Allio ....
On the fourteenth of September' .....

while a long 'snake' of girls, each holding the girl in front around the waist, winds round, under arched arms. Walking around in a circle, we would sing lustily, with a strong rhythm:

'The wind, the wind, the wind blows high
The snow comes pattering from the sky.
She is handsome, she is pretty
She is a girl of a noble city.
Men come courting, one, two, three,
Pray will you tell me who it'll be.'

Then you had to say which boy in the school was your sweetheart. And we started up again:

'Jackie Brown says he loves her
All the boys come fighting for her
Let the boys say what they will
Jackie Brown loves her still.
He kisses her, he pets her, he puts her on his knee,
He says 'My little darling, now won't you marry me?'
The time will come and we shall say:
'Tomorrow, tomorrow will be your wedding day'.

Meanwhile, in the boys' playground, another kind of game was going on. "Very often," said John Annis, "the men of the market would tip a box of apples, or some plums, over into the playground – just to see the kids scrabbling for them!

Alec Witts had vivid recollections of the punishments meted out in Mr. Chapman's time. "They had slates left over from the old Victorian times. If you were late once, you had a slate and had to copy out poetry on it. If you were late twice, you had the stick. If you were late three times, you had the cane across each hand. We never worried about the cane. It was part of life.

The teacher would ask, 'Which are you going to have – the cane or the slate?' We always chose the cane. Because you didn't have to stop in. I was happier than the kids are today – because there was more discipline. Parents did not object to these punishments. Very often, your father would give you another hiding at home for getting into trouble at school."

Albert Haines of Pensham said to me in 1988: "Your father, Mr. Bramford, often caned me. But it did me good. We were brought up to respect other people – not like today, when children do what they like."

On the other hand, good work and good attendance were rewarded. Alice Young speaks: "We had prizes then. You could have your choice of books. I received a silver medal for 5 years perfect attendance. I had a solid silver watch from the Worcestershire County Council for seven years unbroken attendance. I remember sitting in the gallery at school. The gallery went up in tiers."

Nora Bristow recalls: "When I was at school in Defford Road there were no school dinners. We all went home at twelve noon for dinner, until one-thirty. There were always good vegetables in our garden, to make a good dinner for all of us."

Alec Witts spent his dinner-time in a different way: "We were not allowed to stay in school at dinner-time," he said. "We lived at Pensham, so we had to bring our own dinner. We were given two slices of bread and a penny. At dinner time, we would go to the International Stores to buy a slice of corned beef, to put between the bread slices. That was our dinner.

In the Broad Street, we would stand against the bake house wall, where there was a big, black, shiny patch. That was our dining room, because, on a cold day, it was hot against that wall. Then we would tramp round to the market, to see if there was anybody whose horse we could hold. They would give you a penny for that. And then you could go and buy a cup of tea in the market."

<u>In January 1932 a great change took place</u>:

Schools everywhere were re-organised. The National School in Defford Road became Pershore Church of England <u>Junior Mixed</u> School. No longer were the boys and girls taught separately. The 11-plus scholars all went up to the newly-built Senior School (now the High School) in Station Road.

My father, Mr. George Bramford, became Headmaster of Pershore Junior School; a position he occupied for the next twenty years. His teaching staff in 1932 were: Mrs. C. Hallam (Deputy Head), Mr. Addis, Miss Morris, Miss Taylor and Miss Pointon.

Peggy Maple has very vivid and abundant memories of that era. "Mr. Bramford introduced a great many things to Pershore children. He certainly brought a new outlook, which was extremely good for all of us. He was very keen on getting us through our Scholarship Exam. Most of us sat for this exam, for either Worcester Grammar School or Evesham Prince Henry's. I went to the latter.

The classroom at Pershore Junior School was divided by a green curtain, with Mrs. Hallam's class on one side and Mr. Bramford's class on the other. There was an open fire with an iron guard at one end and an old coke stove at the other, for heating. It was amazing that one class did not interfere with the other class.

Your father took Geography. I sat next to Mary Langford and we got the giggles about the Scilly Islands. Your father got extremely cross about it. But we couldn't stop!

I found the greatest interest in the way he introduced the Shakespearean songs to us. He was very keen on teaching songs." His daughter, Margaret, a fellow pupil of Peggy Maple, well remembers learning these songs, taught by her father:

It was a lover and his lass	I vow to thee, my country
Where the bee sucks	Jerusalem
Sigh no more, ladies	The Keeper
Who is Sylvia?	Little Water Wagtail
Cherry Ripe	The Cuckoo

Peggy Maple continues: "When the 'Queen Mary' liner was being built in 1934-35, Mr. Bramford took us outside the school and he pointed out, that, from the school to the old racecourse, further along Defford Road, was the actual length of the 'Queen Mary'. He was trying to convey to the children what an enormous ship it was. That stands out in my memory very much!

Mr. Bramford introduced the Essay on Bird and Tree. I did the Horse Chestnut and the Water Wagtail. Here is my prize; 'Hope's Tryst', which I was awarded for my essay for the Church of England Temperance Society. I'm afraid I didn't stand for my vows!

We did amateur dramatics at school too. I distinctly remember a play with my fellow pupil, Jim Long, as an organ grinder. I was his wife; I was a gypsy with a tambourine. We performed a little sketch, and Wally Buckle was the monkey, because he was the tiniest child in the class. We were probably chosen because we were the tallest children in the class.

We were aged ten and we sang 'Cheri cheri bee,' which was delightful. That concert was performed at the old Mission Hall, to raise funds for the Mission Hall. Mr. Bramford was a member of the Brotherhood there. Other singers took part – Doug Trigg and Charlie Coombe. There were at least six or seven 'turns'. And Mr. Bramford sang, of course. He had a splendid voice."

I was to be Maid Marion in a play about Robin Hood," recalled Peggy Maple. "and Jackie Coombe was chosen to play Robin Hood. Half-way through the play, Robin had to take Marion into his arms and kiss her. Jackie utterly refused to do this! In the end, I had to take the part of Robin Hood, as there wasn't a boy willing. I have pulled their legs about this, since. It was the first year we were all in a mixed class. Your father was very cross about it, but in the end he laughed!

We had to find our own costumes for 'Robin Hood'. I was all right for a hat with a feather in it, because in the '30's, women wore hats with large pheasants' feathers. I found a loose shirt and a little waistcoat. I wore a pair of my mother's silk Directoire knickers – dark green for Robin Hood. I don't know why people laughed on seeing me! She was a large lady, you know. I was tall then, but very thin. The only lads in the play were playing Little John and Will Scarlett.

Another thing your father introduced was outings. He hired a 'bus and took us to Worcester to be shown around the Cathedral. It was the first time for most of us, at the age of ten. We went to the Royal Worcester Porcelain Works too.

Standing outside the Cathedral, who should come past, in a beautiful big, old-fashioned Daimler, but SIR EDWARD ELGAR!

Mr. Bramford cried out, 'Children, children, look who is in that car. It is Sir Edward Elgar, our most famous composer.' We were all very thrilled indeed. Sir Edward was sitting in the back. He had his cigar, and his hat was a grey Homburg. He was a very old gentleman then. I think he died that year. (He died in 1934). We were fortunate to have been with Mr. Bramford, or we wouldn't have known it was Sir Edward Elgar.

Your father introduced HORLICKS into the school for the mid-morning break. I was Monitress, being a big girl. We had to go to the school caretaker for hot water. She lived in the cottage in between the two old schools. We put the Horlicks tablet into a jug and poured hot water on to it. Horlicks people supplied special little beakers with nursery rhyme characters on them. It was a very pleasant drink, especially in winter.

Soon after that, little bottles of milk were sold in schools – one third of a pint for tuppence halfpenny per week. Some children couldn't pay. Your father used to put his hand in his pocket for those children, so that every child had his milk.

The market was all around us. In summer time, when the plums were plentiful, they were dumped by the ton. In the classrooms, we would all be much bothered with wasps. Children used to get under the desk and pretend to be terrified."

Peggy Maple recalled a touching little incident: "A pupil named Jackie Long came to school, unwashed, from Marriotts Hill, in Wellington boots. He was neglected at home – a poor family. He would arrive at school soaking wet. His Wellingtons would be dried out. One day, he fell fast asleep in class, with the sun shining on him. Mr. Bramford sang the popular song of that year over him; 'LAZYBONES' – to the amusement of all the class:

> Lazybones, sleepin' in the sun,
> How're ye goin' to get yer day's work done?
> Never get yer day's work done,
> Sleepin' in the noonday sun.

Jackie woke up. Sadly, he died in his '20's."

Roy Beard has equally vivid memories of his schooldays at the school in Defford Road. "I was born in Church Row. I've been in Pershore all my life. My first day at the old Junior School? I hammered on the door. I was a bit late. Roy Hewlett came to the door. Your father, Mr. Bramford, shouted to Roy Hewlett, 'Who is it?' He answered, 'Roy Beard, Sir.' Your father said, 'Come along in.' I replied, 'Very good, Mister.' He said, 'You call me Sir.'

That was my first encounter with your father. I always think he was one of the best. It's a pity we haven't got any more teachers like him. He instilled into you what was wrong and what was right. He used to say, 'Nothing but the best is good enough.' And, 'Manners maketh man, not money.'

My favourite subject was Geography, due to your father. He would take us out into the playground. The market lorries would be going by – quite a few. Some from Aberystwyth, in particular. He would ask, 'Whereabouts is Aberystwyth?' That's what got me going on Geography. History – no! But now I'm more keen on History than Geography.

If anyone had a particular interest, your father brought it out in a pupil. I remember we sang 'Jerusalem'; one of your father's favourites."

Barbara Hartley said: "Mr. Bramford wanted me to take the Scholarship Exam, but I knew my Mum couldn't afford the uniform for the Grammar School. So I never sat the exam. Mr. Bramford used to say, a long time afterwards, 'I do so wish you had sat the exam.'"

Alas! There were several pupils in those days, whose parents could not afford the uniform, even though their children had passed the Scholarship Exam.

Barbara Hartley recalled: "Mr. Bramford prepared us for the Church of England Temperance Society's exam, instead of Scripture lessons, for some weeks. He likened the body and soul to a car. 'You must feed your soul too. You need inner strength. A car cannot go without petrol. You must keep your body fit, but you must nourish your inner self too, with spiritual things.' The school won the Temperance Shield one year. I received a book prize which I've still got – 'We Three at School'."

Mrs. Hallam, my father's chief assistant, we also remembered with affection. Marjorie Godfrey said: "She was the best disciplined lady in the school. One look from her and you did as you were told. She was a born teacher."

Peggy Maple said: "Mrs. Hallam played the Sousa marches on the piano after Assembly. We all marched out to 'The Washington Post' or 'Liberty Bell'. She was a lovely person and a good teacher. When children made her cross, she got extremely red down the neck, we noticed. Sometimes, we made her cross on purpose."

"Mother Hallam was a Welsh wizard really, wasn't she?," commented Roy Beard. "We used to get the wrong side of her. I think she was good at heart. She used to look around and see who was squinting. I was one of the squinters. The school nurse came round. 'Roy Beard requires glasses,' Mrs. Hallam told her. I always associate her with my sight."

I, myself, remember her frequent catch phrase to slothful pupils: 'The Inspector's at the door!' As a teacher, her most memorable performance was in the Geography lesson. She would, herself, enact the rôle of the Earth:

'You are the Sun, Cowley!' she would exclaim, pointing to a boy seated in the centre of the class. Then, taking up the globe, with a series of pirouettes, each representing a day, this grey-haired ballerina, in her navy blue dress with a white collar, would spin around the entire perimeter of the class, counting, 'One day ... two days ... as her skirts twirled. We held our breath in anticipation of her tripping, rather than in wonder at the motion of the planets.

My sister, Avril, has her own memories of that school: "Growing bean seeds on pink blotting paper; newts and tadpoles in jam jars; a stuffed owl and a stuffed squirrel in glass cases; the visits of a conjurer and a Punch and Judy man; and the super Gray Dunn biscuits for break."

Marjorie Godfrey recalls: "It was always an honour to be chosen as a Monitress. It made you feel important and responsible, to give books out. All the books had to be well looked after."

Laurence Coggins remembers his Art lessons: "Making patterns with potatoes cut in half and dipped in poster paint."

Esme Westcott was in great demand as Goldilocks. She said: "Goldilocks and the Three Bears was always very popular. Because I had long, fair ringlets, they came for me, whichever class was doing Goldilocks!"

Mary Revers relates: "It was the tradition for Mr. Bramford's top class to entertain the Pershore Women's Institute once a year. I produced their play one year. Its title was 'The Sun Man'. However, the boy who took the main part had forgotten to turn up at the W.I. Hall on the night of the play. They sent round for him, but he had gone to bed! So there was only one solution. I, myself, had to play this chief part at a moment's notice!"

"It was a horrible day when the school dentist came," recalled Marjorie Godfrey. "We used to queue up to go into one classroom, where he had some horrific equipment and only a screen around it. The dentist would look at your teeth and either pat you on the head, or you had to have some fillings done. And when the school nurse looked at your hair for nits, everybody at once started scratching."

Mary Stubbs told me: "I still hear from three teachers who taught me in the 1930's at the Senior School (now the High School). They are Mr. Pointer and Mr. and Mrs. Matthews. She taught English; he taught Science. They live at Chippenham, Wiltshire. Mrs. Matthews loves my letters! Last Christmas, I sent them a tea towel of Pershore. They were delighted. 'That's brought back all our courting days!' she said. Mr. Pointer lived at Wychbold. His wife died. He's got married again. He's in his 80's and now lives in Wales."

"On my way to the Senior School, I used to feed our pigs and hens," said Roy Beard. "We lived at The Furlongs, had allotments and kept pigs. I used to share the kitchen waste from the Senior School with Jack Pointer, our teacher. Jack Taylor, another schoolmaster, had poultry. I used to sell him some pullets."

"At the Senior School," said Marjorie Godfrey, "my sister, Edith Twigg, became Head Prefect. Then I became Head Prefect after that. I was Netball Captain too. I thoroughly enjoyed school. We had a lovely big field up there, in Station road, for football, hockey, etc. To have such space was gorgeous, after the Junior School in Defford Road. It was cramped there.

We had to walk up Station road. If you knew anyone with a bike, you tried to get a lift up there. My sister, being older than me, used to sail past me on her 'sit up and beg' bike. It was ¾-mile from the town. About eight 'buses would arrive from the villages, bringing all the children."

PRIVATE SCHOOLS IN PERSHORE IN THE 1930's

Malcolm Meikle said: "My first recollection of Pershore, is of going to school at 7, Broad Street, where Miss Brightman ran a nursery school. It later transferred to a schoolroom behind Elliott's chemist's shop. My very first term of real school, was with Miss Wiley, in Bridge Street, up the alley, opposite the Mill. Miss Wiley played Colonel Bogey and we marched once round the playground, then up the stairs into the schoolroom."

My sister, Avril Bramford, was taken to Gore House School, number 27, Bridge Street, for her first-ever day at school, when she was five. The school was owned and run by the Misses Brickell. Avril was there for three years, until she began at the Junior School, where her father was Headmaster.

There were few nursery schools in those days, whereby three and four-year olds could be gradually immersed into a community of other children. To be left alone, with strangers, in a big, dark, old house, was too much for five-year old Avril, then a dainty, shy, little girl. Like many another child, she cried on her first day.

She remembers: "Miss Edith Brickell was plump and motherly. Miss Nellie was thin and dour and had a twitch. Their friend, Miss Louise Stephens, lived there too, and was always kind to the children. Brother Charles Brickell, with his bicycle, kept well in the background. The blue-uniformed maid, May, was tall, angular, red-faced and very solemn.

The upstairs schoolroom had old-fashioned desks, a huge shiny map of the world on the wall and old blackboards. The children did a lot of marching round to music in those days. Otherwise, it was all very dull. Writing was just laborious copying about farms and animals and the countryside. For Drawing, you copied pictures of girls in gardens, with dogs. For Geography, you copied the map of the British Isles. You had to recite a different town and its county, every day. Popular ones were 'Redcar in Yorkshire' and 'Barrow-in-Furness in Lancashire'.

Playtime was in the garden but <u>not</u> on the grass. The big girls hugged the little girls, because there wasn't much else to do! There was one outside loo. But if you were taken short in class, upstairs, you were allowed to use a marvellous Victorian porcelain loo, with a highly-polished wooden seat.

Fees were about £5 per term in 1935. There was five shillings extra for stationery, to allow for the superior quality exercise books, with their thick blue covers and red and green lines. The bill arrived on beautiful, crested notepaper.

The school's Christmas party of organised games, was held in the Brickell's front room, as a special treat. They always had 'Passing the Parcel', to music. The parcel, usually containing a toy car, was always won by the same boy, Michael Edwards. Why? Because he was the Brickell's godson!"

LEY School in Bridge Street is still going strong, after nearly 60 years. Miss Lois E. Young, who founded her LEY School in 1938, had been, until the mid-thirties, a governess. She began a little school, with six children, at the back of Spiers' basket shop in Bridge Street. Then she had a room behind Swann's, the chemist. Finally, she moved to 62, Bridge Street, because she owned number 64, and LEY School was born.

Miss Young's pupils grew from 6 to 24, aged 4 to 11. Mrs. Kettle, her assistant, taught there for 23 years and retired in 1971, as did Miss Young. By then the school had 42 pupils.

Miss Young told me: "We did country dancing in the school yard. Many children came from the villages, so they brought sandwiches for lunch. Later, there were enough pupils to have dinners sent in from the Manor House café. The girls did raffia craft work and cross-stitch. The boys made doormats out of canvas and rug wool. For games, they used a field near the river. One severe winter, they skated on the river!"

Chapter four

WE EARNED OUR LIVING

In Victorian times, a lot of home industry went on in Pershore – glove-making and stocking-making. "Before the First World War," said Kitty Haines, "people were almost self-supporting, with their own allotment and pig. They had a peg rug in front of the fire, but only on Sundays. On other days, they had a sack bag for a rug in front of the fire. I used to make peg rugs by using strips of coloured rags, knotted into clean sacks. I've still got the pegging needles. We got hold of the newest sacks we could find from the Mill. Sugar bags and flour bags we used.

There were several COTTAGE INDUSTRIES then. The Townsends and the Spencers, in Batchelor's Entry, often came round and asked, 'Have you any old clothes or rags for pegging?' They would take anything. Nothing went in the dustbin. There were no dustbins! You had to get rid of your own rubbish then."

Blanche Dufty told me some fascinating details about gloving in Pershore, in Victorian times: "In the 1860's and '70's, my mother used to live along Three Springs. She and her two sisters did the gloving. She made gloves for Queen Victoria's children, out of beautiful kid. She had a gloving box, to keep all her silks in, and pieces cut off gloves. And she kept this box to show us, when we got old enough to appreciate what she'd done. The gloves were up to the elbow. And they had got to be perfect. She embroidered all the backs of the gloves with fine silk in the most delicate colours – lovely shades of pink, blue, lemon, jade. How she threaded the needles, I don't know. They were so tiny for fine silk. And she didn't wear glasses.

It was a home industry organised by Fownes of Worcester. It was hard work for very little money. The gloves were taken down in dozens to the Three Tuns Hotel. A man would call for them and take them away. If there was one stitch out of place, he could tell. He held the bundle of twelve pairs of gloves and flicked through them as quick as lightning. He would throw out the imperfect ones. That pair had to be made again.

My mother used to do these gloves on a brass 'donkey'. It kept the shape of the glove and gripped it. There were gussets between fingers in them days. That took some doing. I never saw that brass 'donkey', 'cos she let someone else have it.

They were called 'The Three Graces', my mother and her two sisters. Because they didn't do anything else – just sit in the parlour and make these gloves. They daren't do any housework because of their hands, which must not get rough. And 'The Three Graces' were always dressed so nice!"

THE POSTMAN

"My father was a postman," said Esme Westcott. "Previously, he was a hairdresser, but in the First World War, lots of businesses went to the wall and his was one of them. In 1918, he took on Post Office work and he did hairdressing part-time. On the Bishampton run, he had a Post Office bicycle. Even the town run was large. It was the space between the houses that took time to cover. It was the long drives, right up to The Mount and back, carrying a very heavy load.

He used to go out about 5 a.m. until 10.30 a.m. He was free then, until 5.30 p.m. when he had to go back and stamp all the letters, by hand, until 7.30 p.m. But if a telegram came in the meantime, and if the telegraph boy had gone home, he had to go out to deliver the telegram. And that could be to anywhere.

He used to say, 'I've missed my station in life. I should have been a solicitor'. People used to ask him to write letters for them and decipher letters. He would collect medicines at the chemist's for the villagers, who would pay him, and he brought back the money to the chemist."

Laurence Coggins said: "The villagers around Elmley Castle and Bricklehampton welcomed their postman. In those days, it was George Smith from Cornmore. He would collect prescriptions and bring you your medicine that same afternoon.

He would put a bet on a horse for you as well. Villagers used to reward him with a couple of cauliflowers, or some rabbits. He came round here for years."

FACTORY WORK

"I used to work at the Pomona factory – the jam factory," said Lucy Conn. "That was in the First World War. Mr. Baynham owned it then and, afterwards, Mr. Rolls. It was the only factory in Pershore town then. We dried vegetables; parsnips and carrots for the troops in the war, and packed them in big cans. They made a lot of pulp from plums. That was used to make jam for the troops. The pulp went into barrels.

A man, me, and another woman – we had to stack these barrels of pulp on top of each other. You had to roll them up. The numbers on the side of the barrels told you what year the pulp had been made. The hours we worked? From six 'til two, or two to six p.m. Then from six p.m. 'til six a.m. in shifts. Mrs. Dancox and Mrs. Dolphin worked there too. There were lots of women workers there."

The Atlas Works, owned by Edward Humphries, had been employing Pershore people ever since the 1850's; first, on the site of the Pomona factory and later, on the site near Pershore railway station (see Footnote). Everything agricultural was produced – threshing machines, tractors, ploughs.

"I worked at the Atlas Works during the First World War," declared Blanche Dufty. "There were other women up there too. I went as a painter. They were making destructors for the forces in France. Women had to paint their chimneys. But the grey paint had lead in it and it got on my chest. So, I asked if I could have a different job.

I was put on engraving. You had to put the different names on lorries for the forces. That was a skilled job – cutting out all the letters, with very little instruction. I was proud to be the first woman engraver in Pershore.

But we only got the same money as the men, and they thought

we worked too fast! I was picking up £2.10s. a week, from 6.30 a.m. 'til 7.45 p.m. I did that work until the fellow came back for his job. I said to him, 'Thank goodness you've come back.' 'Why?' 'Because I'm absolutely fed up of this!'"

"I worked at Fisher Humphries (the Atlas Works) in the 1930's," said Jack Heeks. "The foreman said to me on the first day, as he felt my arms; 'You're just the chap we want. The blacksmith wants a striker.' Then I became an apprentice. We made threshing machines and straw balers. I worked nights during the Second World War. I was in a reserved occupation. It was only agricultural stuff – not armaments. A lot of it went to France."

BASKET MAKER

"Bob Mann and Napper Cowley used to work for Joseph Spiers, the basket maker," said Cyril Smith. "They were a couple of characters, those two! They were two of the 'Morris Men' on Boxing Day – the 'Napper Joes'. Their work was to go to the osier beds by the river and cut off the canes at the stumps. They would go with their frails on their backs, containing little hooks, with which to do this. They bundled up the osiers into 50 or 60 a bunch. Joseph Spiers had land in Defford Road. There were a lot of springs there and that's where they soaked these osiers – down by the old racecourse."

Walter Palfrey takes up the procedure: "When I was a boy, the old Defford Road School was surrounded by the Growers' Market, with its noises and smells. Behind the boy's playground stood Joseph Spiers' long furnace, which boiled and softened the osiers for basket making. As boys in the playground, we were always aware of the smell of boiling osiers. It was a steamy burning smell. A very sickly smell – like boiling rhubarb. The baskets were made in all sizes and shapes, especially for Pershore Growers' Market. They made bicycle baskets as well."

In wartime, osier rafts were commissioned by the Ministry of Defence, to cover lakes and disguise them from enemy aircraft. Joseph's daughter, Lottie Spiers, kept the Willow Café for many years. She named her final house in Bridge Street 'The Naight', which was the name of her father's osier (willow) island in the River Avon. The word 'Naight' comes from an Anglo-Saxon word, 'eot' or 'ait' meaning 'island'.

BAKER

"We came to Pershore from Worcester in 1924," said Leslie Brookes. "My father's speciality was as a confectioner. So we made a lot of cakes, including wedding cakes. Seven Fancies cost sixpence then. Our rival bakers, Morgan's and Emery's began making cakes, as well."

As a child, I remember Brookes' Cream Horns, Sticky Cushions, Iced Buns, Coconut Pyramids, Maids of Honour, Macaroons .... For a very special treat, my mother might buy some delicious Kunzle cakes, which came from Birmingham. But they cost a lot more than Brookes' Fancies did then!

Leslie Brookes continued: "My father got up at 3 a.m. and he would work until 9 p.m., when he was on his own. I was only a boy at school then. He had to bake and then deliver his bread and cakes, by cart and horse, to the villages, as well as in Pershore.

We had an old-fashioned oven behind our house at number 103 High Street; a half-timbered house. You had to mix everything by hand then – no machines. Two bags of flour were emptied into covered bins, with water and salt added and left overnight. My father would be up at 3 a.m. He used a whisk to knead the dough. He worked 18 hours a day. A loaf cost 2¼d. then. But our lady customers at The Vineyard, in Upper High Street, would only pay us 2d. for a loaf. They used to say: 'We never pay farthings!'

But in the 1920's, a baker was not supposed to dabble in politics – not in Pershore. When we lived in Worcester, my father was a Liberal Trade Unionist, in about 1922. When he came to Pershore, his name was passed on to the local Liberals. But he couldn't canvass or go to meetings, because his work took up all his time. However, someone brought him 100 leaflets to distribute, one night. The elections were coming the following week.

'You must not mix politics with your business!' he was told forcefully, by half-a-dozen people of the town, who were Conservative. 'We do not wish you to serve us any more, as a baker,' they said. And they took away their custom!"

"My father, Jim's, bakery was at 19 Newlands," said Walter Palfrey. "He worked for my uncle, first of all. They took the bread round by horse and cart and also by car. That horse would go up High Street and he knew exactly where my father was going. The horse would go across the street, unbidden, to the next customer!

Jim Palfrey was quite a character. He made lots of people cheerful. On delivery rounds, I could see my father coming down the garden paths and laughing his head off. I knew all the people inside the houses were laughing their heads off too, on hearing his jokes. Dad was always cheerful."

Certain cake recipes were handed down from one Pershore baker to another, for over 50 years. The Handy's bakery, behind Phillips the Grocers, bequeathed special sponge recipes to Baker Hart, who handed them down to Baker Ivor Palfrey.

BARBER

"As a young man," said Laurence Coggins, "I swept up in Les Creswell's barber's shop and did the lathering-up for shaving. Les was my brother-in-law. I had a good grounding, 'cos I had started when I was 11 or 12. By the time I'd left school, I'd been cutting the hair of the boys at Besford Court, where Les had a contract. I enjoyed going to work, 'cos it was so entertaining – a laugh all the time. There were some very funny clients in my shop. They came from all the villages.

One Saturday, they were all merry and bright. The one fellow kept saying: 'Come on, get a move on. I've got to get off.' He didn't care if he had all his hair shaved off. When he was a prisoner of war, it had been shaved off. Herbie Powell came in. I said, 'Herbie, there's a bloke wants his hair cut – just like you used to do it in the Guards'. But the joke was – Herbie had never cut hair in his life before. However, he cut it all off this man's head. They had hid this customer's cap too.

At a quarter to seven that evening, this customer's son came in and asked: 'What was going on this afternoon, Cog? Our old man been in for a haircut? Didn't he have some stick when he got home! And he went to sleep on the sofa and his cap fell off his bald head!'"

BUILDER

"I got a job in the building trade and I've been in it ever since," said Alec Witts. "I was with Tom Simpkins for two years. Then I was a tramp brickie for five years. I used to go round the towns – to Coventry, Gloucester, Longbridge. I always think you get on better with strangers – because there is more respect between you. I travelled by motor-bike. To buy my motor-bike, I lived in a tool shed, on the job, right through the winter. That was at Stoulton, at the motor house. I used to work by moonlight there."

Sid Champken told me: "I was born in Pershore in 1909. I worked for Tom Simpkins on houses. The first house he built, was for Mr. Bramford, the schoolmaster. (The Bramford family enjoyed living in this house in Station Road, for nearly 50 years!). Then he built the Police Station in Three Springs Road. A firm from Birmingham built the Senior School in Station Road. I worked on that. It took about two years to build. They seem to build quicker now. Everything used to be done by hand.

Pershore is five or six times as big as before the Second World War, with all these estates. When the war started, we worked on the aerodrome and I was made General Foreman then. Up to 1939, we were building the new Junior School (Abbey Park Middle School). They couldn't get the timber then, 'cos of the war. So it has flat roofs."

GARDENER

"My father was gardener at The Mount (also known as Pershore Hall) for Edward Humphries," said Blanche Dufty. "I used to be always up there, what with the caretaker's three children I looked after, and with my father being in the greenhouses. He used to grow beautiful grapes and cucumbers, tomatoes and pears. The roses he grew were superb. The 'Tower of London' grew around the front of the house. That was a small rose, which opened out pink at the edges and cream in the middle. He grew great cabbage roses around the tennis court – red and pink.

I always admired a Maltese cross in roses that he did. It was the very, very dark velvet, nearly black rose, and cream in the middle. It was absolutely lovely. Around the breakfast window, there was a rose that I've never seen since. It was a green rose, named 'Marchioneal'. It opened up to a lovely yellow.

My father earned about fifteen shillings for a 72-hour week. Of course, he only got paid if he worked. If it rained, he was sent home for the day, without pay.

On the farm, behind the house, there was a pool for the horses. And the orchards had the most beautiful Blenheims you could see. That was towards Gigbridge. Mrs. Humphries named that the 'Twin Orchard', in the year she had twins.

And then the Deakin family came on the scene, to The Mount, and upset all that the Humphries' had done. All Mr. Deakin wanted to do was to grow fruit for jam. He didn't want the flowers which my father was growing, with tomatoes and grapes. He wouldn't allow my father any coke for the greenhouses' stoves, so Dad had to beg bits of wood for that. And yet, they expected these bunches of lovely black grapes. There was a lovely avenue of chestnuts at The Mount, but they have all gone."

LAUNDRESS

"I was born in Pinvin," said Elsie Barnes. "I don't remember father a bit. But they say he was a good father. I think he was some gardener for Mr. Hooper, at The Croft, Station Road. Then we came to live in this very, very old house in Newlands.

We used to do all the church laundry, we sisters, in Canon Bark's time. We did all the choir surplices for the Abbey. My oldest sister was a genius at that work; Margaret. Canon Bank used to go to Pinvin Church every fortnight. He used to call on us on Sunday morning and say: 'I'm going to Pinvin tonight, so get ready and come with me. And we went with him, in the car, to the service in our old home village church. And do you know, we are, from the beginning of childhood, real church people.

My mother did laundry. As children, we were always given a little bit of housework to do when we come home from school. And my family worked for Colonel Taylor of Birlingham for 50 years, from this house. We done all his laundry work and Mrs. Taylor's. They were nice people. They even had the roof put on this house, at their own expense. Now, wasn't that nice?

We dried the laundry in the garden and we've got a drying shelter on the court outside. Our old wooden mangle is still there. It's a humble home, but it's been a clean one. As long as I can, I shall stop here. But I'm very lonely sometimes, now that my two sisters have passed on. I'm the last one in this world; not a relation anywhere. Quite a few people come in and they have a cup of tea with me. Joan Wicks is a great friend of mine. She comes every Sunday and has tea with me. I says, 'Joan, however do you cut the bread and butter so nicely? She says: 'I was trained to that'."

DRESSMAKER

"In the 1920's, there were several Dressmakers in Pershore," said Nora Bristow. "I can remember Mrs. Tillman, Miss Whatmore, and Mrs. Swain, who made my wedding dress.

But their main work came from doing alterations, in those days. We could not afford new material. Most of my clothes were handed down from my older sister and Mrs. Tillman altered them to fit me. People's clothes lasted longer then, being of very good quality stuff. So the dressmakers either shortened or lengthened clothes and gave them a 'second life'.

If you had relatives with a shop, you were lucky. My cousin in London brought down clothes for us. It was the same for men. They depended on jumble sales. They made their clothes last.

My mother made my Confirmation dress of white crêpe-de-chine. We added a blue sash later on, and that was my Sunday best dress for years! So many people of my generation have bad feet, because they had to make do with other people's old shoes, which did not fit their feet properly."

IN SERVICE

Blanche Dufty was in service at Worcester, before the First World War. She worked in a big house for Dr. Gostlin and his wife. He was a surgeon at The Royal Infirmary, Worcester.

"They came from Diss in Norfolk," said Blanche, "and they brought their own coachman with them. They were very wealthy. Dr. Gostlin would send an old man to the back streets with a stack of envelopes of money for the poor families of Worcester. And his wife was good too. They had no children, but they had four maids, a chauffeur, and a man used to wind the clocks up every week. A man came twice a week to clean the windows. And a man came from the carpet place to take up the carpets and clean them.

The house was opposite the Institute, at 30 Foregate Street. The Mistress was the most particular woman you ever knew. She made me what I am. After I had dusted in the doorway, she would kneel down to see if I had dusted everywhere – to see if I had moved the chair. At the bottom of the stairs was the gong. You always had to put the light on there. It was very dark, coming down the stairs. One day, I skipped dusting there. I hadn't dusted round the beautiful clock. The Mistress rang the bell to summon me. I was 16 then. She said, 'Blanche, don't ever leave that again.' I've seen her going along ledges and looking for dust. I was there for five years.

They had a lot of visitors and dinner parties. My goodness me! We was up 'til about two o'clock in the morning. And you had got to be up again at seven a.m. One day, the Mistress rang the bell 'cos her morning tea hadn't come up. We had all overslept after the big party the night before! When she went on holiday, she bought me a candlestick. 'Many a fall, but you get up', is written on it. She was very, very nice.

They had a huge garden with well laid-out borders and shrubs, as well as the tennis and croquet lawns. We were given pocket money to help with the weeding! I was paid £8 a year, but we were fed and looked after for that. We normally had to supply our own clothes. Mind you, sometimes, the Mistress would take us up to her bedroom and let us select a hat or dress from her wardrobe, to try on and keep. What she didn't realise was, that while the house was empty, the maids used to try on all her dresses anyway!

Sundays were often the busiest days, as we had early morning service to attend at the Cathedral, as well as the evening service there, with the Doctor's wife. We all had to dress up for that."

This disciplined way of life influenced Blanche and other maids everywhere, for good. They were given good food, learnt social graces and were surrounded by beautiful furniture. Blanche remembered the furnishings of The Mount in Pershore. "There were cedar doors and marble wash-stands and a stone lion and unicorn at the top of the stairs. But where are they now? By the pool, there was a stone child holding a basket of fish. Beautiful it was. But it went.

In the Servants' Hall, the fireplace was carved with a motto: 'Waste not, want not'. The eldest son of the Humphries' was good at carving. He done that. And on the stone stairs, was a saying in Latin: 'Every true man loves his country'. I was told that and I've never forgotten it."

Nora Bristow went in service, at the age of 14, to Dr. and Mrs. Kennedy, in Broad Street, Pershore, until 1936, when she married Les Bristow. Nora went first as a nursemaid to Miss Jean Kennedy, a small girl of five. Later on, Nora did everything, include cook. Her hours were busy. Not often did she get a full half-day off. She had every other Sunday afternoon, from 5.30 'til 10 p.m. Her pay was £1 per month, but she had her keep.

Nora speaks: "I wore a navy dress with a white apron, in the mornings. For afternoons, my white apron was daintier and I wore a frilled cap. My mother washed my caps and aprons at home. She used a goffering iron for the frills.

It was a hard life, getting up early to make all the fires, and light the boiler to heat the pipes through the house. Breakfast had to be ready for 8.30 a.m.

The Kennedy's lived at the Manor House at the bottom of Bridge Street, before they moved to Western House. I was terrified of the long, dark, unlit, rambling passages at the Manor House, when I was left on my own. My employers would often be out at night, playing bridge. The wind would bang the trees, which would creak and groan.

But you had to make the best of your job in those days. You had no choice. It did us good. We did not expect life to be easy."

Marion Knight said: "My sister and I came to Pershore in 1929, by train, for my interview at Pershore Cottage Hospital. We were taken to Birlingham, to the house of Miss Dukes, for tea. I remember that Miss Dukes' maid, Lavinia, wore a maid's uniform and a white lace cap with streamers down her back."

ERRAND BOY AND SHOP ASSISTANT

Errand boys of the 1920's and '30's were told to be polite to their shop's customers when delivering goods, to go to the back door and to close the gate behind them.

Jim Dowler told me: "I was errand boy for Phillips' Stores. I earned four shillings a week. From there, I went to the London Central Meat Company, for seventeen shillings a week. Then I went to Mr. Wildbore, the coal merchant."

Alec Witts said: "I went as errand boy to the International Stores. Then I was taken on as an apprentice. But I hated it. There were apprenticeship papers to sign in those days, if you were apprenticed to shop trade as a provisions hand. A young person would not be allowed to sign them today. All the groceries had to be cut up by hand. There was no pre-packing, like today. There was a lot of skill in it, really.

When you served a customer, it was all paid for by cash. The assistant would have to add it all up <u>mentally</u>. Mental arithmetic was a strong point in those days of no computers."

HAIRDRESSER

Rene Giles said: "Mother was taken ill with a stroke, so I did hairdressing at my home. Later on, I cycled to villages, as well as Pershore, to do hairdressing in people's homes. My customers were my friends. They gave me wedding presents."

NIGHT SOIL MAN

"You had to get home early," said Kitty Haines. "If you had been to the pictures and you met the night soil men – the smell was terrible! When we lived in Bearcroft, I was frightened, as a child, to see the men's light going along and them emptying the pans. As soon as the public houses were closed, they began their work. Just turned ten p.m. on a Friday night."

The Night Soil Men were accompanied by a horse-drawn vehicle, which had many names. Perhaps the sweetest of these, was 'the Honey Cart'! Next morning, if you saw a sprinkling of carbolic powder on the road, that showed where the cart had stood.

"In the <u>old</u> houses, down High Street and Bridge Street," continued Kitty Haines, "you only had them once in six months. That was for the 'pits', as they were called. They used to put ashes over the 'soil', in <u>those</u> privies. If you didn't leave the night soil men a drink, there was a terrible mess next morning. But if you left them a drink, it was as clean as a whistle!"

Those were the same men who used to work on the dustcarts in the daytime. They used to have a week on days, and a week on nights. It was Orchard Ditch, where they went to dump it all, by the old cholera ground. It's now Orchard Road, and full of houses!"

Rosie Long recalled: "I was coming home from Cropthorne one evening. I had just started courting my husband at the time. It used to be between 10 and 11 p.m. when the night soil men started going up here in Newlands. But we were late coming home that evening. Pooh! Believe me! There was Mr. Irons, Jack Long and Harry Boulter. Those were three I remember doing that work."

"Our privy had wooden seats and buckets," said Esme Westcott. "Ours had a contraption on the back. You pulled a handle and sawdust came out! It was most intriguing. It did the trick, because they mixed Jeyes Powder with the sawdust – more hygienic. The night soil men dug pits in different places. One was at the back of where the swimming pool is now. It was all open fields then. Pershore was a very small place then."

WORKING FOR MR. A. C. SMITH, THE CHEMIST

Mary Stubbs told me: "In 1939, I left the Co-op Market and went to work for Mr. Arthur Smith, the chemist, in Broad Street. My wage was still 7/6d per week. He was certainly a hard taskmaster, but then that made me thorough. My wage when I left was twenty-five shillings per week.

I used to arrive at 8.30 a.m. and my first job was to sweep the step and pavement. Then I had to clean the brass handle of the shop door and the letter-box and the brass rail that ran along the counter. I had to light the burners for the sealing wax. I then took the ledgers through to the office and entered all the entries from the Day Book.

Once a month, I had to make out the Accounts on pink bill-heads. The biggest accounts went to Derretts of Little Comberton, Mrs. Firkins of Eckington and Mr. Stephenson of Fladbury. These customers had regular orders each month, of all Mr. Smith's own preparations to sell in their stores.

I used to help replenish the stocks of patent medicine, which Mr. Smith made up for sale. There was Parrish's Food, Liquid Paraffin, and Blackberry Balsam, made from blackberries picked on Bredon Hill. The kids brought Mr. Smith these blackberries. A halfpenny a pound he would pay them.

Children were given Cod Liver Emulsion mixed with Blackberry Balsam, and it was lovely to take. If you had too much, it made you a bit squiffy! Mr. Smith also made up health Salts, Plum Preserving Powders and Rheumatic Pills No. 9056, which are still available in powder form from Ogles the chemists, who own his shop today.

Avena Skin Food was mixed on a marble slab with a flat knife, until it was creamy. Then it was put into white porcelain jars of two sizes. It was sealed with a blue and white band and labelled. This product sold very well and was sent to titled ladies all over the country. I learnt to pack parcels to look perfect, as Mr. Smith would not have any job done slipshod.

There were Cow Drenches, Horse Drenches and Powders for Pigs, to mix for the vets. But the worst job was the Foot rot Paste, which was mixed in the cellar. It was mixed in a huge pestle and mortar, which hung from the ceiling and was very heavy. It was a very thick black paste.

I hated going down to the cellar, as there were often dead mice in the paste. I used to pray that Mr. Smith would not send me down for a Winchester of anything off the shelves, for there were huge cockroaches behind some of them. But as luck would have it, I never dropped one of those Winchester jars.

Another job I had to do was to go to the Post Office twice a day, 12 noon and 5 p.m. with the medicines for the country patients. The postmen took out these medicines, which were carried in a huge square leather bag, with a brass plate on it. It was quite heavy.

From 5 to 7 p.m. my evening job was to help Mr. Smith in the dispensary. One job I liked doing was packing up the bottles of medicine and the pills and sealing them with sealing wax. Patients got green medicine when they had 'flu and a red tonic medicine when they got better.

Compliments from Mr. Smith were few and far between, but he <u>did</u> say once, 'Your copper-plate writing is most beautiful, Miss Howes.' It always puzzled me why 'Upper Class' medicines were packed in white paper and the 'Poorer Class' medicines were packed in pale green, thin paper. Perhaps it was just Class Distinction!

Twice weekly, we had all the X-Rays to develop from the Cottage Hospital. Mr. Smith taught me to do this and I enjoyed doing it. The darkroom was situated under the stairs and it was painted bright red. My own office was really a glorified lean-to at the back of the house. My chair used to go through the floor 'cos it was so rotten.

We had two large wooden vats in the back room, in which all the empty bottles were washed. One was filled with hot water and one with cold. We had various young girls to do this job, but no-one stayed long, for Mr. Smith was such a temperamental man.

He used to smoke a foul-smelling pipe. During the war, he sent me out to the Post Office for stamps and also to the tobacconist's, if they had any tobacco, which was short then. I used to queue for more than half an hour to get him an ounce of tobacco. Then he would grumble because I had taken a long time!

Eventually, I was drafted into a job of national importance in the Air Ministry and went to R.A.F. Defford as Clerk of Works Assistant. I met Sydney, who was stationed at R.A.F. Pershore and we got married. Give me the old days every time. Even though the money was less, the times were happier."

CHAUFFEUR TO THE PRIME MINISTER

Blanche Dufty told me of the interesting career of her brother, Arthur Bell. "Dr. Emerson was the first in Pershore to have a car and my brother was his chauffeur. There used to be some big tennis parties at Amerie Court – 'At Home' days. The Emersons were present, driven by their chauffeur. Sir Herbert and Lady Whiteley from Grimley were there too.

Lady Whiteley asked my brother to be her chauffeur. So he gave in his notice to Dr. Emerson and he was with the Whiteleys for over thirty years. He was such a smart man, my brother. He used to take them to London for the London season and to Ascot. He would mix with royalty.

In 1936, the Prime Minister, Stanley Baldwin's, daughter had married Lady Whiteley's son. Stanley Baldwin wrote a letter to my brother: 'We've got to get to the House of Commons today, very quickly, to see about this Abdication crisis.' So Arthur drove the Prime Minister to London from Worcestershire. Two detectives followed behind. My brother knew all the short cuts.

Just at 11 a.m. he got the Prime Minister there – but the detectives had lost the Prime Minister! My brother always laughed about that. He was in the kitchen of the House of Commons, having tea, and these detectives came rushing in. That car he was driving used to light up the Newlands when Arthur brought it there, to see my mother – always at midnight.

Lady Diana Whiteley said, many years later, that my brother Arthur Bell, was the smartest man in Worcestershire. He wore green livery with a cream collar. Their crest was the stag head on the silver buttons. He had a black peaked cap and black leggings. But he didn't want to acknowledge me outside the Guildhall in Worcester, when he was taking her Ladyship there!

He used to tell us about the people he had been with and the swimming sessions at night. He told us of the Prince of Wales (later Edward VIII) coming down and the Duke of Kent and of their capers. Arthur used to hide among the bushes to have a look. He said to the detective: 'I'm doing the same as you!' They were given lovely dinners at banquets.

Arthur drove Stanley Baldwin about a lot, during the Abdication time. And he was a gentleman himself. He had been with them so long. Mr. Baldwin was the M.P. for Bewdley, so he was often in Worcestershire. I was very proud of my brother, Arthur, because he was a gentleman."

THE FIRST LADY MAYOR OF PERSHORE 1991-1993

"I've been a Councillor since 1982," said Betty Hughes. "During my ninth year, I was appointed Pershore's first Lady Mayor; in May 1991. You are allowed two years' term of office. I've really enjoyed my years as Mayor. You get an involvement with a cross-section of the community. Each committee is different.

I am Patron of the Perscoran Brass Ensemble and President of Pershore Operatic and Dramatic Society. I'm a governor of one of the local schools. Jack Heeks and I visit local churches – Eckington, Birlingham, Wick. My logo, as Mayor, has been: 'Unity within the Community'. To do that, you have to understand village life too. The villagers must feel that they belong. The Evesham Mayor is looking towards the youth, like me. I take an interest in the local Cadets, and girls can now join Army Cadets. We must encourage the youth. They are our future."

FOOTNOTE

Edward Humphries made the wrought ironwork for Pershore railway station and the gas lamp standards for Pershore town.

The wedding of Edwin Smith and Ellen Payne in the 1890's. He was Custodian of Pershore Cemetery, as was his son Cyril Smith in later years.

Elmley Castle about 1910

63

7—Opening of the new Central Market. Mr. A. Beynon, proprietor.

9—Holy Cross Parish Council support Pinvin's request to the Great Western Railway Company to start a motor bus service between the station and Pershore.)

9—Cup and medals of the North Cotswold Football League presented to the winners, Pershore Rovers.

10—Mr. D. E. Tower obtained a first class prize for his exhibit of bottled fruits, at the Royal Agricultural Show, at Shrewsbury.

12—Special Services for the 110th Anniversary of the Baptist Sunday Schools.

13—The County Licensing Committee renewed the order as to Pershore continuing a "populous place"

14—Registration of the new Central Market with a capital of £1,000.

14—The District Council informed the Cropthorne Parish Council that they were unable to proceed with the Housing Scheme on account of the price of land.

19—Dedication Service at Bredon Church. One of the new windows was given by the Bishop to commemorate Bishop Prideaux, a predecessor of his in Cromwellian days.

19—Death of Mrs. Margaret Knight (23), daughter of Mr. and Mrs. Ballinger, Croft Cottage, Pershore.

21—Property auction sale at Pershore, the Coach and Horses, Pinvin, being sold for £610, and Gore House, Pershore, was withdrawn at £750, and the butcher's premises, owned by Mrs. Kings, were withdrawn at £350.

21—Dorothy, second daughter of the late Mr. Charles Field, of Pershore, and of Mrs Field, Gloucester, was married to Mr. C. Southern, of Gloucester.

21—William Bayliss, of Evesham, was killed by the Bristol express at Wadborough siding, his little grandson having a marvellous escape.

22—Conference of parishioners with regard to making Pinvin and Broughton separate benefices, and raising the living of Pershore.

22—Death of the 5 year-old son of Mr. and Mrs. Salter, of Hopney Cottages, caused by drinking boiling water from a kettle.

25—The "Diocesan Magazine" announced that Sir Richard Temple, of Kempsey, had kindly consented to return the old 12th century font, which was discarded from the Abbey about 70 years ago.

26—The united Church choirs of Wyre, Fladbury and Throckmorton, had an outing to Weston-super-Mare

27—Rick fire at White House Farm, Charlton. Damage estimated at about £200.

31—Abberton and District Fruit and Vegetable Show, opened by Mrs. Eyres Monsell. Very successful.

AUGUST.   1914

1—Harvest reports prove present season's crops to be fairly satisfactory, and considerably better than its immediate predecessors.

3—Bank holiday. Bredon Agricultural Show was quite a success.

4—England declared war on Germany as from 11 o'clock to-night, in consequence of the violation of Belgium's neutrality. Worcestershire Territorials recalled from camp at Minehead.

5—Intense excitement on the news that war had been declared. People began to lay in stocks of foodstuffs, and the price of goods advanced enormously. Sugar was 5d. per lb., butter 1/6, and bread advanced 1d. per loaf. Banks were closed for 5 days.

5—Mobilisation of troops. Territorials and Yeomanry left for Worcester.

5—Meeting at the Music Hall. Major Checketts attended to enroll any volunteers who had served under the colours.

6—Horses bought in the Pershore district by Mr. G. Dudley Smith, of Strensham Court, who held Government compulsory powers.

View of Pershore from Marriott's Hill, before the 'new' bridge.

Entrance to The Square, Pershore about 1910.

Broad Street, known as The Square, in the 1930's.

65

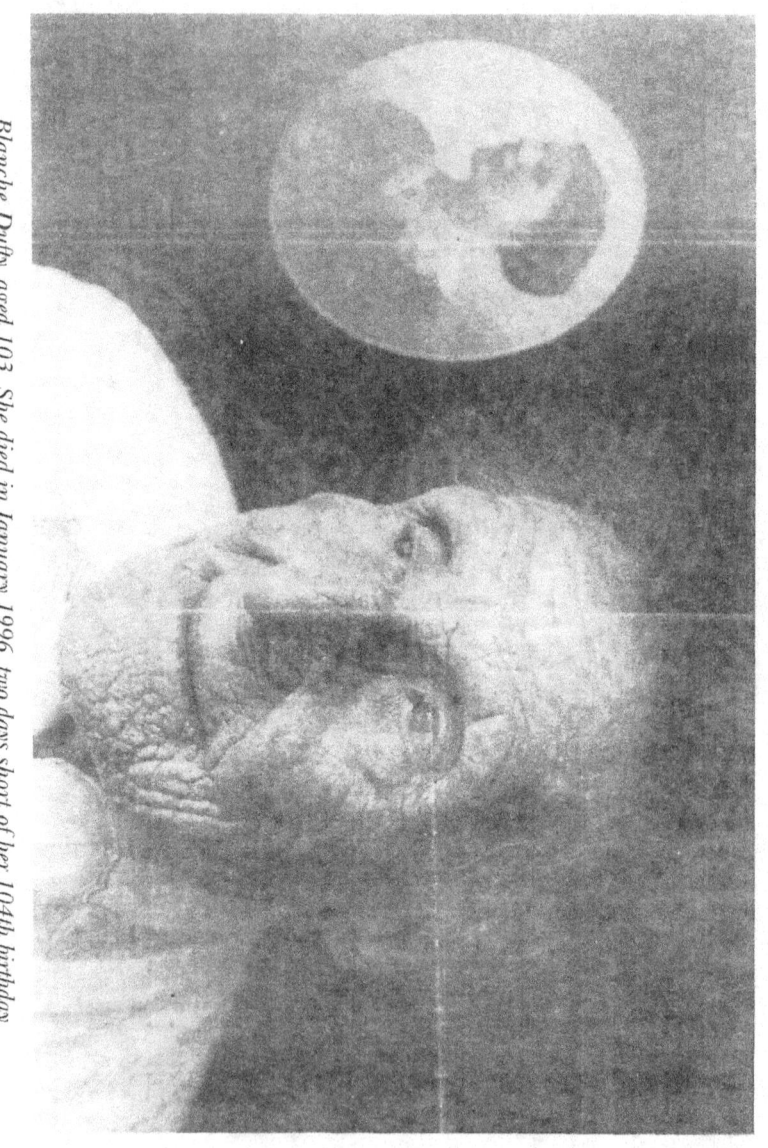

Blanche Dufy, aged 103. She died in January 1996, two days short of her 104th birthday.

Pershore Postmen on parade c. 1936. They wear their War Medals. Head Postmaster, Mr. Rogers, wears a morning coat (and top hat, not shown). His little son is in front . Second and third from right are Albert Champken and Ralph Willis. Note the telegraph boy, far left.

Lyn Westcott grafting a fruit tree in 1937.

George Heeks uses an early form of Rotivator on the Westcott Brothers' Fruit Farm at The Ford, Pershore.

George Heeks picks apples at his employers' fruit farm, The Ford, in the 1930's.

SHOPS

Shops in 1931 – from the Official Guide Book of Pershore

H. C. Swann M.P.S.
Abbey Pharmacy

A. V. Derrett
High Class Baker
Post Office Stores, Wyre Piddle. Tel. 62

Charles Hiskins
General Draper
London House, High Street
The best brands of hosiery stocked.

The Avon Restaurant
Bridge Street
Proprietor: Miss J. Salmon
Accommodation for Commercials and Cyclists. Good Beds.
Terms Moderate. Teas. Cold Meats a speciality.
Pork Pies and Sausages. Best Confectionery and Tobacco.

K. Kettell
52 High Street
Saddler and Harness Maker.
Walking Sticks. Dog collars supplied and engraved.

G. Phillips and Sons
42 High Street
Family Grocers. Established 65 years.
Our motto "Quality and Service". Tel. 61

D. T. Trigg
Broad Street
High Class Ladies' and Gents' Hairdresser

E. D. Cornelius
18a High Street
General and Fancy Draper and Milliner
Hosiery and Baby Linen a speciality

Christine Bloxham
Ladies' and Children's Hair specialist
Agent for all leading makes in knitting wools
Inspection invited!

Epicam – Epicure Ham Co. Ltd.
Hams are cured using a very old recipe, handed down. Hams are rubbed, daily, by hand, in various pickles, for six weeks, imparting a mellow and delicate flavour.

Devilled Epicam a very high-class relish, which is quickly becoming the essential to all <u>real</u> picnics. This delectable sandwich filler is unique.

Chapter five

WE WENT SHOPPING

In the 1920's and '30's, Pershore, like small towns everywhere, had numerous small shops and no supermarkets. The shopkeepers became personal friends of their customers, in many cases. The town's population in the early 1930's was only between three and four thousand.

Each shop had its own special smell. In those days, a boy was given sixpence on a Saturday morning, to spend as fourpence for a haircut and twopence for the cinema. A halfpenny worth of chips went a long way.

MISS GLADYS HARRIS was a pale-faced lady with glasses, who, for generations, kept a General Stores in Broad Street. It was a tiny shop, with stone flags for the floor. The door was always open, regardless of the weather. Miss Harris used to sell everything – even pomegranates. In the 1950's, she would sell black bananas for sixpence a bunch.

Ethel Rock recalled Miss Harris as a kind person and generous to her customers. "Miss Harris used to say to my son, 'Well, how is your Mum? She can have her sweets on us.' 'Er never charged the full price of sweets to many kiddies. 'Er was ever so good to the children. My daughter, Margaret, went to chat to 'er for about 'alf an hour. Miss Harris said to 'er, 'You can have your sweets cheaper, 'cos you work in the Cottage Hospital. I loved Miss Harris."

MISS CORNELIUS had a draper's shop in High Street. It was a long, narrow shop with long counters, and chairs to sit on, while she talked to her customers. Walter Palfrey remembers: "She would put everything back on the long shelves before she turned to you to serve you. People had all the time in the world in those days. Miss Cornelius would wrap everything she sold in paper and tie it with string."

In those days, you could take a small selection of dresses, blouses or skirts home, 'on appro' (approval) to try on at home and bring back the next day. Ethel Rock said: "We used to have all our clothes from Miss Cornelius. Many people who saved money in the Shoe Club for Christmas would go to her shop for underclothes – dear, but good stuff. Miss Cornelius would be in that shop even when she was feeling ill."

Those were the days of long 'combs' or "Chilprufe" combinations, for men and women, to combat the non-existence of central heating in houses. Girls wore "Liberty" bodices over their vests and thick 'gym' knickers. Men wore long flannel pants and hand-knitted woollen socks, which needed frequent darning. Corsets, suspender belts, and thick lisle stockings were frequently worn by women and girls.

MISS NEWICK kept a fruit and florist's shop in Bridge Street. She also had a snack bar for cups of tea and lardy cakes. She greeted you with "Hello-o-o." Miss Newick told me: "I kept open until 10 o'clock at night. Some of the customers who came late were employed on the fields. Mine was the only shop open really late – for any emergency, such as tea, sugar, and eggs. I had no holidays. My parents depended on me.

My father used to make the wreaths and crosses – the florist's work. My mother helped him wire up the flowers. It all takes time. You have to use a thin wire for the stems and a thicker wire over that. Delicate stems like violets would snap off, unless you used very thin wire. If an urgent order came in, Mother and I did the wiring of the flowers and father did the making up. It was a full time job for me."

MRS. WINWOOD in Bridge Street, had a fruit and vegetable shop. "She used to make all sorts of wine," Esme Westcott told me. "She got us to go out and pick dandelion heads for her, and blackberries, elderberries, elder flowers, cowslips. She used to give us three whole pennies for a peck basket of what she wanted for her wine. (A peck is about 7 or 8 pounds weight). I don't think I was allowed to know what happened to the wine. I certainly never tasted it. Perhaps that was because I signed the pledge when I was eight years old!"

MISS SALMON kept the Avon Tea Rooms in Bridge Street. She also sold cooked meats, boiled hams, pork pies. (See CHARACTERS chapter for more about Miss Salmon). Alec Witts said: "Miss Salmon was a fussy woman. She had to be down on us kids. She was a very old-fashioned woman. We used to swear she took a sausage out of the window, feather-dusted it and put it back!"

THE INTERNATIONAL STORES in High Street, had once been the Bell Hotel. In the ballroom, behind the shop, the rafters were painted gold. Harry Watts, the wheelwright, had his premises behind the Stores.

PROTHERO'S the grocers, was on the North corner of Broad Street. If customers kept coming in the shop, Prothero's would keep open, until perhaps 7 p.m. Some of the assistants would cycle to different villages each day, to take orders. They baked their own bread. The shiny, blackened bricks of their Hygienic Bakery wall, lining the North side of Broad Street, offered welcome warmth, on a cold day, to generations of passers-by and children, waiting for a bus.

PHILLIPS the grocers, in High Street, (now Feasts), opposite the Working Men's Club, "had beautifully polished floors and all the packets of food were hand-wrapped," Walter Palfrey said. "Harry Phillips and Mr. Howard served in that shop for years and years. They would always blame each other if things went wrong. They would weigh out sugar, tea, coffee, etc. on a flat blue 'sugar' paper and parcel it up, tucking the corners in. There was no sellotape then! They patted the butter into shape with wooden bats."

<u>MOORE'S</u> (later Harrington's) was a high-class draper's shop, where the Midland Bank is now. Blanche Dufty said: "My son was errand-boy for Moore's. They sold beautiful linen. The other day, I gave a friend a table-cloth that I had had from their shop. The table-cloths kept beautiful for years."

Ruth Brant remembered: "Harrington's had brown lino on the floor – very shiny. In winter, they had little round stoves which used to give out very little heat!" Walter Palfrey recalled: "The shop assistant pulled the cord and a box shot across to the cash desk and back again with your change. There were old wooden counters and chairs. You could sit down at the counter in a leisurely way."

<u>BROWN'S THE IRONMONGER'S</u> is still a hardware shop, facing Broad Street. Rene Giles recalled: "The Browns were such an airy-fairy family. Ma Brown would say to me: 'Have you got anywhere else to go, Mrs. Giles?' 'Yes.' 'Well, while you've gone, Daddy (or Da) will look and find it for you.' The shop was in a real pickle. But they were a lovely family, really."

Walter Palfrey said: "The whole shop was complete chaos. <u>They</u> knew where things were, but how any stock-taker would know. It was a family business. They all came forward to serve you. Those verandas over the Brown's shop and over the chemist's next door, were lovely vantage points for watching all the parades through the streets."

<u>HISKINS, THE DRAPER'S</u> in High Street. "I used to ask for sixpence worth of those bits for making patchwork. They'd got all day to serve you in them days."

<u>LANE'S BOOT AND SHOE SHOP</u> in High Street. Blanche Dufty told me: "Mr. Lane always kept me a nice pair of boots, or shoes, off my Shoe Club Card, at school. We paid into this Shoe Club card sixpence a week. If I hadn't got quite enough money on my Shoe Card, he'd put a special pair in the window, for show, until I could pay for them. He let me have a pair of

button-up-to-the-knee boots, even though I couldn't pay in full for them. My mother was a sweetheart of his!"

"MONKEY" MILLER in High Street. "They had everything in clothes," said Roy Beard. "They came from the Banbury area. Mrs. Miller used to wear a man's cap and smoke a pipe. They parcelled your purchases up with brown paper and string. You would buy some trousers and a jacket and they would throw in a cap, or a tie, 'for free'."

THE MISSES GRUNDY in High Street, were very ladylike in their confectionery shop. "As children, we went there for broken biscuits. They even had a special Christmas Showroom, displaying Christmas cakes. To us children, to see all these goodies, was like entering the grotto of Father Christmas himself!"

H. C. SWANN, THE CHEMIST in High Street (formerly Dowty's now Cook's). The Swanns were a musical family. They formed their own family orchestra, with the grandfather, Mr. Sumner, conducting. Ella Patricia Ardern one of the Swann daughters, remembers her father's shop. "Our chemist's shop was two shops together. You walked from one shop into the other. Our large house, behind the shop, was rambling. It had a front staircase and a back staircase – good for playing 'Hide and Seek'!

From our double bay window upstairs – our sitting room – we could watch people shopping and all the street events. Our mother never needed to go shopping, because the grocer, the butcher, the baker, the greengrocer, all delivered to the house. We had an apple loft to store our apples from the garden."

MRS. KETTELL'S shop was a Saddlery, on the corner of Church Street with High Street, and had a lovely smell of leather. John McCormick, who worked there, made very good handbags and purses, too.

<u>MRS. BRANT'S FISH SHOP</u> in Newlands, is remembered by Jack Heeks, because there was a big slot in the counter. "When you paid your threepence, (twopenny fish and one pennyworth of chips) she used to throw your money down the slot and you heard it chunk into a drawer. There were no tills then."

<u>MRS. BARBER</u> of Church Street sold vegetables. You walked <u>down</u> a step into her shop, which had a stone floor. It was so dark in there, you could scarcely see Mrs. Barber.

<u>MOSELEY'S</u> in High Street sold shoes (later Lennards). In the 1920's the popular 'Lotus' and 'Delta' shoes cost 16 shillings and ninepence a pair.

<u>SWEET SHOPS</u> There were several. Mrs. Mence's was in High Street. Mr. Butt, the tobacconist in High Street, also sold sweets. "He was rather severe and wore a brown overall." Mrs. Twigg took over Brookes' shop in the Newlands and sold sweets. Mrs. Nutting in Broad Street made home-made sweets.

Jack Heeks remembers names of some of the sweets you could buy in those days: Coconut Squares, Lucky Bags, Cayley Suckers with liquorice sticks, Jelly Babies, Humbugs, Raspberry and Pear Drops .....

Betty Tuffin remembers the simply <u>delicious</u> ice-cream made by Mrs. Brooks in Newlands. Betty would be sent across by her grandmother to buy a basinful of ice-cream for sixpence.

At one time, there were six butchers in Pershore: Elkerton's in Bridge Street, the London Central, the Co-op, Wood's, Brown's (all in High Street) and Bick's (later Annis) in Newlands.

<u>THE KOSY TEA ROOMS</u> in High Street, were owned by the Misses Fitz, a pair of elderly ladies, who also sold sweets. It was not 'til after the Second World War, that there appeared THE GREEN DOOR CAFÉ, run by the Misses Butterworth. A little later, there was THE WILLOW TEA ROOMS kept by Miss Lottie Spiers. That café had a <u>blue</u> door.

Chapter six

WORKING ON THE LAND

The Vale of Evesham has long been noted for its market gardening, and for its vegetables and orchards. But the growing of crops depends on skilful management and reliable workers on the ground. And in time of war, allotments are valuable assets.

Ellen Willis told me: "The land in Pershore was all owned by the Coventry's. There were orchards everywhere, as far as the railway station. That's how Coventry Terrace and the Coventry Arms pub got their names."

Cyril Smith said: "There was a sheep dip in Defford Road. The farmers used to bring the sheep in hundreds. I remember great flocks of sheep coming past the cemetery, down to this sheep dip. There was another sheep dip in Head Street and a cattle market as well. It was opposite the Mission Hall in Head Street (now St. Agatha's Hall)."

Ethel Rock said: "Pershore Fruit Market always had nice fruit. We always went there at Christmas-time for the apples for the children. Some lovely apples, especially Blenheims. My husband worked for a Mr. Poole. He had a lot of Bramleys, Worcester Pearmains, Russets. They used to store them.

The Pooles lived in London and they left the work entirely in the hands of my husband. We had to pick the fruit and beetroot. Turnips we tied and Swedes we done. Then we did radishes and onions. We had to do 240 radishes for tenpence. The land was behind the Abbey Garage, near the jam factory. The ground was called The Furlongs. Mr. Tarrant of the Abbey Garage took over the factory with the garage."

"Nearly everyone had an allotment." Said Nora Bristow. "They would bring barrows of produce to market to earn a few pounds to pay for coal, or the doctor's bill. Women worked on the land for extra money. My parents, the Collins, had some land at Stocking Brook – fruit trees. Earnings from this fruit helped to pay bills."

Fanny Newick told me: "We had a fruit and florist's shop in Bridge Street, in the 1930's. My father rented the kitchen garden from the Benedictine monks at the Abbey House. The house originally belonged to the Hudson family. My father supplied the monks with produce from that kitchen garden. They were too busy with their own monastic work, you see. Father also rented the greenhouses and the small flower beds. Mr. Berry had the orchard attached to the ground. He used to keep pigs."

Ethel Rock said: "We used to go pea-picking in the morning, at about four o'clock 'til about twelve dinner-time. We could earn between twelve and twenty shillings a day.

I went plum-picking up to Mr. Westcott's at The Ford, in Station road. We had quite nice times up there. We used to go hop-picking at Wick. We walked everywhere. We've had some good times!"

Blanche Dufty said: "Mr. Deakin at The Mount wanted fruit for canning – raspberries, logans, strawberries. Acres and acres was put out. I picked them with my mother. The land there goes down to Broughton.

At half-past three in the morning, I used to start out and knock up a woman on the corner. I got a prop and knocked on the bedroom window. We used to tiptoe up Priest lane, so as not to wake people. And we were down on the fruit farm at 4 a.m. You knocked off at 10 a.m. You were lucky to earn five shillings. Deakin's jam factory was at Wigan and Torrington."

Esme Westcott said: Pershore Co-op Market was full of produce in the old days. It was an auction market. There was great competition. They reckoned there were certain places on the floor, where they got a better price – either first, or last, but not in the middle. There was a great scramble.

In the season, they used to start queuing outside our family house in Abbey Place, at about half-past five in the morning.

The queue of drays and horses would stretch right through

Broad Street and down to the Bridges. The sale started at 11 a.m. But rows and rows of produce just didn't get sold. When there was a glut, I've seen piles of plums as high as a house, just dumped. They used to burn them, because of the smell, at the back of the market.

Drays used to take all the produce up to Pershore railway station, often during the night, in August. Whole trainloads of produce used to leave Pershore. The market provided transport to the small growers who couldn't afford a horse and cart. Their little loads of produce were put out on the roadside, in villages, and it would be safe. It would stay there all night, until next morning, when the transport would pick it up and bring it to market."

There were some very big growers in the area. Mr. Alan Mumford, at Three Springs, Mr. Bligh at Benedict's by Tyddesley Wood, Mr. Whitely on Holloway Hill and Mr. Duncombe Gibbs at Pensham.

Charles Clemens told me: "I worked at the Co-op Market for a time. I booked the stuff in as they brought it in. Mr. Mumford was on the committee. 'Wagger' Coombe was one of his men who worked on his fruit farm. When I was in the army, 'Wagger' and I were in the same regiment. We used to talk about Mumford. 'Oh yes, he would have things just so. You must measure things out and be sure you don't vary it.'"

Laurence Coggins said: "Yes, that regular queue of drays all down Bridge Street – but nobody with the horses – they were all in the Millers Arms. Each horse would move forward automatically. The drivers in the pub would judge just how long it took their dray to reach the market and nip round to unload the produce there.

The Millers Arms was a very busy pub for market gardeners. It was a meeting place. They did a lot of business there. If someone from Elmley wanted some sprout plants, he would go there on a Wednesday and would be sure to meet a grower from Drakes Broughton or Birlingham who had some."

Nora Bristow told me: "My husband, Les, worked at Doug

Trigg's, the hairdresser, in Broad Street. On busy Wednesdays, farm workers came into the shop for a shave and haircut, while their farm dray moved slowly up Bridge Street and Broad Street towards the market – pulled by the horse, who needed no driver. One horse would always wait outside a certain pub, whether his driver was inside it or not."

George Clark from Lower Moor said: "I was an agricultural worker – cabbage cutting, sprout-picking. You would take all day going to market and be in debt if your stuff was not sold. Trains would take plums to Manchester and Liverpool. But they're grubbing up all the plum trees now. I remember a plum called 'Jimmy Moore', and a 'Heron', and 'Early Rivers'. 'Warwickshire Drooper' was a golden plum, the last of the season. In winter, a lot of land workers were laid off and on the 'dole'."

The Pershore Co-operative Market was established in 1909 and the Central Market, behind the Abbey Garage, in 1914.

Jim Dowler said: "My father was a market gardener, on his own. He had been wounded at the Battle of the Somme and had a shattered arm. So we children gave him as much help as we could, after school, on his ground.

Father used the donkey-cart to bring his vegetables to the Central Market. There was quite a class distinction between the two markets, and the people who went there. In the Central Market there was Socialism and in the Co-op Market there was Capitalism."

Fanny Newick said: "My father went to the Co-op Market as a buyer for our shop in Bridge Street. My duty was in the shop. Buyers came to the market from all over – from the North and from Wales. They liked Pershore produce; it was fresh and good."

"I worked at the Co-operative Market for 7/6d per week, in 1936." Said Mary Stubbs. "I was in the buying and selling department, under a very strict lady called Miss Healey. You certainly had to work hard, because she kept her eyes on you the whole time. But that hard training made you very thorough.

In the summer we worked very long hours. We never went home until all the books were balanced. In fact, for five nights a week, in high summer, we worked until one, two, or three o'clock in the morning. We had to be back at work for 8 a.m., but we enjoyed it. Some weeks, we took home £3 per week with overtime.

We were always chaperoned home in the early hours, by the young men of the market office. The biggest laugh was, that the same old spinster who trained us, used to <u>time</u> the boys who took us home. If they took more than ten minutes, they were really in hot water! But it was a happy life and we never grumbled."

THE WEATHER

Jim Dowler remembers: "Summers were hotter. We used to get a bad winter every ten years. We had more snow at Christmas-time. My mother used to say: 'When we were kids, our parents used to turf us out on a Christmas Day, to go for a walk in the snow. We walked up to the station to see the trains.' We got more floods then. Church Row was flooded."

"When I was born, in 1892," said Blanche Dufty, "my mother told me the River Avon froze over and they took a horse and wagon over and it didn't crack."

Esme Westcott recollects: "Before going to school, we used to walk to Wick for skimmed milk, because it was cheap. My mother believed in skimmed milk – I don't know why. We used to fetch two half-gallons of it for our large family. It was in four small cans.

I remember the beautiful September mornings, when the cobwebs were all shimmering in the sun. The winters did seem particularly cold, with cold winds. We had big scarves tied round and pinned behind our backs, in the biting East wind. That would be in the late '20's, early '30's.

In the 1940's hard frosts, the telegraph wires were twice their size. You could see icicles hanging from the trees. In that terrible snow of 1947, Pershore was cut of for three days. It was the drifting that caused the problem. In 1963, the Avon was frozen over and people walked <u>on</u> the river, as far as Wyre Mill. As a boy, my father walked from Pershore to Tewkesbury <u>on</u> the Avon – in the 1880's or '90's."

HOP-PICKING AT MEIKLE'S WICK GRANGE

"I went a few times. It used to make you hungry, the smell of the hops." Jack Heeks recalls: "You saw children asleep in the hop fields at Meikle's. The smell of the hops lulled them to sleep. When the crib was full, they would bushel up. The Dudley people came down and lived in the outbuildings. Some of them stopped behind in Pershore and didn't go back home."

Fanny Newick recalled: "The hop-pickers came from Dudley and Old Hill, in a special train. A wagon and horses went up to Pershore station for all their luggage and the hop-pickers walked from the station to Wick. They brought their own utensils for cooking. Hop-pickers brought good trade to local shops."

Malcolm Meikle told me: "Hop-picking is now in history, on our farm. The hop-pickers came from the Black Country in special trains, to Pershore, or to Suckley and Alfrick. We housed them in huts. They were given blankets. Every Sunday, they were given a ration of potatoes and oil for their lanterns.

In the war, my mother had to collect the ration books for these 150 to 200 people. She bought all the food in bulk and portioned it out from the garage. The local grocers couldn't cope with the influx of all these people – extra rations for four weeks. Derretts, the bakers, came here to sell bread and cakes to them.

Evangelistic Missions would come and preach the Gospel here during the week. They had a captive audience of hop-pickers. It was always a tradition that the pickers robbed the local orchards. Their luggage was always reputed to be that much heavier than when they came. They had a bit of a sing-song to finish their time here.

Each grower of hops had an agent – a hirer in the Black Country. She would give everybody there a shilling when she signed them up. There were two other sources of labour; gypsies, and a small contingent of local people from Pershore. Pretty well the same families year after year. Traditionally, they used to go on strike on the second day, for more money. But labour relations were really quite good after that."

THE LAND ARMY

Avonbank became a hostel for Land Army girls in the Second World War. Betty Hughes recalls the Land Army girls who came from London to Peopleton. "They came knowing nothing of the conditions of work. One farmer put them to clean his field of thistles. They had open-toed shoes on and their feet were crippled afterwards. They hadn't got their proper uniform then. Some of them took to the work and stayed on after the war."

Ellen Willis recalls: "The Land Army pre-fab was opposite Hurst Park, in the fields. We used to go over there, me and my family, during the war. They showed films in the evenings and we were invited across there. It was just like a little cinema. We saw 'The Way to the Stars' and it was FREE."

FOOD IN TIME OF WAR

Alice Young told me: "The 1914-18 war? Our boys all went to that war. There was rationing. But we come through. And, do you know, I think we were better for it. The rationing done us all good. For a treat on a Sunday, mother used to stew some rhubarb with an extra drop of milk on it and with bread and butter. We used to think that great! That was our Sunday tea. My mother was a cook before she was married, at Stanhope

House in Bridge Street. That's the house where those steps go up and down. I used to love to run up and down them."

"There wasn't much meat in the Second World War," said Ellen Willis. "We had rabbits for meals. The milkman, Mr. Pinchin from Wyre, came in a cart with a horse and brought eggs. Derretts the baker from Wyre and Brookes the baker from Pershore – they all had carts and horses in those days."

Peggy Maple reminisced: "During the war, I was at Bulford, on Salisbury Plan, nursing. I said to our cookie, 'Don't we ever get greenstuff?' 'No,' was the reply. We only had a little root vegetable, or it was tinned peas. I was reduced to growing lettuces in tin cans. I was determined to get some greenstuff for a better diet. We kept our lettuces well watered and they were green, but they never hearted. We used to cut them off and take them down to breakfast, my friend and myself. She was nursing with me."

At Hall Farm, Bricklehampton, Marjorie Revers said she always enjoyed cooking. In the war, when meat was rationed, she made rabbit stew and roasted pigeons with bacon. The farm-hands missed their CHEESE very much, as it was rationed.

Nora Bristow reminded me of the food people had in the 1930's. "Beef and lamb were too dear. Instead, we had poultry, or pork from our own pig. We would cook rabbits in a pot on the hob. We exchanged chitterlings and faggots with our neighbours. They were wholesome and not dear. Bacon and beans were salted for the winter. Eggs were put in isinglass, to preserve them over winter. For tea, we made toast at the fireside and spread dripping from meat on it. We toasted pikelets and spread them with lard, flavoured with rosemary – to save butter."

GYPSIES AND CARAVANS

"When I lived at Bricklehampton," said Laurence Coggins, "there was an orchard at the bottom of our garden. There

84

used to be 15 or 20 caravans in there. People with no homes used to sleep in the farm buildings. They were called 'Dudley', or 'Brummy', or 'Yorky'. They came year after year. Quite tidily dressed at the start – then rougher and rougher – then they vanished for another twelve months!"

Malcolm Meikle said: "My father used to refer to gypsies as being 'an essential nuisance'. They were 'essential' for the picking of the peas, beans and hops."

"We were potato picking at Allesborough Farm," said Ethel Rock. "A woman working there had a caravan. She said to us, 'If you would like to come in and have a cup of tea ...' So we went, the three of us. Everything in that caravan was brass and it was brightly painted too. It was beautiful. Her name was Mrs. Lock. She was a nice woman. She used to travel to various places to work."

"My grandmother was a gypsy," said Alec Witts. "Gypsies kept very much to themselves. They were mainly horse dealers. Today, they are not real Romanies.

My grandmother was superstitious. She would say: 'You mustn't bring a piece of wood into the house if it's already burnt. If you did, the Devil would dance on the chimney-pot.' 'You mustn't bring hawthorn or white flowers into the house.' If there was a thunderstorm, she used to cover all the mirrors up and take all the knives and forks off the table; anything that shone, because it would reflect the lightning.

It was a different world in the 1920's. You lived off the land. The women went out on the land, pulling onions. We used to follow the binders round, when they were cutting corn – to stook it. Haymaking was done by hand. Each season had its occupation."

Chapter seven

PERSHORE PLUMS

Alec Witts told me: "The Pershore Egg Plum was discovered in Tyddesley Wood. It was a sport. It was developed from there. There used to be a red flag on top of the mound in the wood, when they were firing on the rifle range. It was down one of those rides it was found, by a man who lived in Church Street, Pershore."

It is widely claimed that George Crooke, landlord of the Butcher's Arms, an inn in Church Street, Pershore, discovered this famous plum, in Tyddesley Wood, in 1833. It was first planted in Gigbridge Lane orchards.

"There's no better plum," continued Alec Witts. "It is British, so it is not 'pushed'. It's a good jam plum; it's everything. There's one stage of that plum when it's very like a peach. When they go gold, that beautiful gold, they go dry then. They are best when they are just changing from green to yellow."

WHERE DO WE GROW THE YELLOW PLUM?
WHY, PERSHORE, WHERE D'YE THINK?

Esme Westcott told me a great deal about plums. "On our 24 acres, at The Ford in Station Road, it was all plums. We had about 20 varieties. We would be picking from early July to October. I can well remember our varieties, in crop sequence:

Early Laxton and Prolifics.
Herons, Pershore Egg, Pershore Purple.
Laxton Bountiful, Victorias, The Green Gages.
The Cambridge Gage. The Ontario Gage.
The Monarch. The Czars. The Severn Cross.
Wye Dale. Marjorie Seedling. Then the damsons. More plums:
Belle de Louvain. Purple Diamond. Apricot Gage.
Warwick Drooper.

But with all those varieties – most of them very nice plums – people only seemed to know the Victoria.

The old people knew that the Pershore Egg Plum was useful for anything. It makes jam, wine, tarts; you can pulp it – anything. But, unfortunately, it has gone out of favour. It's a shame.

All the other plums had different flavours, different skins, different colours, different stones – flat, smooth, rough, pear-shaped. They split open, or they cling to the plum. Most of them were grafted off the Yellow Egg Plum.

If they were a red variety, they were grafted on Pershore Purple. If they were a light-coloured variety, they were grafted on Egg. You would have to get a scion off someone who had an odd tree, then you would graft it on to your tree. There are all sorts of odd plums about that have come from odd stones growing.

Lots of people claim their grandfathers discovered the original Pershore plum growing wild in Tyddesley Wood. I always understood it was a Mr. Martin who found it. It certainly is a very good stock to graft from."

"We were busy all the year round," said Esme Westcott. "You have to take all the dead wood from off the trees, and all the mummified plums. Then there's the pruning, which has to be burnt. Any trees with silver leaf have to be taken out altogether and burnt.

In spring, there is the spraying programme, and the fertiliser. Then you have to mow between the trees. When the crop begins, you have to prop all the trees, to distribute the weight. If you want quality, you have to thin out the plums.

We never had 'Pick Your Own' schemes because the cost would be very high. When we picked, we had to insure the pickers – on ladders. 'Pick Your Own' schemes would be very hazardous.

Our orchard was planted row-by-row for pollination purposes. The Egg plum is the perfect pollinator for everything. You would put a row of special dessert varieties by a row of Egg plums. You have to oversee the picking, to watch that people are not picking green Victorias and saying they are Egg plums.

We had some 'travellers'. Quite a strong-looking man and his brother. We said it would be all right for them to come and work to pick our plums. But the next morning, he brought his wife and wife's sister and his grandmother and grandfather and his cousins – a whole gang of them! We said, 'We have only got these two rows. When you've done those, you will have to go.'

His wife was pregnant. But then I saw his wife at the top of a very tall tree, up a ladder, with a basket around her waist. There was this strong man standing at the <u>bottom</u> of the tree, holding the ladder. I expressed surprise. But he said, 'It's all right Missus, I'm holding the ladder'!

Our pickers were normally young people waiting to go to college, aged 16 to 18. And we've always given preference to choirboys and Girl Guides, in view of our past interest. We preferred older ones, of course. But you need one or two men. We never had to advertise. One family with six children kept us going for years and years. Their name was Boyce, from Wyre Piddle."

Apple and pear orchards were also prominent in Pershore and district, in the old days. Much cider and perry was made. There was a cider mill and bakery at the back of the Plough Inn.

Marion Knight told me: "There was a cider mill by Amerie Court, to which Colonel Taylor and Colonel Porter from Birlingham brought wagons of apples to make cider for their workers on the land. Cider was very much the drink of farm workers then."

The house of Fred and Marion Knight, 'Lyndhurst', was built in 1932, on a pear orchard. Their piece of ground was very, very fertile, because the 'applus' (apple cores and skins) was dumped there, after the apples had been pressed for cider in the stone presses.

From John Knight's brewery, beside the White Horse Inn, people could buy the pulp, after brewing, to feed to pigs.

Chapter eight

MONKS, VICARS, ORGANISTS, CHOIRBOYS

The monks came first! They were Benedictines. The original monks had arrived in Pershore in 972 A.D., when King Edgar's charter gave extensive estates to Pershore Abbey.

"The monks of the 1930's, who lived at Abbey House, terrified us," protested several Pershore residents. "Let me explain," said Betty Tuffin. "In the 1920's, the monks in their black habits, were friendly. They walked down Newlands, two-by-two. They would talk to my grandmother. But they went away to Nashdom Abbey and another order came, dressed in grey habits. People didn't like the 'grey' monks as much."

Fanny Newick told me: "The Abbey House originally belonged to the Hudson family. It was in the Abbey grounds. The Benedictine monks came into some property at Nashdom Abbey in Surrey, on condition they went there to live. The Council later took over the monks' empty property at Abbey House. It was deteriorating badly and was infested with rats and mice. The house was then demolished. It was unsafe. People couldn't live in it."

"The monks used to frighten us children to death," said Kitty Haines. "During the First World War, there were no street lights. As we went past the Abbey grounds in the dark, the monks used to rattle chains on their gate.

We would be returning, as a gang of children, from Guides or Brownies. We lived at no. 7 Bearcroft. Mrs. Gould would be waiting for us to come home and she stood by the gate. She shouted to the monks: 'These kids' fathers are fighting for you lot in the Forces, and all you did was to put on women's skirts to keep out of the Army.' And it was the truth. They rattled those chains on purpose, to frighten us, because we were children."

A similar experience was related by Freda Hutley-Reade. "After the Girls' Friendly Society meetings, we used to run fast up Church Walk, because the monks would peep over the wall and make signs to frighten us off. We used to walk down Orchard Ditch to collect acorns for me Dad's pigs. And the monks would frighten us off again, as we went past Abbey House where they lived."

Blanche Dufty remembers: "Round the wall of Abbey House, there used to be wisteria. A woman who lived by my mother, used to do the monks' washing. Her niece had to take this washing up there. She used to get me to go with her, 'cos she was frightened of them. There was big doors, before you walked over the courtyard.

One day, these doors slammed and I said, 'Oh dear, they've got us.' And they had a donkey there. They had prayers going on at one and two a.m. We were woken up by that. But you got used to it. They had a pond where they fished.

My friend and I used to cycle to Worcester to see a play. We would arrive home in Pershore at midnight. My friend lived in the Broad Street. She would go and find out if she were locked out. If so, she would come back and sleep at <u>our</u> place in Newlands.

One night, - a lovely moonlight night, she was going down Church Walk. All of a sudden, these monks looked over the churchyard wall, with their hoods on. And she started to laugh and couldn't stop. <u>She</u> saw the funny side!"

Jack Heeks also remembered the monks, with mixed feelings. "Pershore in those days was a bit weird. We had gas lamps. There were seven Benedictine monks in the monastery, near the present bowling green. The bell tolled at 10 p.m. for prayer. They used to walk in procession towards the Abbey, these hooded monks. You couldn't see their faces. When we were returning from the pictures, it was a weird sight.

There was a ten-foot wall, and behind it was the monks' kitchen garden. It is a car park now – near the bowling green. The monks would only go out shopping for the meagre things. They were pretty well self-supporting. They had a greenhouse.

They would fish in the moat for carp. In my schooldays, when we had a hard winter, which was pretty frequent then, the monks had already gone – 'cos we used to skate on that moat. Fred Horton took over their vegetable garden."

CANON LAWSON

"If ever there was a saint on earth, it was Canon Lawson," said Blanche Dufty. "He instructed me for my confirmation. When all this illness was going on at home (my sister had T.B.), he always came to visit us every morning.

Later on, my daughter had diphtheria and was in the Sanatorium. He would go up there, to Three Springs Road, every day, and find out how she was. And he would say prayers for my mother and my husband, both of whom were ill at the same time. My son, at five-years old, was struck with double pneumonia and pleurisy. He wasn't expected to live. Canon Lawson used to kneel down and pray for him. He was a good man. My son recovered.

Whenever I walk by that gravestone near the Abbey, which bears Canon Lawson's name, I always think of him. He once bought a pair of shoes for my son – which he badly needed. He paid for me to go to Birmingham to fetch my son home from hospital. You never forget that kindness."

CANON GRESFORD JONES

He had been a Bishop in Uganda and was Vicar at Pershore Abbey in the early 1920's. Alec Witts recalls: "Once a week, the Vicar would come into the old Defford Road School to give a Scripture lesson to the older pupils. That was Canon Gresford Jones in my time. The Scripture was more of a History lesson in those times."

Charles Clemens had vivid memories of <u>Mrs</u>. Gresford Jones, the Vicar's wife. "She was a real Christian. When you shook hands with her, you had a thrill. She was a Christian from head to foot.

One Saturday, there were signs that we were going to get a high flood in Bridge Street. Some gypsies were trapped in Weir Meadow. Two young Bobbies had told them the day before: 'You'll get flooded out by morning.' 'Oh, no, we shan't' was the reply. 'All right,' retorted the policemen, 'but don't say we didn't warn you.'

At four or five in the morning, there were should of 'Help!' from those gypsies. Both these policemen had been in the navy. They borrowed a flat-bottomed boat from the Mill. They had a rope and rescued those gypsies, two at a time.

Later on in the day, Mrs. Gresford Jones heard of the incident. She went up to the Police Station. 'Where are those gypsies who were marooned?' she enquired. She was told they were camping out, further along Three Springs Road, which was all fields in those days. She arrived at their camp: 'Now,' she said to the gypsies, 'I want eight of you to come with me. I've got dinner ready for you at the Vicarage.'

There was a nine-month coal strike, which badly affected me as a coal merchant. We had no work coming in. We had no coal to buy or sell. Mrs. Gresford Jones came to see us. Jim, my son, was four then. He knew we had got only three biscuits for our tea on Sunday. He went to get them and offered them to Mrs. Gresford Jones, as she was our guest. She took one and said, 'Thank you.'

But she must have summed up the situation, because on the next day, someone knocked on our door and went away. On the mat was a wrapped box of chocolate biscuits. We each ate one. That was Mrs. Gresford Jones. She was a gem. She always took action.

Only three years ago, in 1984, I met her again, walking along the bank of the river at Pershore. And I shook hands with her. There was something about her that no-one else had got. You got a thrill. I guarantee she held my hand for ten minutes. She was so pleased to see me. Not long after, she died. Her husband wasn't a Christian, but his wife was. Because she lived it."

CANON BARK

"I liked him. He married me and my husband and christened our children," said Mary Stubbs.

"I had a lot to do with him, being in the choir," said Edwin Hill. "He was a huge man and quite frightening. He had a high-pitched voice. Canon Bark was a very clever man and a musician – a Bachelor of Music. He gave organ recitals in the Abbey.

Canon Bark always made the boast that he visited every one of his parishioners once a year. And he walked it everywhere. Or he would ride his 'sit up and beg' bike."

"He always looked so stern," remembers Rosie Long. "At Evensong, in wartime, he would have all the lights turned off, save the one above him, to save electricity."

Walter Palfrey said: "Canon Bark always wore his black cassock and mortar-board in the street, with its tassel in front of his nose. He had rather big feet, which he turned outwards. He walked at about ten-to-two.

One day Canon Bark came out of the Post Office and Jack Hemming was nearby. Someone said to Jack, 'Have you seen Canon Bark?' Jack replied, 'Oh yes, he's just gone down to the Bridges to turn round!'"

Some people used to say, "If Canon Bark goes up the church tower's narrow winding steps, he has to fold over his feet." But he is also remembered for saying, 'I can't have 31 people on the Church Council – it's too many.' So he got rid of several aged members, including old Jimmy Ford, who had a long white beard.

CANON R. H. MURRAY

Dr. Murray, Canon of Worcester and vicar of Pershore from 1928-1938, was an historical figure in more senses than one. "He was a good Vicar, but not really cut out for the cloth," was one comment I heard. "He was an outstanding man," said

Charles Clemens. "He was Scots-born and he'd got a Scots and Irish twang – mixed."

"He came from Ireland, but he dared not go back to Ireland," said Leslie Brookes. "He was actually a British agent out there. He was always afraid the Sinn Fein were going to get him.

His wife was the daughter of the Lord Chief Justice of Ireland. She had had a breakdown because of the 'Troubles'. When they were in Ireland, they used to sleep with their revolvers under the pillow, so Canon Murray told me.

He caused quite a furore when, in about 1937, he started telling people that Hitler was determined to crush Britain.

He had his contacts in the Secret Service, apparently. The establishment wouldn't take any notice of his warnings. They were making too much money out of scrap metal, which they were selling to the Germans."

(Author's note: All this sounds only too familiar today: even as I write, this very week, in February 1996, has seen the docklands bomb shattering the Irish ceasefire, and the Scott Report on Arms to Iraq).

"I'm sure Canon Murray did translations and codings," continued Leslie Brookes. "He was a very, very clever man."

My own memory of Dr. Murray (Doctor of Literature) was of a jolly man. He laughed a lot, moved quickly and jerkily and had an Irish sense of humour. I think he chose the two Irish curates we had then at Pershore Abbey. In those days, each of the fifteen or so, villages in Pershore Deanery had its own Vicar! And curates were plentiful too.

The Abbey then was cold and not well lighted. It was bare – not comfortable and well maintained, as today. There were no colourful altar frontals in modern collage, and embroidered kneelers, as now. High walls surrounded the Abbey grounds. The monastery and monks were still there! The Victorian vicarage, with no central heating, must have been cold too.

At a summer play, enacted by an amateur company, outside, in the Abbey grounds, I remember Dr. Murray sitting in the front row and roaring with laughter. He laughed especially, when a motionless girl in the play, representing a white statue, was stung by a wasp, and dashed off, unravelling her white wrappings meanwhile.

In those days, when Pershore was a very small town, Vicars used to visit your home at least once a year. Canon Murray drove his care to Pinvin to visit a couple who had just celebrated their 50th wedding anniversary. They gave him a glass of their plum wine. They told him it wouldn't hurt him at all. And Canon Murray could drink a drop of wine too!

After drinking their health, he said, 'Congratulations on your marvellous achievement!' The old lady replied, "We've been married 50 years and we've never had a disagreement.' Canon Murray responded, 'Oh, how dull!' So they gave him another glass of plum wine.

He said goodbye and went out to his car. But the wine had a paralytic effect upon him. He had to sit in his car for an hour, before he dare drive home. He never touched plum wine after that!

Alice Young said: "I used to like Canon Murray. We'd got a dish of rice pudding on the table, when he called one day. And he said, 'Carry on! Eat your pudding.' I had a round table with three splayed legs. When he came in, my children, Jean and Ken, had got under there, out of sight. They'd got some butter and sugar – eating something – because, in those days, children were seen and not heard. And Canon Murray thought it all a great joke."

John Annis remembers Canon Murray when John was a choirboy in the Abbey. "He would often come into the Abbey wearing tennis shoes. He enjoyed playing tennis. He would drive out of the Vicarage gate too fast and, once, he had two serious accidents at Pinvin crossroads. In his new car, the accelerator and the brake were located the other way round from his old car – hence the confusion. At least, that was Canon Murray's explanation."

"Oh yes, he was a nice fellow, Murray," said Charles Clemens. "He would often come into the Abbey while I was playing the organ. He would slide on the long organ stool and talk to you while you were playing. Well you can't play <u>and</u> talk! So I used to stop playing.

He stopped me one day between the two churches and talked about someone who had got a divorce – rare in those days. He said to me, 'Can you understand? It rebounds on people.' But he must have foreseen his own divorce later on."

Esme Westcott recalled: "Canon Murray was a very literary man. His sermons were short, but memorable, especially when he brought in history (he was a historian) and when he spoke on the Incarnation."

He used to say, 'I always limit my sermons to twelve minutes.' So you can imagine what he said to one of his curates who once gave a forty-minute sermon! He was Chairman of the Working Men's Club in Pershore, too.

Dr. Murray was a scholar. I still treasure a signed copy of his book, published in 1936 at 3/6d. by John Murray – doubtless a relation. The book is entitled: 'The King's Crowning.' It was written to anticipate the Coronation of Edward VIII on May 12th 1937. Against this date, in the book, my mother, Meg Bramford, has pencilled 'No'. It was, of course, George VI who unexpectedly and dramatically stepped into the shoes of his brother; 'the King who was never crowned'.

The book is well researched and very readable. It deals with all the coronations we have ever had. The Introduction, by the Very Reverend Foxley Norris, Dean of Westminster, and a friend of Dr. Murray's, begins: 'Many people can write history; a few people can write history that is accurate; a very few people can write accurate history that is also alive, entertaining, and original. Dr. Murray is one of the very few.'

"He had travelled widely," said Betty Tuffin. "He would come and talk for hours to my father when he was ill. I think Canon Murray's frequent jokes hid his private sorrow. His wife was mentally unbalanced and he had a sad home life."

Alice Young remembered: "During his last wonderful sermon, he spoke about how the people of Pershore had treated him. 'JUDGE NOT, THAT YE BE NOT JUDGED'. His wife was in a mental home. He had had a very sad life."

Peggy Maple said: "He was the first clergyman in England to take advantage of the new law on divorce, brought in in the '30's. So he knew that he had to resign his living here. It was quite a scandal at the time."

I believe Pershore people still like Dr. Murray, even after his dramatic departure in 1938. There was some sympathy for him. As a teenager, I walked home from the Abbey on the Sunday we had heard the belated news of his divorce. My companion, an elderly lady, said to me, 'Now we know just why Dr. Murray preached that sermon on his last Sunday.'

THE REVEREND HODGINS AND THE REVEREND BINGHAM

In the 1930's, two of Canon Murray's Irish curates were fond of sports. The Rev. Hodgins played rugger and the Rev. Bingham, hockey. Alice Young, daughter of the verger at that time, recalls: "I used to have to fetch the Rev. Hodgins to come to the service. He hadn't got up! The curates lived at Southern House in Broad Street.

One Friday morning, when the service was in St. Andrew's, the two Miss Woodwards were sat there in church, and Miss Lipscombe from Pensham. I was ringing the bell. I could ring the bell as well as a man. Eleven o'clock come. Miss Woodward comes up to me. I was in the belfry. 'Alice, do you know who's taking the service today?' 'Mr Hodgins.' 'Go and see if he's in the vestry.' Nobody there.

So I went down to Southern House to find out where he was. 'A nice thing for a clergyman!' I thought, 'You'm in for it!' He come to the door in his dressing gown. 'Do you know you've got a service at 11 o'clock?' Oh, he didn't know where to put hisself. I think he only half dressed, but his cassock and surplice hid the rest. He did get a ticking off over that!

Then there was the time he had that motor-bike and ran into a herd of cows, up Station Road. He was critically ill in hospital.

97

Canon Murray was good to him. The curates stayed quite a time in those years and they visited people in their homes then.

You remember the Rev. Bingham used to have his hair waved? He come one morning for 8 o'clock Communion, to take the service. He was in the vestry, sitting in his chair and waiting for the clock to strike eight. I had stopped ringing the bell and I went into the vestry. I said to him. 'Good God: what have you got a hair net on for?' 'Oh!,' he said, 'I'm glad you reminded me, Alice.' He was a nice fellow. He was a paratrooper in the war – a Padre. And he got killed in Italy."

MR. CHARLES MASON, *Organist*

He was known as 'Quimmy' Mason, because he was always quivering. Charles Clemens told me: "Mr. Mason was called up in the First World War, but he was never sent to the front, because he was too nervous and unpredictable. Instead, he was made army organist in Rouen Cathedral in France. There he played for services for the troops who were preparing to go to the battlefields."

"Mr. Mason's organ-playing was close to our hearts," said Edwin Hill. Edwin had been a choirboy when Mr. Mason was organist and choirmaster at Pershore Abbey in the 1930's. "He was a wonderful man. He was such a kindly person," said Edwin. "He used to lodge with the Summertons in Defford Road, so he and I would walk along together to choir practice or the services.

And if we choirboys were good, we used to get a sweet. If we were bad, we would get a good telling off." I heard too that Charles Mason played the piano for Miss Lawson of Broad Street, while she was dying.

MR. CHARLES CLEMENS, *Organist*

"I was a schoolboy organist!," said Charles Clemens. "I used to play the piano at school for an evening hymn, or some old songs. And Mr. Chapman, the Headmaster, was very fond of my playing.

One afternoon, in 1906, when I was aged twelve, a man came into the school and went up to the headmaster. Mr. Chapman called me out and said, 'I want you to go with this gentleman and play for a special service at Drakes Broughton.' I think it was a wedding. This man had come with a pony and trap.

Now I didn't like horses, even though we had them at home in the coal trade. So it was quite an adventure to travel with this man in a very high trap with a high-stepping horse. But I can't remember how I got back after the service.

My first place as organist, was at the churches of Defford and Besford. I used to cycle to Defford in a morning on Sundays and back home for dinner. Then to Besford in the afternoon and back home for tea. Then to Defford again for Evensong. Three services on Sundays and a choir practice once a week. And for all that, I received £5 per year.

When I first played at the Abbey in Pershore, Mary Baker, my first piano teacher, was present. I played Handel's Largo. Mary Baker came up afterwards and said, 'Charles, did I teach you to play Handel's largo at the speed you took it? Because 'Largo' means 'slow'. And you were racing through it!'" However, Charles Clemens eventually became organist at Fladbury Church and stayed there for 42 years.

MR. LESLIE BROOKES, *Organist*

Leslie told me: "I started on the piano when I was seven, at Worcester. I was about ten when I had lessons with Mr. Mason, on the organ at the Abbey. When I was eleven, he used to leave me to play for the last hymn at Sunday school services. Then he allowed me to play for all the hymns at Sunday school.

After that, I played the organ in several nearby churches – at Little Comberton, at Peopleton, at Wick ..." Now, in 1996, at the age of 80, Leslie is still regularly playing the organ, for services at Wick, and at the Baptist Church in Pershore.

CHOIRBOYS

They had to be dedicated to their task of being present in Pershore Abbey three times each Sunday and for the Wednesday evening practice too. No wonder they sucked sweets during the sermon.

As a child, I remember how splendid the Abbey choir looked on Easter Day! They would be wearing freshly laundered surplices and posies of primroses pinned to those surplices – an old custom. The three Miss Barnes of Newlands did all the laundering for the Abbey. In those days, the Abbey choir would consist of at least ten men and sixteen boys.

It was the custom for the choir to ascend to the top of the Abbey tower at Rogation-tide (on a usually cold Wednesday in May) to bless the crops. At each side of the tower, a prayer was said and a hymn was sung, as the choir looked towards the fields and farms.

Roy Beard said: "We choirboys wore stiff collars. They weren't very comfortable!" Lyn Westcott said: "The choirboys were paid five shillings every quarter. Our money was wrapped in paper and sealed with red sealing wax, just like Arthur Smith the chemist did, with his medicines. Choir outings were quite jolly days out. Usually, we went to Weston-super-Mare. We lost a boy once and had to go looking for him."

Alice Young said: "In the old days, choirboys went carol singing to all the big houses. They were always asked inside and given an orange and some mince pies. Mrs. Wyn Marriott was always generous to them."

A VERGER'S DUTIES

Alice Young, the youngest child of William Need, verger at Pershore Abbey for 46 years, was kept busy helping her father in the Abbey from an early age. At the age of 90, her memories of this were still vivid. She told me: "My earliest memory, at the age of three, was of having to go in the Abbey and dust the pews.

I went along with my parents. Dad told me off if I hadn't dusted under a book. Later on, I used to clean that brass eagle, the lectern, every week, for quite a few years of my life. If my father noticed any finger marks on it, I'd got to rub them all off.

I used to like St. Andrew's when it was used as a church, before it became a Hall. The times I've cleaned and polished all the tiled floor there. We used to use St. Andrew's quite a lot then for services – and always for a Harvest Festival."

The glass doors at the West end of the Abbey are a memorial to William Need, Alice's father. They were made by Joseph Howes, a Pershore carpenter. He also made the vestry doors and the new pulpit. He renewed the oak outer doors at the West end. Alice Young's son, Kenneth, a choirboy, sang a solo: 'I know that my Redeemer liveth' from Handel's Messiah, at the funeral of his grandfather, William Need.

Joan Wicks told me, in 1986, that she had been cleaning the cross and the candlesticks on the High Altar for nearly forty years: "I use my own materials too," she said. "But you see, to me, it's an interest. I like to do it and I can manage it. I still clean the silver in the Wick Chapel too and I clean the Churchwardens' staves."

BELLS AND BELLRINGERS

In 1893, the Curfew Bell was rung at Pershore Abbey at eight o'clock in the evening, from November 5th until Candlemas Day (February 2nd). It was a signal to townspeople to return to their homes.

As a child, before the First World War, Alice Young remembered ringing the Curfew Bell. "It was an old tradition. But you wouldn't get them out of the pubs at that time! You had to ring that Curfew for fifteen minutes. Then you had to toll the date on another bell. And that was my job. I used to love it when it was the 31st of the month, 'cos I could keep on pulling! I've tolled the big bell for funerals, for an hour, many a time.

For the 'Passing Out Bell', Dad had to go up into the belfry.

It was three times three for a man and three times two for a woman. Then you tolled the tenor bell from the bottom, every minute.

The Pancake Bell? Jack Workman used to ring that at 11 a.m. on Shrove Tuesday. A Pancake Bell was rung in St. Andrew's too, as they were once separate parishes, with separate parish Councils and separate Churchwardens.

The tunes on the Abbey Carillons? There were two barrels, one for each week of tunes. Dad had to go up into the tower to change the barrels once a fortnight.

There was a muffled peal if one of the bell ringers had died. And they always did a muffled peal for New Year's Eve. Dad and the other bell ringers rang the muffled peal from 10 p.m. 'til midnight. Then Dad used to crawl under those bells and take the leather buffs off the tongues of the bells. That meant they were ready for the bright peal, to bring in the New Year. It was quite dangerous to crawl under those bells.

The bell ringers never got no pay. Father, with another ringer, used to go round all the big houses in Pershore and Wick on a Boxing Day. They would collect for the bell ringers. They had a notebook and wrote down the amounts people gave."

THE ABBEY TOWER

Going up to the belfry was quite an adventure for Alice Young, as a child. "I went up with Dad and the other bell ringers. Just before the lantern tower are the lime pits, where you go over like a wooden bridge. Then there are metal steps all open at the back. You could slip straight through! I never dared look down! But I didn't mind when I was up in the 'cage' at the top. My brothers could all ring. And my husband, Alan, was a bell ringer for a long time."

Esther Marshall of Broad Street, said: "Long ago, in the summer, my friends and I often took our picnic tea, up on top of the Abbey tower. When the buttercups were out, the river meadows looked beautiful."

THE ABBEY EMBROIDERY GUILD

In the 1960's the Abbey Embroidery Guild made a great many tapestry cushions and kneelers for the 'old monks' seats' and altar rails. They are still there and have worn well. They depict the vegetables and fruits of Pershore's market gardens – carrots, onions, tomatoes, beans, leeks, plums, apples, pears, strawberries, blackcurrants, damsons. There are kneelers, which portray a variety of gardening tools, and two rather special wedding kneelers.

Ruth Brant was one of the embroiderers. She said: "We made about three kneelers each, in the end. Mrs. Hammond, who lived at Pensham at the time, got us interested. We had to go and see Mrs. Bramford and Mrs. Euphie Lees to see if our work was up to standard, before we were entrusted to start the actual kneelers. We used to visit Mrs. Hammond every Monday at her flat in Britannia Square in Worcester, for a good many years, to do our embroidery. I made a leek kneeler, I remember."

THE FRIENDS OF PERSHORE ABBEY

As a choirboy, John Annis remembers two significant services in the 1930's in the Abbey: "The very first service of the Friends of Pershore Abbey was held in 1932. Dr. Farncombe of Endon, Wick, founded the 'Friends'. Many dignitaries were present, including the Poet Laureate, John Masefield, who read some of his poems from the chancel steps.

This service was broadcast on the wireless and was a seven days' wonder to the townspeople. Wires were strung between the Abbey and a tall telegraph pole in church Walk. The vestry was used by engineers, who filled it with the paraphernalia of broadcasting of those days. There were row upon row of accumulators - wet batteries, which were an essential component of wireless in those days. The music for the service was highly acclaimed. So the choir and the organist were pleased!

Another service, which was most spectacular, was held by the

Knights Templar, a Masonic order. Their colourful robes and regalia were magnificent and the Abbey was packed.

The Vicar of that time, Dr. R. H. Murray, took time to explain to us choirboys, all that would be going on in the service. He kindled our interest, as he was, himself, an historian."

ABBEY PAGEANTS

Several pageants have been held in the Abbey over the years – both Biblical and historical. With the start of the annual Pershore Festival in the 1960's, plays too, were held in the Abbey. One spectacular play was 'Murder in the Cathedral' by T. S. Eliot. The Rev. John Hencher, the curate of the time, who had been an actor, took the part of Thomas à Beckett.

"I enjoyed being in those pageants," said Ruth Brant. "I was in two pageants. For my part as the Virgin Mary, I wore a dress that Vivien Leigh had worn at Stratford-on-Avon. The Vicar, Dr. Moore, hired the costumes from Stratford – from the Royal Shakespeare Company."

THE MISSION HALL

Alice Young remembered the Mission Hall (now St. Agatha's Hall) in Head Street, as it was before the First World War. "At the back, there used to be a huge gymnasium. Ever since I was a child, they used to hold a parochial supper in the Mission Hall in January. It was free. I went there and helped Miss Handy and Miss Ridgeway to cut up the sandwiches."

John Smith told me: "I recall being told that the Mission Hall was provided for the poorer inhabitants of the town, who had no 'Sunday best' to wear to the Abbey."

Leslie Brookes had heard the same explanation. He said: "People reckon it was built for the folk around Head Street and the Newlands who couldn't dress well enough to go to the Abbey. It was the old snob attitude and I haven't much time for that.

My mother was from a Salvation Army family. But she was a C. of E. Sunday school teacher at Worcester before coming to Pershore. She liked plain services. So she felt more relaxed going to the Mission Hall than to the Abbey – which, I'm sorry to say, in the 1920's, was very cliquey. You had to live in a place for a long time to be accepted.

There was a lot of class distinction then. 'You haven't been to the Abbey services, Mrs. Brookes?' 'No, because we go to the Mission Hall.' 'Oh, that isn't for people like you. That is for the lower classes. You are trades-people.'"

SUNDAY SCHOOL

Sunday school in the 1920's and '30's was attended by a great many children. It was held in the old Defford Road School and you walked to the Abbey, two-by-two for the service.

Miss Handy and Miss Ridgeway were in charge for many years. Nora Bristow recalls going to Sunday school twice a day and that it was always bitterly cold in St. Andrew's, where they met. "I started going to Sunday school when I was three-years old," said Mary Stubbs.

"I want you to see my little chapel in memory of my two sisters," said Elsie Barnes. Beside the fireplace of her old house in Newlands, in a recess, was a colour photo of Pershore Abbey, flanked by two white candles, unlit, in brass candlesticks, a silver chalice, a palm cross, a crucifix and a photo of all three Barnes sisters. "The oldest was Victoria and the other one was Harriet," said Elsie. "And every night of my life I pray to my dear sisters passed to rest, in spirit."

THE ROYAL MAUNDY MONEY

Joan Wicks felt very honoured to receive the Maundy Money from Her Majesty the Queen, in Worcester Cathedral. She told me: "In 1980, when I was 79, the Vicar from Pershore Abbey came to me and said, 'How would you like to see the

Queen?' I thought he was just going to give me a ticket to sit in the Cathedral. He said, 'You may be chosen by our Church Council to receive the Maundy Money in Worcester Cathedral. The Queen will be 54, so there will be 54 men and 54 women selected.'

He asked me lots of questions about what I had done. I told him about my cleaning in the Abbey (for over 30 years then) and that I had visited people in hospital and shopped for other people. He asked me how much pension I got. When I told him, he said, 'However do you manage?' I said, 'I manage very well, because I don't drink or smoke.'

A letter came from Buckingham Palace to say I had been chosen. I was very excited about that, of course. We had to be in the Cathedral at 8.30 a.m. on the day before Good Friday. I was allowed two friends to accompany me. We went in a little bus to the Chapter House to assemble. I was with the last ones, my name being Wicks. The Almoners showed us to our seats.

The High Almoner had this lovely gold plate piled with the little leather bags, which held our special money – a red bag and a white bag for each person. We had to hold our hands out and the Queen placed the money on our palms. It was a lovely service and, afterwards, we chosen people were given free coffee and cake in College Hall. It was a long morning!"

A past Verger of Pershore Abbey, Mr. Jim Ritchings, was similarly honoured by the Queen, on the same occasion, in 1980.

Chapter nine

WE ENTERTAINED OURSELVES

PERSHORE FAIR

The annual Fair has ancient origins. It was always held on June 26th, the day of St. Eadburga, granddaughter of King Alfred. Pershore Abbey is dedicated to St. Eadburga. This saintly lady is to be seen in a window of the South Aisle of the Abbey. She is shown washing the clothes of her nuns, while they sleep.

The Fair was held, originally, in the churchyard of the Abbey. In mediaeval times, people at the Fair used to trade in kind – an exchange of different foods and goods. Then it gradually became an amusement Fair and moved to Broad Street. Now it has moved to the Weir Meadow. "The first night's takings, from the stalls in Broad Street, were always for Pershore Cottage Hospital," said Freda Hutley-Reade.

At Fair time, in the early 1800's, any person who hung out a bush at his door, had the privilege of selling ale without a licence, during the three days of the Fair. Leslie Brookes recalled this custom: "On Fair Day, people were entitled to put a sheaf of straw outside to show that they were selling drinks inside. We used to have a little stall outside our bakery in High Street, on Fair Day, where we sold brandy snap."

Pershore Fair was traditionally known as a Horse Fair. Because the cuckoo is rarely heard after the end of June, an old saying goes:

> Cuckoo comes in April
> Sings a song in May
> Buys a horse at Pershore Fair
> And off he rides away.

Sid Champken told me: "The Horse Fair was held on the ground where the Police Station is now, in Three Springs Road.

In the evening, outside the Star Inn in Bridge Street, you would see all the gypsies selling horses to each other – the most exciting thing! These horses would be running up and down the street, piebalds and all, and the sparks would be flying from their feet. There was no traffic then."

"It was a mad time," said Alec Witts. "The gypsies rode up and down the street, with carts and horses – like the old chariots of the Romans!"

The grand entrance of the Fair people into Broad Street, on the evening before the Fair Day, was a most exciting sight, as I well remember. Their trailers and steam engines and caravans would be all lined up and panting in anticipation. They queued up in Bridge Street, High Street, Defford Road and Church Walk – all ready to dash in when the Abbey clock struck eight.

The Chief of Police, Inspector Airey, would be standing at the corner by Prothero's with his cane held high. When he lowered it, and police whistles blew, that was the signal for the rush into Broad Street, from all four corners. Everything happened. The Fair people all took up their places and built up their stalls. Some would fight for their pitch, with poles.

"Strickland's steam engine was the strongest to enter," said Sid Champken. "He would swing round the corner and stake his pitch." "As a lad of 10 or 11," said Walter Palfrey, "I used to watch Strickland's putting up their roundabout by the Baptist Church. I got more fun out of that, than going to the Fair. It was a terrific roundabout, with an organ. Lovely!" "The Ginny horses was the big attraction," said Jack Heeks. "There was also the cakewalk – shaky, jumpy, rocky."

Ethel Rock had happy memories of the Fair. "We was all young girls then and there was some smashing Fairs. They're not the same today. I liked to go on the swing boats and the horses. A man come from Worcester. He was called Dickie Pratley and he had old crocks, pots and pans. We used to smash his china. There were coconut shies, gingerbread stalls and ice-creams, of course."

Living at no. 7 Broad Street, Elwyn Wilson, the doctor's wife, was in the middle of all the noise and bustle of the Fair. She told me: "All the stalls and caravans were on the pavements. Late at night, when we were in bed, the Fair people would cook their peas and chops under our window. They would come and get water from our house, to cook their potatoes. They were friendly people, living right outside our door and it was all very interesting, every year."

Esther Marshall experienced a close bond with the Fair folk: "Living in Broad Street, we got to know the Fair people very well and liked them. They spent a lot of money in the shops and never gave any trouble. The mother of one family was a Pershore girl, and she had run away with the Fair people when she was 17.

We had the day off from school, and my friends and I would be in the swing boats all morning and visit the caravans. The Fair opened at 2 p.m. We were allowed to stay up until midnight, much to the envy of those who lived far away."

My own mother, Meg Bramford, once took on the role of a fairground lady. Malcolm Meikle told me: "One year, there was a 'Save the Avon' charity evening at Pershore Fair. The Fair people said they would give us this benefit evening – but we had to man the stalls and collect the takings ourselves.

I have this vivid picture of your mother, Meg Bramford, sitting in the booth at the bottom of the Big Wheel, collecting the money. Elwyn Wilson was on the dodgem cars booth. Another Mrs. Wilson, of the fairground family Wilson, was telling Elwyn about the Licensed Showman's Ball at the Grosvenor Hotel in London, and how she gets dressed up for the ball."

THE FORESTERS' DAY AT WICK HOUSE

It took place annually, before the First World War and Blanche Dufty remembered it well: "The Foresters were a sort of men's club. They helped each other – like a sort of insurance. There was a procession, to Wick House and back. We had banners and a little band. When we got there, we had games and a lovely tea, laid out on trestle tables. It was served by the local gentry. The Hudson family lived at Wick House. Then there were donkey rides and races. It was our annual school treat."

PERSHORE FLOWER SHOW

It was a very important occasion. There had been a Pershore Horticultural Society since 1846, but the Show was organised in earnest in 1875. Blanche Dufty recalled it all, with her usual enthusiasm: "It was a marvellous day, generally in August. The church bells would ring. People came from miles away, by train, to Pershore station. So they had to walk down to the town and the Abbey bells would guide them!

You could go up on the Abbey tower for twopence and stay as long as you liked. Thousands of people came. The Show was held in the Abbey grounds and there was a great big marquee. My father, being a gardener – he always had the day off. Wonderful flowers, fruit and vegetables. We don't see them like that today.

The greatest thing was dressing up for the day. We spent ages putting on our Sunday best, and we made a point of wearing a large hat. I wore a see-through dress, which my sister had made – pink under-slip and gold underneath.

My eldest brother had given me my first ring – and wasn't I proud of it! I was a bit vain in those days. I noticed the publican's wife, next door, eyeing everyone through her window. So I pretended to finger my hair, just to give her a good look at my ring!"

Alice Young described the scene. "Bells were ringing all day long. My mother used to replace my father, the verger, in the Abbey, 'cos he was one of the bell-ringers up top. Mother had to stay in the Abbey all day, because visitors had to pay threepence to go round the Abbey.

On Flower Show Day, we had a picnic ham at home, which Mother had boiled. So we kids had to help ourselves. Then my brother Jack and I replaced Mother in the church, while she came home to have her dinner. There were lots of runners in the races. That barometer over there was won by one of my brothers for a half-mile. Jack, the youngest, was in the Birchfield Harriers and he won a lot of prizes."

Blanche Dufty has the last word on the Flower Show: "The historical pageants were wonderful affairs and there was also paintings, carvings, fretwork and needlework. It was nearly always fine weather. And it was hot weather in them days. At night there was fireworks and dancing. A very big day!"

PERSHORE MUSIC HALL

It was behind Phillips the grocer's shop in High Street. "The Phillips' and the Huttons used to give concerts there. They did Gilbert and Sullivan operas. Mrs. Charlie Phillips had a lovely soprano voice," said Alice Young. In 1917, Walfords' Welsh Maids Tour sang there. Blanche Dufty remembered hearing eight Welsh girls who sang beautifully, accompanied by a clown. Vesta Tilley had once performed there.

THE YELLOW BOB TROUPE

Jim Dowler told me: "They were like pierrots, the older ones. Their costume was green with yellow bobbles down the front. They were Pershore people, organised by Captain Attwell of the Church Army at the Mission Hall.

We used to go round village halls and the Cottage Hospital, mostly for charity. We did sketches and songs. It was in the early '30's. Mr. Bert Annis was one of us. He had an old car and would take three or four of us to the villages. Or we went by motor-bikes and side-cars.

Miss Newick was one of us. She had a lovely voice and sang mostly opera. Old Mr. Rann, Master of the Workhouse, always sang 'I like a doughnut with jam in'. The comedian was Bert Shepherd. Leslie Brookes was a comic too. Whenever we went on to do a turn, we drank a little glass of parsley wine, just to give us a bit of courage. That wine was home-made, by Nellie Cornelius out of Nogains." There was a lot of 'home-made' entertainment in the 1930's, as we shall see.

THE FOUR P's CONCERT PARTY

Esme Westcott told me about this: "In the 1920's, ordinary people got together and went round the villages to entertain. We did songs, recitations, monologues and comedy acts. I was only a very small child, about three-years old. My little song used to go down well:

> What a little thing am I
> Hardly higher than the table
> I can eat and I can sing
> But to work I am not able.

It had three verses. I was dressed in a little silk frilly dress. Captain Attwell took me and my big sister to the concerts in the side-car of his motor-bike.

Sometimes I was on the back of the motor-bike with my big sister holding me on. She used to play the piano in the concert. The Four P's stood for 'Pershore for Peace, Progress and Prosperity'. Or, when this symbol was taken for Pershore Growers' Market, it was 'Pershore Plums Properly Packed.'

THE BABES IN THE WOOD PANTOMIME

Esme was in this too. She said: "When I was about ten-years old, a proper performing troupe came to Pershore. They wanted local people in the show. It was done on the stage of the cinema. My brother and I were picked to be the Babes. Two of my sisters were in the chorus line.

I think we were each paid the fabulous sum of half-a-crown, which was a great deal of money in those days. It ran for a week and was well-supported by the villages. That was just before the changeover from silent films to sound."

OTHER PERFORMERS

Ella Patricia Ardern remembered the Swann 'Family Orchestra', of the early 1930's. "My mother played the 'cello, my father the clarinet. We three daughters played violins and our grandfather, Mr. Sumner, conducted us. We were joined by Marjorie Pettifer on the piano, and her brother, John, on the timpani. Miss Shepherd from Edwards' shop was another violinist with us and Mr. Venn was on the double bass. We played in village concerts, along with plays performed by local schoolchildren."

Jack Heeks remembered: "We went to the Magic Lantern shows at the Mission Hall. Ebenezer Jones, who lived in Mason's Ryde, played a tin whistle very well. He also played a violin."

Alice Young recalled. "I was in a concert as a child. I was Widow Serpolio and I had to sing a song. I wore my mother's black apron and her shawl, with a bucket and brush. And a gang o' boys sat in front, poking fun at me."

Jimmy Parker, from Hurst Park, was the leader of Pershore's brass band. "Mr. Sumner and Dad started it for boys," said Rene Giles. My father used to have boys in the sitting-room to teach them the cornet. One came every Sunday morning for a lesson. Mother used to get most annoyed!

My father came from a very musical family in Shrewsbury. All his brothers and sisters played in the theatre there. Dad could play the piano, the cornet and the trombone. When they had the Pershore Flower Show Day, father used to conduct the brass band in the Abbey grounds. I would go and watch him."

LIVING WHIST

This was organised by a Women's Institute President in about 1932, and there had been a previous version in 1922.

Women and children were dressed as playing cards and performed in the Abbey grounds. Trumps were called. A hand was played, and the cards moved accordingly, interspersed with graceful dances. I remember my mother, Meg Bramford, was Queen of hearts. She danced, with others, a gavotte, to Handel's Water Music. Being a little girl, at that time, I was merely the two of Clubs.

Esme Westcott, also a young girl, was the two of Spades. She described Living Whist: "All the 'cards' shuffled round in the centre of the arena, while music was played. Two ladies then picked the cards they wanted. The four suits dispersed to the four corners.

As I was the Trump card on that occasion, I marched proudly into the centre and led out the King and Queen."

LIVING PICTURES

Several times, this form of entertainment was produced by Miss Nancy Matthews at the Women's Institute Hall. A large gold picture frame was erected on the stage, with a black velvet background. People chose the picture they would represent. Each tableau was shown three times, Miss Matthews' little hand-bell signalling the drawing to and fro of the curtains. Subjects varied greatly. Mr. Bligh, from Benedicts, Tyddesley Wood, commented skilfully, and with humour, on each picture, whether it was the work of a great master or folksy and funny.

My sister, Avril, still remembers the thick white taffeta dress and hair ribbon she wore for 'The Age of Innocence', and the white lace dress and white paper flowers she held for 'Lilies'. She was also 'The Child Samuel'. I was dressed as a little Victorian girl, in church, wearing a purple skirt, a red cape, black button boots, a 'pork pie' hat and holding a fur muff. For 'My First Sermon', by Sir John Millais, she sits bolt upright. For 'My Second Sermon', she slumps on the bench and slumbers peacefully. My sister and I were 'The Princes in the Tower', dressed in black velvet. My father, George Bramford, was 'The Pied Piper of Hamelin', followed by a group of dancing children. Bearded Jimmy Ford and old Miss Wrench were 'Darby and Joan'. Miss Wrench was also an excellent choice for the advertisement for Mazawattee Tea.

'The Last Trump' showed four card players – Mr. Grundy, wearing a blacksmith's leather apron, Brian Lane, the verger, Doug Trigg, the barber and George Bramford, the schoolmaster. There was great fun behind the stage, as many performers were in two or three pictures. They had to change costumes in a very cramped and crowded room.

In 'Mrs. Jarley's Waxworks' in 1940 or '41, we were <u>animated</u> pictures. Maurice Banbury, the dentist, was Jarge, Mrs. Jarley's son. He wound us up to move in a mechanical fashion. Such were the home-grown entertainments we enjoyed, long before the advent of television.

CHORAL SOCIETIES

Pershore has had several of these over the years. In 1919, Pershore Choral Society's conductor was Miss Fanny Stephens. They gave concerts in the Three Tuns Hotel ballroom.

Leslie Brookes said: "I was twelve when I joined the Choral Society in Pershore, in about 1926. They let me in at half fees. I used to stand by Captain Hutton. I could get down to bottom 'G'. That was good experience. Later, in the 1930's, I joined the Male Voice Choir. Mr. Sumner was conductor and your father, Mr. Bramford, was our accompanist."

Margaret Taylor said: "I joined the Women's Institute choir under Miss Joan Phillips. We got bigger. One day, Joan said: 'I think we ought to have some men in our choir.' So we found some men to join us and, in 1949, we called it the 'Pershore Choral Society'. Our first venture was The Messiah. We thought we were doing wonders. Now it is a very big Choral Society. Joan Phillips was conductor for 34 years."

DANCES AT THE THREE TUNS HOTEL

"My husband was M.C.," said Blanche Dufty. "He used to do a lot of dancing in India, when he was in the Army, in the First World War. At the Three Tuns, we used to take the floor for special dances. We learnt all the latest dances from London – the Waltz, the Veleta, the Lancers. I would rather dance in a set. We won a prize for the Waltz. My favourite was the Veleta."

Rene Giles said: "There was always a dance on Thursday nights at the Tuns, and Police Balls for charity. One night, there were as many as 400 on the floor. And there was a slope in the floor which was getting dangerous."

THE PICTURE HOUSE

"It was our main entertainment," said Rene Giles. "For silent films, Fanny Hunt used to play the piano there. She would really thump out the music! One could go twice a week, because the programme changed half-way through the week."

In the 1940's, my sister, Avril, remembers the scent spray being used over the audience in the interval. On Saturday mornings, there were children's serial films like 'The Headless Horseman'. That was when the Picture House had become the Plaza cinema.

CIRCUSES

"I remember circuses in the Weir meadow," said Cyril Smith. "Before the circus, Cowboys and Indians used to parade through the town, with their horses, to advertise their circus. There were wagons drawn by horses. It was just like the Wild West."

THE NOT FOR JOES/NA' FA' JOES/NAPPER JOES

They were groups of Pershore and district Morris dancers, who went about the towns and villages for ten days, around Christmas and New Year. The big day was Boxing Day. One team was still performing up to the Second World War. I well remember them visiting houses in Station Road and dancing for us on our back patio.

Bill Scarrott related his memories of these dancers to Dave Jones, founder of Hereford Folk Club and Bromyard Folk Festival. Before the First World War, Bill Scarrott started dancing with the Not For Joes when he was eight. That was two years before he left school, at the age of ten.

"The men in those dance teams were brickies, carpenters, plumbers, fellows off the ground, farmers," he said. "There wasn't the work about at that time of year. There were eight men in each team. They were accompanied by a fiddle, concertina, and sometimes, a tambourine, triangle, tin whistle, or bones. They performed stick dances in two lines, facing each other. Their name originated from an old Victorian Music Hall song, which they sang in a wide variety of versions. They would make up their own verses."

Bill's version was:

> Not for Joe, not for Joe,
> Not for Joseph if he knows it.
> Not for Joe, not for Joe,
> Stick 'im in the garden, let 'im grow.
>
> If I 'ad a penny, I'd buy a penny gun,
> Fill it full of powder and make the coppers run.
>
> Oh! Not for Joe, ...

"For their costume, they wore ordinary trousers, tied at the knee, and ordinary shoes, unpolished. A woman's flowery blouse was decorated with long strips of rag, threaded through, like ribbons, all over. On their head, an old trilby hat, and they blacked their faces and hands with burnt cork.

Bunches of bells were tied round the waist. The 'collector' carried a pig's bladder, with which he struck dancers and onlookers alike. The Napper Joes would walk to the villages to perform and even as far as Malvern and Ledbury – on foot. It was companionable and it was a way of earning money, at a time of year when there was no work and therefore, no pay."

"I was one of the Napper Joes," said Jack Heeks. "We

dressed up in women's clothes and went round the pubs and to the big houses – usually on Boxing Day. We went to the villages as well – Stoulton, Drakes Broughton, Birlingham. We always sang the Napper Joe song and banged our sticks together. It was handed down to us."

'Nobby' Clark from Lower Moor said he had danced with the Napper Joes at Wyre Piddle, Fladbury, Charlton and Cropthorne. "For New Yearing," he said, "we used to start walking the streets at about four o'clock in the morning. If we saw a light on in a house, we would sing and then be asked into the house. We would walk around the table three times. Christmas Day was carol singing, Boxing Day was Not For Joeing and New Year's Day was New Yearing."

Alice Young has a less favourable memory of the Napper Joes, before the First World War: "They were organised from the White Horse Inn. As kids, we were frightened of them, with their black faces. They had been in all the pubs and they were three-parts drunk. I would run a mile from a drunken man. And they had the thickest sticks they could get."

In the 1980's, Dave Jones, of Putley, Herefordshire, recreated the 'Not For Joes' in Herefordshire. They now dance under the name of 'The Old Wonder, Not For Joes'.

THE CORONATION, 1937 *(George VI and Queen Elizabeth)*

"I can remember the Coronation in 1937 in the Village Room at Wick," said Malcolm Meikle. As children, we were given the choice of penknives or money boxes with the King and Queen's heads on, and also a mug."

Marjorie Pettifer was Britannia, in the grand procession through the streets of Pershore. Tom and John Pettifer drilled a group of children into Toy Soldiers. My sister, Avril, was one of them. They paraded to martial music, wearing red uniforms and bearskin hats, cheeks rouged and carrying wooden guns.

Programme of Events in PERSHORE
for the CORONATION in 1937

Carnival Parade - ORDER OF PROCESSION.

Police
Band
British Legion
Brittannia
Foresters
Chamber of Commerce
Fire Brigade
Mayor's Coach

Abbey Garage	Car	Crown

Heralds

Jester

Carnival King and Queen and Court

Messrs. Clemens & Son	Lorry	H.M.S. Courageous
Mr. F. Bomford	Decorated Car	
File of Pedestrians		
Mrs. Pettifer	Lorry	Playing Fields
Mr. Brookes	Van	
Baptist Church	Lorry	Linked Empire
Mr R.C. Edwards	Decorated Car	
Mrs. Pettifer		Toy Soldiers
Mrs. Harrington	Lorry	Milk Bar
Mr. A.H. Brown	Van	
Miss Roberts	Lorry	Hospital Sick Room
Mr. J.A. Knight	Decorated Car	
Drakes Broughton	Dray	School Children
Cycles & Perambulators		
British Legion	Lorry	Peace and War
Messrs. Clemens & Taylor	Van	
Mr. Rowley	Lorry	?
Mr. H. Price	Decorated Car	
Mr. T. Simpkins	Lorry	Trade House
Messrs. Checketts Bros.	Van	
Central Market, Ltd.	Lorry	National Mark
Mr. Stokes	Decorated Car	
Cheltenham Gas Co.	Lorry	Own Trade
W.C. Jones	Van	
W. Fearnside	Dray	Empire Greetings
G. Phillips & Sons	Van	
Co-operative Fruit Market	Lorry	Peace & Security
Bruton	Car	Public Want
John & Mac		After the Coronation
Police		

- - - - - - - - -

Presentation of Keys and Crowning of Carnival King and Queen

King - Gordon Bancks, Esq.: Queen - Miss E. Jaynes: Maids of Honour - Misses I.Leach, B.Overd
Mayor - W.T. Chapman, Esq; Cardinal - J.S.Irwin Esq.; Jester - T.J.Checketts, Esq.

119

4.30 - 7   Children's Tea and Sports at local schools

6.00   **TOY SOLDIERS' DISPLAY**
AT CRICKET FIELD

Produced and arranged by Mrs. A. Pettifer, Miss M. Pettifer and Mr T. Pettifer.

Song "Toy Town Parade" ..... Neville Brown and John Simpkins and Soldiers Chorus
Inspection, Mr. T. Pettifer.

Song "Toy Town Artillery" Neville Brown and John Simpkins and Soldiers Chorus

Conductor, Master Michael Edwards

6.00   **TEA for Older Persons** (65 years upwards)
AT THE ANGEL HOTEL

6.30   **PUNCH and JUDY SHOW** AT CRICKET FIELD

6.50   **Scholars' PHYSICAL DRILL**   "   "

7.00   **FOLK DANCING**   "   "

Under direction of Miss Gardner

1.	Circassian Circle	5.	Jenny Pluck Pears
2.	Gathering Peascods	6.	Huntsman's Chorus
3.	Flowers of Edinburgh	7.	Durham Reel
4.	Newcastle	8.	Ribbon Dance

7.30   **PUNCH AND JUDY SHOW**
AT CRICKET FIELD.

8.00 to 9.00 **DANCING and COMMUNITY SINGING**
IN BROAD STREET
Conductor, J.M. Carroll, Esq.

9 - 2   **DANCE at ROYAL THREE TUNS HOTEL**

THE WOMEN'S INSTITUTE

The W.I. movement was founded for instruction, as well as entertainment. It was in 1916 that the Pershore W.I. was formed. Mrs. Rusher, wife of a Pershore doctor, of The Paddocks, Worcester Road, became President. Subjects of early talks at meetings included: 'Bad Drains' and 'Knitting for soldiers at the Front'. Members numbered 106. An ex-Army hut was purchased and erected in Priest Lane for their meetings.

In 1929 and 1930, during the General Strike, the Women's Institute did much good work in Pershore. At their meetings, members contributed eggs for the 'Egg Roll Call', thus ensuring that Pershore Cottage Hospital received an average of 250 eggs each month.

A Christmas party was given to the Inmates of the Poor Law Institution (now Heathlands). A collection of clothing was sent to miners' families. The W.I. Hall was used as a welfare centre, where babies were weighed and their progress assessed.

W. I. members' catering and organising skills were much in demand during the Second World War in Pershore. A canteen for servicemen was held in the W. I. Hall every night of the week. Records show that, on one occasion, 1,000 servicemen were served in one evening! That was when Pershore and Defford aerodromes were at their busiest. W. I. members became expert salvage collectors. Many helped with Pershore Services Comforts Fund.

The highlight of those war-time years, was the W. I. 'Canners' Club'. A canning machine was purchased and installed in the Hall. Great quantities of fruit and vegetables were preserved in cans – a useful addition to families' war-time rations, in spite of the shortage of sugar.

Pershore W. I. Drama Group flourished in the 1950's, with Mrs. Vera Evans as producer, among others. The play 'Nine 'til Six' mirrored the lives of shop assistants in the dress department of a large store. 'Sanctuary' was set in a convent in France, during the French Revolution. Catherine Parkes was the Mother

121

Superior. 'The Old Fool' was even more ambitious, and included husbands Walter Palfrey and Jim Gardener in the cast!

Betty Tuffin played the role of a schoolgirl of 13 in this play, even though she was then aged 30, and was expecting! At a rehearsal, Walter Palfrey had to give the 'schoolgirl' a slap. "He slapped me so hard," said Betty, 'that I nearly fell off the stage. And the cast were most concerned about me!"

French's plays for women were often performed by Women's Institutes in the 1930's. One of them, 'The Umbrella Ladies' was the speciality of Mary and Marjorie Revers of Bricklehampton. Mary explained the sketch to me. "We sat at either side of the stage <u>under</u> large closed umbrellas, which were copiously draped with long skirts. Attached to the spokes on top of the two umbrellas were masks of old ladies, wearing large bonnets.

We began as two <u>thin</u> ladies but, in time, first one, then the other became fat. This was done by opening our umbrellas very slowly, conversing all the while." Village audiences enjoyed this simple, but amusing, sketch.

PINVIN DRAMATIC SOCIETY

This was an ambitious group, which flourished in the 1930's, performing a Shakespeare play annually in their Village Hall, with great enthusiasm. Miss Walters and Nancy Willis were producers. I well remember seeing their 'Merchant of Venice', 'Merry Wives of Windsor' and 'A Midsummer Night's Dream'.

Pinvin residents, Frank Westcott, Leonard and Kath Coates, Mrs. Spalding, Charles Harriss, were regular actors in this Society. Pershore people joined them. I well remember seeing Charles Harriss, a market gardener, playing Shylock. Mr. William Westcott, fruit farmer, of The Ford, who was also an artist, designed and painted their scenery. "For 'The Merchant of Venice'," said his son, Donald, "he constructed domes and even a moving gondola."

My sister, Avril, then aged ten, was the Fairy who talks with Puck, in 'A Midsummer Night's Dream' – 'Over hill, over dale ...

' The curate, the Rev. Smythe was Bottom, and he later married Puck. I recall two of the 'Workmen' actors elbowing each other good-naturedly. They were the Pinvin Boucher brothers and their real-life work was undertaking!

The following summer, I borrowed Bottom's larger-than-life ass's head for our version of 'The Dream', at Worcester Girls' Grammar School. This papier maché head had been stored in fruit-grower Leonard Coates' barn in Pinvin. I transported it home, gingerly, resting on my bicycle bars. A few days later the ass's head travelled with me by train, to Worcester, in the guard's van. Its tennis ball eyes were goggling. So it had a double success. A device inside it could waggle the eyelids too!

PERSHORE DRAMATIC SOCIETY

This was formed after the war and flourished in the 1950's. They took their plays round the villages. Eve Elliott said: "We had an enthusiastic group and we did one play a year. Bob Ashworth produced. We performed 'Arms and the Man', 'The Holly and the Ivy', 'Night must Fall' ..."

Avril, my sister, remembered that when they used the Plaza cinema for their plays, there was no accessible loo. So they brought a chamber-pot and stowed it under a chair. Backstage was dusty. The men used the projection room to change in.

Walter Palfrey said: "It was great fun, our Dramatic Society. We had previously put on shows at the W. I. Hall. One night, in the Plough Inn, Dennis Hartwell, Manager of the Plaza cinema then, said to me, "Why don't you use the cinema?' The Alcester Managers of the Plaza agreed. The 'flea pit', or 'chicken run' seats, at the front, cost sixpence and the 'posh' seats, at the back, 2/6d in those days.

We men in the Society had to go down to the cinema on the Saturday night and unscrew all the seats at the front and back. We took the front ones to the back and the back ones to the front. We took the screen down too.

Dennis Hartwell gave us three nights – Monday, Tuesday

and Wednesday. We had to put it all back again after our last performance. It took us hours. We slept in the posh seats in the end, before we went home. The cinema patrons who came on a Monday, were quite astounded at there being no film. But they all came in and saw our play instead. It was somewhere to go!

We were very ambitious. Our first play was 'The Chiltern Hundreds'. Harry Stubbs came to see us. He was the Vicar in 'The Archers' then. He thought we were very good. Eileen Gardener was the producer."

POPULAR SONGS

I have always been acutely aware that a popular song can conjure up, for each one of us, the unique atmosphere of a particular occasion or era. Here are the titles of songs of the 1920's and '30's, harvested, at random, from my memory:

Tiptoe through the tulips
The Wedding of the painted doll
The Broadway Melody
The Destiny Waltz
Have you ever seen a dream walking?
Lazybones
Your must say 'Yes' to Mr. Brown
Everything's in rhythm with my heart
Dancing on the ceiling
In your Easter bonnet
Love is the sweetest thing
Night and Day
I'm in the mood for love
My heart stood still
What'll I do?
Nice work if you can get it
On the good ship 'Lollipop'
Animal crackers in my soup
A nightingale sang in Berkeley Square

I told every little star
Miss Otis regrets
Don't forget, dinner at eight
Cherry Blossom Lane
September in the rain
Room 504
There's a small hotel
The Love Bug
Smoke gets in your eyes
These foolish things
Love walked right in
The way you look tonight
Dancing cheek-to-cheek
Deep Purple
All the things you are
Waltzing in the clouds
It's foolish, but it's fun
On the Isle of Capri

RADIO

As schoolgirls, we would listen eagerly each week, to radio programmes like 'Monday Night at Seven', and 'Henry Hall's Guest Night'. From the radio, we would learn the words of the very latest popular song, to sing it on the school train to Worcester.

Chapter ten

RADIO, ELECTRICITY AND WATER COME TO PERSHORE

Three brand-new commodities arrived in the town, within the short space of about seven years. Each was to transform entirely the lives of the townspeople, by making the daily round more comfortable, and also by broadening their horizons.

"Radio came and people had these tall masts," said Leslie Brookes. "Mr. Clemens let me have some wire and a crystal and a pair of head-phones. It cost me about half-a-crown altogether. That was in 1926 or '27, when I was about eleven."

Charles Clemens told me: "I had the first valve set that was made. Arthur Taylor came to see me. He had been on board ship as a radio operator. They used crystal sets. The range was 50 miles in daytime, 500 miles at night.

Arthur said: "Let's start up and make crystal sets. He was a nice lad really. He wasn't afraid of anyone. If we had a difficult customer, he would say: 'Leave it to me.' Some of them could be rather nasty, if some little thing went wrong with their set.

I was sitting listening in and, suddenly, I heard a voice talking. I was so excited. Up to then, we had heard only dots and dashes – never a voice. I turned to run downstairs and tell them about this, forgetting I still had the head-phones on. I pulled the set off and broke the valve. I had to go to Birmingham to get another one!

I knew nothing about radio. All I knew was from reading. I had a nice magazine, 'The Model Engineer'. It gave you all the history of radio and I used to take it in weekly. When Arthur came, he had the theory of transmitting. He had been to North Wales to be trained before he joined up. He had to be efficient in transmitting and reading Morse.

Then his father took him to Glasgow for his first trial on a boat as an operator. It was a ship that went round the coast, training radio operators. Arthur got on well with the Captain. You travelled First Class in those days, if you were a radio-op. But Arthur told me: 'We were lowered to Third Class when every ship had to have a wireless operator, after the war. There were more of us!' After ten years, Arthur came home and saw me, in 1922.

My wife always said Arthur Taylor was a perfect gentleman. He was the ideal man for the job. We did all the work in that big room at the back of my house, next to the Plough Inn. Arthur never would walk in without knocking and saying: 'Is it all right, Mrs. Clemens?'

I used to like the Rev. Willis of Defford – a Christian. He used to make up crystal sets for the widow ladies living alone in Defford and he would put up an aerial for them.

There was no licence in those days. We used to save him parts to make a crystal set. He would knock at my door, open it, and say: 'Is the Professor about? You must be a Professor, 'cos nobody else knows anything about these radios!' But Arthur Taylor knew much more than me, because he had worked on a liner.

Arthur and I planned to give a talk and display, on RADIO, in the Mission Hall. It was a packed house. We couldn't get hold of a famous speaker, so Arthur said he would talk about 'Radio on Ships', and how it worked at sea. He did a demonstration of the Morse alphabet before he started, and he used a blackboard and chalk. Arthur said he would talk for an hour, because we couldn't get a sound out of the transmitter at first, that evening.

At last we got Rugby. It was the biggest radio station in the world then. It went out to every ship in the world. We switched on Rugby, which was transmitting all the telegrams to ships. One telegram I shall never forget: 'Return at once. All forgiven.' Not all were as dramatic as that. But, you see, that transmission was private in those days.

Arthur said to me: 'You won't give me away? I could get hung for this!' All the audience could hear was dots and dashes, with

Arthur on the head-phones you see.

He was translating for them from the Morse Code, and disclosing the actual words of the telegrams going out to ships!

About 1920, the only wireless station working in this country, was in Essex. It was run by Captain Eckersley. When the BBC had advertised for an engineer, he had put in for the job, but they had turned him down. So every night, he ran a talk, on this station in Essex.

Roy Beard takes up the story: "When I was about nine or ten, I was very friendly with Jim Clemens, who was about my age. He had a lovely train set in his house, next to the Plough Inn. What always fascinated me there, were the radio sets, and everything connected with them. At home, we had just a three-valve crystal set. It involved a large battery and an accumulator, which we had to have charged up each week. We took it to Mr. Charles Clemens for this.

In 1942, Clemens and Taylor had just taken over the Wireless Supply at Malvern. Malvern seemed at the other end of the world to me – sixteen miles away. They needed an assistant there, so I was taken on.

Mr. Clemens Senior said to me: 'Try it for five weeks and let me know, Roy.' I forgot to tell him how I liked the job. I've been working there ever since, for the same firm, more than fifty years on!

Michael Clemens, the grandson, owns the business now. He still can't get over me, and my life's job there. He has branches now in Barnards Green, Upton, Evesham, Broadway and Chipping Campden. Mr. Clemens Senior didn't believe in Apprentices. Jim, his son, did."

Appropriately, Roy Beard has the last word: "In 1947, the first television set to be seen in Pershore, appeared in the window of Clemens' shop, next to the Plough Inn. There was quite a crowd of people on the pavement, watching the screen. And the pavement there is narrow. Eventually, the police complained that Mr. Clemens was causing an obstruction. This particular T.V. set had to be taken out!"

ELECTRICITY

(by courtesy of The Shropshire, Worcestershire and Staffordshire Electric Power Company).

Electricity came to Pershore in 1926-28. When it was being installed in the town, Walter Palfrey remembers seeing trenches dug in Church Walk, and skulls and bones dug up, near the Abbey and the monastery. But the villages around Pershore had to wait much longer for electricity. Most villages around Pershore had electricity by 1954.

The Evesham Journal heralded the coming of this novel form of power with great enthusiasm:

September 12th 1925
The ELECTRICITY will be turned on NEXT MONTH in Evesham. The power station erected this year at Stourport, will feed a vast network of overhead power lines, which will afford every facility for rural supplies of every description.

January 1925
The power lines will run from Redditch, through Crabbs Cross to Astwood Bank near Feckenham, Inkberrow, the Lenches, to Evesham. The line will continue to Broadway. Further extensions will be made through Hampton, near Cropthorne, to Pershore and on to Upton-on-Severn.

The high-pressure line will be reduced for a single farm, by means of a transformer. A low-pressure line will be run along the hedgerows to the farms, where the current may be used for lighting, heating, cooking and all other work on a farm, such as timber-cutting, chaff and root-cutting. The coming of the power will be a boon to people who are rather isolated.

October 1925 PERSHORE – Practical Electricity.
A start will be made in November to revive the Continuation Classes, which were of great utility to the town before the war. A class in Practical Electricity will commence. Mr. Arthur W. Smith (chemist) is officiating as Hon. Local Secretary.

BIRMINGHAM POST September 1925
At a Trades' Exhibition in Bingley Hall, Birmingham, Mr. V. W. Dale spoke on 'The Use of Electricity in the Home'. He said: "Regarded, until comparatively recently, as a luxury, electric lighting is now within reach of the democracy. It offers the safest, cleanest, most convenient and cheapest illuminant. Permanently sprayed lamps, in handsome colours, can introduce decorative lighting in the home. People are only just beginning to realise the extraordinary effect of colour upon the mind. It can produce cheerfulness morbidity, or any other mental condition desired, by the scientific colour psychologist.'

BIRMINGHAM POST August 1925 Shop Window Lighting and Dressing
At the Drapers' Summer School at Oxford, Mr. Evans of London (of D. H. Evans department store in Oxford Street?) said that a survey of shop windows throughout the country showed that 46.8 per cent of drapers' windows were poorly lighted. Their slogan should be: 'People buy where the light is bright'. Excellent lighting could be obtained by the use of window reflectors, with 100-watt light bulbs spaced one foot apart. Additional attractiveness could be obtained by the use of coloured lighting.

January 1926 Pershore Working Men's and Old Comrades Club
The late Mr. Harry Workman left £250 to be used for the better lighting of the Club. He anticipated them getting their own electric supply, with their own engine and battery, but the outlook today was for a public supply.

EVESHAM JOURNAL Advertisement 1926.
Electrical Cooking and Baking Demonstration in the S.W.S. Showroom, 18, High Street, Evesham. All ladies interested are cordially invited to attend. FAMILY COOKER (6 – 8 persons) costs £19.15.0d.

EVESHAM -179-
ELECTRICITY SUPPLY

The Shropshire, Worcestershire, and Staffordshire
Electric Power Company.

ELECTRIC FIRES ON HIRE at a rental of 3/-
PER QUARTER. JUST THINK OF IT—HEAT
AT A TOUCH OF THE SWITCH.

APPLY FOR FURTHER PARTICULARS

District Office :—

BEWDLEY STREET, EVESHAM.

2 2 MAY 1926   'Phone : 265 EVESHAM.

Tewkesbury is feeling the pinch of the Coal Strike and there is scarcely any coal in the town. The Tewkesbury Gas Company has again come to the rescue and has supplied more than 200 householders with coal. We remember the usefulness of the Gas Company during the last coal strike. 3 1 MAY 1926

Ironic!

EVESHAM
ELECTRICITY SUPPLY

The Shropshire, Worcestershire, and Staffordshire
Electric Power Company.

THE ELECTRIC IRON will allow you to do
your ironing under a shady tree IN THE GARDEN.
What could be more welcome THIS HOT WEATHER.
Call at our District Office and hear how it can be done.

2 7 JULY 1926

1926

District Office :—

BEWDLEY STREET, EVESHAM.

'Phone : 265 EVESHAM.

EVESHAM
ELECTRICITY SUPPLY

The Shropshire, Worcestershire, and Staffordshire
Electric Power Company.

IF YOU WOULD LIKE to enter a Competition for a
£2,000 ALL-ELECTRIC HOUSE, call at our nearest District
Office and ask for Entrance Form and further particulars.

1 3 OCT. 1926

District Office,

18, HIGH STREET, EVESHAM.

'Phone 46 EVESHAM.

131

WATER

"Water came to Pershore in 1932," said Leslie Brookes. "My mother got into trouble, because she complained that she had come from Worcester, where they <u>had</u> got sanitation – but not in Pershore. When we had visitors come to see us, they had to go out to the earth closets. Sewage was taken to Orchard Ditch, where the Plum Tree pub stands now. All that ground was allotment and market garden before the Abbey estate was built."

I learned more about Pershore's need for a sewage scheme from Leslie Brookes: "In the 1930's slump, a delegation went to see the Chairman of the local Council. They were led by Mr. Grinnell of Priest Lane. He was foreman at Fisher Humphreys. They were out of work. They thought it was wrong they should be getting money for nothing – just for signing on the 'dole', when Pershore wanted a sewage scheme.

So they went to see Dr. Emerson, the Chairman, in his big house, 'Pershore House', opposite the Post Office, where solicitors' offices are now. The men told him they were prepared to work for the same money that they were getting for 'dole'. They said they were tradesmen, but were willing to work on a sewage scheme and take labouring jobs.

Dr. Emerson ordered them out of the house. 'Pershore exists very well without sewage and water,' said he, sourly.

Mr. Grinnell reminded Dr. Emerson that <u>he</u> could afford to pay a man to pump the water, by hand, into the tank on <u>his</u> roof. It was well-known that Dr. Emerson had his own septic tanks in the garden and they led into the river. So the delegation departed, frustrated and desperate."

In 1931, Pershore still depended on wells and pumps for water, as it had done for centuries. Nora Bristow said: "We had no bathroom, so we bathed in a tin bath by the fire. In hard winters, our pump would be frozen."

The devastating smell from the cart of the Night Soil men was an accepted weekly occurrence. Marion Knight recalls:

"Coming home from the pub, my husband, Fred, on hearing the jangle and sloshing of carts, would avoid them, by turning along another street and going another way home. The smell was powerful and nauseating.

As there was no back entrance to many houses, the Night Soil men had to carry the buckets through the sitting-rooms. They used to say, that any coppers in their pockets turned green – caused by the powerful gas given off from the night soil."

Ellen Willis told me: "I came to no. 31 Hurst Park in 1928 and I've lived here ever since. The best pump for drinking water was here, outside my back door. You could use the other pumps for washing, but not for drinking, because the ground round the area was salty. So everyone in these 32 houses came daily, for their drinking water, to this pump.

We were all very friendly then. Before my son, Peter, was of school age, he liked to help pump the water at this pump, when people came with their buckets. It was enamel buckets then. In 1932, it was wonderful to be able to turn on the taps inside your home, at last!"

Marion Knight began nursing at Pershore Cottage Hospital in 1929. The District Nurses (the Sherwoods) lived in the Cottage Hospital then. Marion was taken, by a District Nurse, to see twins born in Ganderton Row; then a very poor group of cottages, with just one pump in the yard.

But the Cottage Hospital itself only had a pump for water! There was a tank in the roof and a man pumped the water, to this roof tank, twice a day. When there was a drought, water from the river was brought from the Brandy Cask pub in port-wine barrels, by horse and cart. "This water," said Marion, "was used for sluicing bed pans and cleaning floors – and it smelt strongly of wine!"

Later on, a windmill at the back of Nogains, near the Hospital, was used to pump water for the hospital. Then, with the arrival of the S.W.S. Electricity Company, it was arranged that an electrical apparatus should be installed, to pump water from the well, to the hospital tank.

There was a grand Opening Day for this event. General Sir Francis Davies was on the committee. "But on the big day," said Marion, "the new mechanism went wrong. The water was being pumped <u>back</u> into the well, because the valves had been put on the wrong way round!"

Marion Knight continued: "Mr. Percy Feek was Treasurer of the Hospital. He paid out one shilling a week for the nurses to take a bath at the Three Tuns Hotel.

Laundry was done in the Hospital by Mrs. Dunsby every day. She was the mother of Mrs. Roberts, who kept a shop next door to Faggs. The laundress was paid £1 per week. She turned up her sleeves and wore armlets. She starched the collars and cuffs of the nurses' uniforms."

I, myself, well remember the joy of the Bramford family, and our neighbours, when we had decent plumbing and water on tap in our houses. We had come to Pershore a year before, in 1931, from Overbury, where water <u>was</u> on tap from the rills of Bredon Hill. We always said the water followed us <u>over</u> Bredon Hill! For Pershore's water did, indeed, come from the Holland-Martin estate on Bredon Hill. It came through Eckington. Later on, it came from Worcester also, to the reservoir on top of Allesborough Hill.

There was a Deed of Grant dated 24th May 1932, between R. M. Holland-Martin of Overbury Court (1), the Overbury Estate (2), and Pershore Rural District Council (3), 'the benefit of which vests in the Authority.' This was a grant to run for 999 years and which gave Pershore R.D.C. the right to take 120,000 gallons per day maximum, at fourpence (old pence) per thousand gallons, so long as certain conditions were met. The annual rent was £1.

Chapter eleven

HEALTH, ILLNESS, REMEDIES

Good health is a very precious asset. But it depends so much on a number of variable things – family history, diet, weather, stress, being employed, liking your work, harmony at home, a balanced outlook .....

I admired Elsie Barnes' spirited reply to my query: "How old are you now?" "Well, Margaret, to tell you the truth, I never bothers to think. I'm well turned sixty. (She was about 78!). I never bothers to keep a statement on me age. It's me health I keeps more looking to. But one thing I can say, Margaret, I've got a wonderful young brain to keep everything in order."

"A lot of people won't believe us about this cholera ground in the Orchard Road area," said Kitty Haines. "It was the burial ground they had to set aside during the cholera epidemic in 1854. Twelve trees were planted to mark the spot. As children, we used to say there was the best blackberries in that ground – but we was too frightened to pick them!

Several Pershore people had relatives in that ground. There were no coffins. They were buried at night, because they couldn't get people to handle the corpses. People were very superstitious then. The bodies were wrapped in sheets. A horse and cart came round, at night, to collect them."

Blanche Dufty remembered the scourge of T.B. before the First World War. "My youngest brother had T.B. and was cured in Knightwick Hospital. My sister had T.B. and Dr. Rusher was attending her. But the medicine was just coloured water. It was too late. She was so full of life. She would say: "What have I done to have this?" Dr. Emerson could do nothing.

That's how I came to be a maid at a doctor's house in Worcester. My poorly sister had been a maid there before me. I was replacing her. The Worcester doctor and his wife thought a lot of her and brought her anything she wanted. He would ask my sister: 'Lily, is there anything you want?' 'Yes,' she would reply, 'Put a new pair of lungs in me!'"

The Fever Hospital was in Three Springs Road. "There used to be a lot of scarlet fever in Pershore," said Kitty Haines. "It was because of the drains and the sewerage being so outdated. The outbreaks would start among the poor families in Head Street and Newlands. There would be six or seven in a family then, and no Family Allowances."

Ella Patricia, the youngest daughter of Mr. Swann, the chemist, was once told: "Don't go down the entry in Broad Street (Ganderton's Row) because there's an infectious disease there."

My sister, Avril, remembers a neighbour, young Dick Beaumont, being taken, wrapped in a red blanket on a stretcher, to the Fever Hospital at Knightwick. When she visited him, with his mother, they could only speak with him through an open window.

Esme Westcott told me: "In the 1920's, you had to pay for all your medicines and for the doctor. It was 2/6d a visit for the doctor. Before the First World War, the midwife in Pershore went out in a pony and trap, with the doctor. There were no cars in that day. Everybody called her 'Ford' (never 'Mrs.')."

Mrs. Swann, the chemist's wife, used to say: "When we began, in the 1920's, our sick customers – workers on the land – came to the pharmacy for medicines to be made up, because they could not afford to go to the doctor. Many of them could not even pay us for their medicines. So they paid us in <u>kind</u>. They brought us pheasants, poached from the wood, bread, eggs from the farms, etc."

"It wasn't found out until I went in the services in the war," said Leslie Brookes, "that I had had polio as a baby and rheumatic fever. If I played football, which I loved, I was out for the count. When I was twelve, Dr. Kennedy told my parents I should have to walk up the stairs one at a time. And not to think about putting me to any work. But I haven't done so bad! I did lots of exercises and deep breathing."

Doctors' prescriptions were sometimes doubted, as this comment by an elderly lady living in Newlands shows: "I've got this blooming arthritis that's caught up in my neck. Doctor's given me some tablets to take. But I don't like taking them. I wonders if they're <u>drugs</u>!"

Marion Knight told me about Pershore Cottage Hospital in 1929. Marion was born in India. She lived there until she was eighteen, having been at school at Simla in the Himalayas. Her father had been with the Governor of Bombay and later with the Governor of the United Provinces. She came to England to train as a nurse.

Marion spoke: "This year (1995) the Cottage Hospital has celebrated its 100th birthday. There was a service in Pershore Abbey and a tea party in St. Andrew's. The hospital cost £1,000 to build. Lady Coventry opened it. Mr. Ganderton of Perrott House, Pershore, gave £500 towards the building. He was a wool merchant. Ganderton Row was named after him, and also a ward at the Worcester Royal Infirmary.

Wages for nurses in 1929 and the early '30's were £60 per year. In 1929, when I went to nurse there, there were thirteen beds. In 1895, it had opened with two beds and a cot. The cot had been given by Miss Allen. The Allen's were chemists before Arthur Smith. There was a brass plate on this cot. I know, because I polished that plate on that same cot. The cot was still there after 35 years."

There was a Private Ward upstairs in 1929 – but no lift. So, after operation, the other nurses and myself had to carry the patients, on stretchers, up the stairs! Standards are lower today in hospitals. There are no caps, or aprons for nurses and no nursing as such. There is no personal touch, or attention to details."

Nora Bristow said: "Remedies were home-made in the 1930's, to save money. You paid 7/6d for a visit to the doctor. But food was more wholesome then. We had our own eggs, chickens, pig, and good home-grown vegetables on our allotments."

Here are some of the old remedies that Nora Bristow recalls:

<u>IMPETIGO</u>   Drink nettle tea.

<u>STYES ON EYE</u>   Place a wet tea leaf gauze bandage on the eye.

CHILBLAINS   Put your foot in a full chamber pot. It is a sure cure. Or, rub a raw onion on chilblains. Vaseline was used a lot for sores and bruises.

CUTS   Put iodine on, as an antiseptic.

BURNS   Use bicarbonate of soda – painful at first.

ARTHRITIS   Drink hot cider vinegar and honey.

SORE THROAT   Glycerine, honey and lemon juice. Also, butter and brown sugar, mixed together. My Aunt Winifred's remedy for a sore throat: wear an unwashed stocking round your neck all night in bed.

POULTICES   Imagine a piping-hot cloth, steeped in mustard and bread, or linseed and flour, being applied to your chest, or back, for several minutes, to relieve bronchitis or cure sores!

The District Nurse, who came to our school house in Overbury, when my sister was born, taught me this rhyme:

> Here comes Nurse with a red hot poultice,
> Slaps it on and takes no notice.
> "Ow!" says the patient, "it's too hot!"
> "No!" says Nurse, "of course it's not!"

ANCIENT WORCESTERSHIRE CURES AND RECIPES

To cure Fits Dry and powder the green leaves of mistletoe and take as much as will lay on a shilling in a glass of cold water.

The Itch Take the juice of celandine.

Nothing (dated 1738) Take the whites of 3 eggs and 3 spoonfuls of raspberry juice. Beat it all one way, until it come to a great blob.

The best sandwich of all, is made of the blue sky, the green fields and the fresh air in between.

A class at the old Defford Road School in 1929, with their teacher, the formidable Mrs. Webb.

A class at Defford Road School, Pershore, in 1931

Outside the old Defford Road Junior School in 1933.
Headmaster, George Bramford with his staff. From left, Miss Cooke,
Miss Taylor, Mrs. Hallam. The Co-operative Market is behind.

George Bramford, Headmaster of Abbey Park Primary School, Pershore, retires, aged 60 in 1950. Mary Revers, on his staff, presents a pair of bowls. Others in photo: Meg Bramford, Jim Gardner, Deputy Head, and Percy Feek, Chairman of School Governors.

PHOTOS

Schooldays at LEY School, Bridge Street, Pershore, founded and led by Miss Lois Young.

Pershore Brotherhood Male Voice Choir c. 1932. Their conductor, Mr. Sumner, carries his hat.

Pershore Abbey Choir and Churchwardens, 1950's, with Canon Bark centre. Sitting next but one to him is Rodney Baldwyn, organist.

Nativity Play in Pershore Abbey, 1961.

*The Three Kings. Left, John Harriss, centre Harold Orchard,
right Gearge Bramford.*

Ruth Brant as The Virgin Mary.

"Monks" of Pershore Abbey in a pageant, "Christianity comes to Pershore" in 1949. From left: Audley Bloxham, Donald Westcott, Brian Montandon, unknown, Bill Pugh, Lyn Westcott, unknown.

Chapter twelve

TRANSPORT AND CALLERS AT THE DOOR

In the 1920's many people still walked to work. They could not afford to buy bicycles. It was quite normal to walk to the villages around Pershore to visit relatives and friends.

One Pershore lady, as a girl, walked from Pershore to Sedgeberrow, via Ashton-under-Hill, and back again, and thought nothing of it. Postmen walked from Pershore Post Office to the villages. They delivered, not only letters, but also medicines from Arthur Smith, the chemist, for his village customers, and brought back empty bottles for him to refill.

Laurence Coggins said: "In winter, a lot of men were laid off if they worked on the land. They had to go three times a week to sign on the 'dole' at Captain Hutton's office, opposite Heathlands – the Labour Exchange. Miss Peggy Phillips was his secretary, In snow, they were laid off, but were expected to go to Lower Moor or Wick – on foot, to do a job there!"

Rene Giles told me: "In the 1930's and '40's I often walked from Defford station to Pershore from the Cheltenham train. My mother walked to a funeral at Great or Little Comberton and thought it quite normal."

Alec Witts has lived in Pershore since 1919. He said: "Pershore then, was an old, slow, country town. They were a community on their own. They only went outside when they had to. We went to Worcester by horse and cart then, to buy grains from Spreckley the brewers for feeding pigs."

Leslie Brookes' father, the baker, had a delivery cart and horse for the bread. They were kept at the back of the shop, in premises rented to his father. They travelled, in the '20's and '30's, as far as Wick, Pensham, Fladbury, Moor, Wyre and Pinvin, delivering bread. I well remember this lofty, dark green cart, with big wheels and long shafts, between which the horse trotted. Leslie or his father would be high up, holding the reins.

"My first bicycle was a second-hand one," said Blanche Dufty. "My brother and another fellow made this bike up from a garage. But I was always having punctures. I used to ride to Worcester on half days. Then I bought a green bike off a friend. I used to go to Birmingham on that. I would stay the weekend with my sister there. I would cycle with a couple more friends. That was a better bike, so no punctures.

We would set off early in the morning. We would go the back way, through Alcester and cut the towns off. You felt your legs wouldn't go any further – but you never got off those bikes, once you'd started. It took about three hours to Birmingham. I cycled to Bromsgrove too and to Cheltenham a lot. I went shopping for my mother in Worcester – all on this marvellous bike!"

"Cars were few and far between in the 1920's," said Alec Witts. "Mr. Bickerstaff, the coalman, had a coal dump in Pensham. He had an old

T-Model Ford. It wouldn't go up the hill forward. He had to reverse it all the way up the hill! The schoolmaster, Mr Chapman, had an Overland. The only place you would see such cars as that one, was in gangster films! It was a marvellous sight for us to see."

Alec Witts continued: "I myself travelled by motor-bike. I paid £45 for a brand-new 250 Triumph motor-bike – a terrible sum in those days. There were only English bikes on the road, in those days.

Everything in the country was English. The country was very poor. After the slump of the 1930's, they brought in a scheme called 'National Mark' – a Union Jack. You looked for the mark on everything you bought. That was right up to 1937-38 and was to prevent foreign goods coming in."

In the 1920's, the return bus fare from Pershore to Worcester was tenpence. In the 1930's, the Midland Red ran frequent buses between Pershore town and its railway station, which was then a thriving, busy station. Trains were used then, to carry plums and other produce to big cities.

As for rail travel, it is well known that such important families as the Hudsons, of Abbey House (and later, Wick House) had objected to the railway being brought too close to the town, so Pershore station was sited as far out as Pinvin.

Jack Heeks told me: "The fire engine used to be pulled by horses in the 1920's. They were kept at Partridge's Mill. And the fire engine was kept further up Bridge Street, where Belle House is now and the Town Council offices."

Betty Hughes said: "I worked as a telephone operator in my younger days. The old Telephone Exchange was situated over the present Post Office. When a Fire Call came through, the operators had to turn a handle for one minute, to ring bells in the firemen's houses to wake them for an emergency."

An unexpected visitor, which hovered over Pershore in 1932, was the Graf Zeppelin, a German airship. As a child, I remember seeing it, with awe, from our cottage in Hurst park. Later, elsewhere, a British airship, the R101, came down in flames, and that was the end of airships.

CALLERS AT THE DOOR

"Before the Second World War," said Nora Bristow, "butchers, bakers, grocers, delivered their goods to their customers' houses, by bicycle, van, or horse and cart. Wards from Evesham came in their van, labelled ONWARDS, carrying all household stuff and, above all, paraffin for lamps. My mother cooked with paraffin, as there was no gas or electricity up Holloway then. Milkmen measured out the milk by ladles, into your jugs, from their milk float, drawn by a horse. Greengrocery came on a bicycle."

I was told: "Harvey Marshall cycled around villages, selling Distilled Peppermint in bottles. This was a cure for all. He also sold home-made sweets and herbal remedies. Mr. E. Winkett cycled round villages selling triangular peppermints which he made at home."

Betty Hughes told me of visiting tradesmen coming to Peopleton. "Men came round with bars of salt, on trucks, from Droitwich. We used to keep these salt bars on each side of the fireplace, and cut up the salt and put it in our jars as we needed it. 'Monkey' brand soap was also sold from house-to-house. That was used for cleaning – cutlery, for instance. Knives were made of steel then.

Leslie Brookes, the baker, came on a bicycle. On Good Friday, he would shout, 'Hot Cross Buns!' Palfreys came with their bread cart, and also Harry Page, the old local bakers from White Ladies Aston. You had to fetch the milk from the farm."

My sister, Avril, remembers several callers and trades people who called regularly, when we lived for a short time at Hurst Park, and then in Station Road. Mr. Howes would come on his bicycle, to collect the grocery order for Phillips the grocer. He would wear a brown overall and write it all down in his notebook. The 'Corona' man would leave a crate of four bottles – Ginger Beer, Orangeade, Dandelion and Burdock, and our favourite one, Cherryade.

Davenports would bring 'Beer to the Home'. A knife-grinder would wheel his machine on the grass verge and there he would sharpen your knives. The District Nurse, riding her bicycle, would call at certain houses to visit new babies. A talkative tailor from Cheltenham would call twice a year, to measure you for a new suit.

You put your 'W' card in the window, if you wanted the Walls Ice-cream man to call. He came on a tricycle, from Evesham, and sold twopenny 'bricks' and penny 'fruitos'. The 'Snofruit' tasted of the cardboard in which it was wrapped.

Our aunt, Flo Bramford, who had been born in 1892, always called the ice-cream man 'the Hokey Pokey man'. In her young days, all ice-cream men were Italian and they called out, 'Hokey Pokey, penny a lump'. You took out a cup for their ice-cream. (Hokey Pokey is said to come from the Italian 'Ecce poco' = here is a little).

There was also the Night Soil men's weekly visit, until the water came in 1932. Hearing, for the first time, their strange rumbling, their scraping and low voices, I had thought, as a child of seven, that they were 'late gardeners' who were still gardening, on a midsummer night!

The roadman, sweeping the paths and gutters, was a familiar sight. Road works brought the Night Watchman, with his hut and fire in a brazier. On one occasion, my uncle got him to wake us up at 4 a.m. so that we could set off early for Weston-super-Mare. And we all remember, with nostalgia, the Fish and Chip van, which arrived conveniently, at lunch-time on Saturdays, with its inviting aroma and smoking chimney.

Chapter thirteen

SNAPSHOTS OF VILLAGE LIFE AROUND PERSHORE

"There were five of us children in Lower Moor," said George 'Nobby' Clark. He was born there in about 1898. "At weekends, my mother used to send us on a message to our Gran's at Pershore. We would go through Wyre and down by the meadows along the river and out by the Pomona Works (Jam factory). Then on to Nash's Passage, off Broad Street, where Gran lived. We all had wells then, but no water on tap.

Wages were very low. Father was working at 18 shillings a week to keep seven of us. He worked on the land at Chadbury Fruit Farm. There was just one shop-cum-Post Office in Lower Moor. A man from Harvington came with a dray, selling paraffin for lamps and other goods. We went to 'Eversham' once a month or so, by train, from Fladbury. The fare then was fivepence return.

We used to walk to school at Fladbury. The Headmaster was Mr. Gordon Bancks, the father of Gordon Bancks the solicitor. For entertainments, there was local football, and a Working Men's Club in Lower Moor, to play billiards. There was an occasional dance, at sixpence a time, with a pianist.

As boys, we used to go bird nesting – collecting birds' eggs. We went rowing on the river, but I never swam in it. It was dangerous.

I used to sing in the church choir at Fladbury. We went twice a day on Sundays, when we were lads. In the morning to Fladbury church, in the afternoon at Lower Moor and Sunday school as well. Father was very strict that way. We walked everywhere. The first bike I had, I paid for in instalments – about 3/6d a month. Thirty shillings a week wasn't a lot of money. You paid your mother £1, you clothed yourself on ten shillings and that was it. We didn't starve, but we lived rough. We got by."

"I like a village," said Charles Clemens. "I was asked to be organist at Fladbury church in the 1920's. I went initially for five Sundays, and I stayed for 42 years, as organist. When I left, they gave me a Royal Worcester china dinner set.

I cycled every Sunday to Fladbury from Pershore, where I lived - 4½ miles there and 4½ miles back, in all weathers. Later on, I went in for a motor-bike and side-car. One morning, I had no petrol It was rationed. So I had to use the bicycle again. The choirboys were all waiting for me at the gate and when they saw me on the cycle, they cheered. Ice and snow were never too bad in Fladbury.

The choirboys were a bit of a headache – they always are! I've been a boy myself, and I knew what they did. But they were country lads and easier to handle than Pershore ones.

The Reverend Sylvester was the Vicar at Fladbury. He was a nice fellow, but he couldn't sing – not a note! He would say the responses in the services. People used to come to church just to look at him – he was so nice-looking!"

"I was born at The Kennels, Wood Norton, near the hall where the BBC is now," Rosie Long told me. "We walked from Wood Norton to school at Fladbury. It took more than half an hour. When my mother wasn't working at Craycombe House, I had to have my dinner at school. We took our dinner with us. At first break, we were given a cup of hot cocoa. Mother used to come and fetch me from school.

Then we moved to Charlton. My mother's step-mother lived in our house after we left. She had all these cats. There must have been eight or ten of them. As we opened the back door, they would shoot up the chimney, one after the other. And they stayed there until we came away. They were wild!

When we lived at Charlton, I went to school at Cropthorne. We were at Fernhill Farm, down by the railway. We had to walk over the railway, up to Cropthorne School. It's a good mile and a half each way, along a lonely lane.

Among my teachers, I remember Miss Revers from Bricklehampton. She took the Infants class and taught

Singing. I liked Needlework, which Miss Hyde took. I was 14 when I left school, in 1927. My mother was pregnant with my sister. So I had to stay home to help look after the boys. I had four brothers. Then I went into service. I'm 80 now."

Mary Eulalie Revers of Hall Farm, Bricklehampton, was born on Christmas Day 1900. She has taught many generations of village children and Pershore children, throughout her long life. Her name, Eulalie, means 'Yuletide', thus evoking her birth on Christmas Day. The doctor present at her birth, suggested this appropriate name to Mary's mother.

In 1912, the Revers family moved from Staffordshire to Laverton, near Broadway, Worcestershire, to her grandfather's farm. After that, Mary's parents kept The Mill inn at Elmley Castle. Only in 1927 did they move to Hall Farm, Bricklehampton.

Mary went to the village school at Elmley Castle, then became a pupil teacher at Bricklehampton School. This school closed in 1922. So Mary went to Cropthorne School as an Infant teacher for 22 years. In 1945, Mary Revers came to Abbey Park School, where my father, Mr. Bramford, was Headmaster.

Mary went to college in Birmingham for one year, to become a fully qualified teacher. She returned to Abbey Park School as Senior Mistress, in 1946 and remained there until 1966. During those years, she taught all the music throughout the school. She has always had many piano and organ pupils.

In November 1991, at the age of 91, Mary Revers was awarded the British Empire Medal for "her contribution to the Church of England and to village life, which has been outstanding". Also mentioned in the citation: "She has been a church organist at Little Comberton and nearby churches for over 70 years; a member of the Women's Institute since 1929; a member of the British Legion and a member of the Church Council for many years".

The medal was presented by the Lord Lieutenant of Worcestershire, in Little Comberton Church. They all went to

The Mill inn afterwards, to celebrate. Hereford and Worcester Radio taped and broadcast Mary playing the organ. She received congratulations from the Royal School of Church Music and from the Bishop of Worcester. She was presented to Princess Margaret when she visited Evesham.

Hall Farm, Bricklehampton, the home of Mary Revers, was built in the eighteenth century. It belonged to Bricklehampton Hall and provided the residents in the hall with milk, eggs, etc. Hall Farm's present dairy was once a Laundry for the Hall. Hall Farm was once two houses. The linking passage can be clearly seen. Their cellars are very deep.

"I was born at Hampton by Evesham," said Ellen Willis. "My father was a market gardener. He used to shoot on Bredon Hill. I was friendly with the Vicar's daughter. Every year, I used to go to her birthday party at the Vicarage. During the First World War, in Hampton, we went to the Parish Room, opposite the Vicarage, to knit for the soldiers.

At school, we had concerts. At the end of each concert, we had all the flags of the nations. I think I represented Portugal. Our teacher, Miss White, was Peace. Britannia was there too. We all walked up to the Abbey Manor (it's a hotel now) and we did a concert there for the wounded soldiers."

"I was fourteen-years old when I went as organist and choir-master to Wick church," Leslie Brookes told me. "Some of the choirboys there were bigger than me. I had to have the Sexton in, to keep them in order! There were about fifteen children in the choir in those days."

"The big houses of Wick made quite a contribution to the life of Pershore," commented Malcolm Meikle. "The Hazelwood family, who were the forerunners of the Hudsons, lived at Wick House. Part of Wick House (now demolished) was certainly very old. There was plaster work there dating from the time of Sir Christopher Wren, in the 1660's. It may have been Elizabethan before that. There was a very ornate fireplace too.

Some Pershore Abbey stone was in Wick House – some bosses

and a lovely little angel bracket. But I'm afraid they weren't saved. It is supposed they came originally from the collapsed North transept, because the Hudson family had lived in the Abbey House previously. They probably had those carved stones in their garden there! The angel bracket was visible in a Wick resident's garden for many years after Wick House was pulled down.

Colonel Hudson died in about 1941 or '42. There is no record of the sale of Wick House then. The house was pulled down because it was empty. It had been leased to a school at the end of the 1940's. this school failed and some boys set fire to it. The house was derelict and was pulled down."

"There is a legend about my own home, Wick Grange," continued Malcolm Meikle. "A book about the Hudsons of Wick, contains a note explaining how the Grange came to be altered, from a half-timbered thatched house, to what it is now. Mrs. Farmer, a widow living here at Wick Grange, wanted to marry George Hudson of Wick House. She was told, that if she smartened her house up, he might marry her. So she engaged Samuel Whitfield Daukes to design a new house for her. However, George Hudson didn't marry her, so she had to mortgage her house.

The architect, Samuel Whitfield Daukes, became quite well known in this part of the country. His father had been a mining engineer in Dudley. Daukes had designed the Abbey Hotel in Malvern, Cirencester Agricultural College and the re-vamping of Witley Court. He also designed St. Paul's College at Cheltenham. He lived at Diglis House, Worcester.

These buildings of his have a lot of castellations on the top. But Daukes could also work in the Classical style, as at Witley Court. It is thought he designed Mount Pleasant too (known as The Mount, or Pershore Hall). It is much more ornate, so was built later than Wick Grange. The Mount was built in 1862 for Edward Humphries. *(see Footnote)*.

We presume that Wick Grange was restored in about 1853, which is the date on the weather-vane of the stable block. My parents came here in 1922 or '23. I discovered the grave of that previous owner, Mrs. Farmer, in St. Andrew's churchyard. It is one of the few left there.

The past owners of Wick Grange were clearly only farmers. Wick Manor owners were clearly gentry. They owned the bulk of the village. Historically, ours is one of the few pieces of land they have never owned.

As a child, on Flag Days, I used to go to Wick House and Avonbank (now Pershore College of Horticulture). Mrs. Wynn Marriott would be sitting in the morning room at Avonbank. She would buy her Alexandra rose. We had Sunday school trips at Avonbank, in the shrubbery at the back. Avonbank used to contain furniture from India and China, because General Marriott had served in India.

At Endon, another big house, just up the road from here, lived Dr. and Mrs. Farncombe, who were very much to the fore in civic matters locally. Dr. Farncombe founded the Friends of Pershore Abbey, in 1932."

Margaret Taylor told me: "My husband, Arthur Taylor, was a jeweller, as you know, and so was his father. His father came from Sedgeberrow and was one of a family of seven. In those days, they had to serve a very long apprenticeship for watch-making and jewellery. They had to make little parts for repairing clocks and watches.

In the 1880's, Arthur's grandfather was a schoolmaster in the village of Dumbleton. The schoolchildren had to walk to school, from Sedgeberrow to Dumbleton – four miles each way. They took their lunch to school, of course. The schoolmaster himself, cycled daily between Sedgeberrow and Dumbleton."

"I went to Elmley Castle School," said Laurence Coggins. "There were about 30 children in school then, in the 1930's. We had a maypole on the 29th May every year and a May Queen. They still have it now – quite a big occasion. It has been filmed once or twice."

"I delivered groceries to the villages, in wartime, as a schoolboy," said Edwin Hill. "I worked for the International

Stores. I used to make enough money to clothe myself. I've clothed myself since the age of eleven. The wages were seven shillings a week, for working evenings as well. Quite a lot of little 'tips' too. At the age of fourteen, you got fifteen shillings a week.

We delivered to most of the villages on a Saturday. I'm thinking of a lovely farm at Little Comberton. It is Old House Farm, and there was a lovely family called Pitcher. It was baking day on Saturday mornings. Even in the war, I saw this beautiful long scrubbed kitchen table, where the lady of the house was busy kneading her dough. You would have to lay the grocery out on the table, check it off and they would pay you. If you were very, very good, there was a threepence for you as well!"

"We lived in Peopleton," said Betty Hughes. "I was in the church choir. We had little concerts in the village – mostly magic lantern shows. Mr. Harcourt Fowler came round quite a lot to entertain us.

One old lady used to make 'pig-swill'. We children had to strip all the hedges of elm leaves and fill baskets with them. She would put them in a huge tub to feed the pigs. But the elm leaves had to be pressed down by us first – to earn our pennies, you see,"

Rosie Long talked about Besford. "I went in service to a Mrs. Harris at a farmhouse at Besford. I went as a general servant and nanny to the children. There were six children there. Three of those same children, now grown up, came here to my home in August last, for my 80th birthday! Those three still live at this farm. They went to school in Worcester, eventually, by the train.

I used to love helping to make the butter. It they got stuck on the land, when it was harvesting time, Mrs. Harris would let me go out with the farmhands. Usually, I helped in the kitchen and she got a governess for the children."

"The Besford Court boys?" said Roy Beard. "They used to march them from Besford Court to Pershore on Saturdays.

They would come over Besford Bridge, down Holloway and Newlands and go to the Plaza picture house. They had mud on their boots from walking across fields. It was a long way in winter.

The boys used to fill up most of the front seats in the Plaza. It was twopence on a Saturday. A lot of them were orphans or homeless. Jack Hemming used to help them when they left the Court. He did a lot of good for the down and outs."

"The Besford boys wore khaki shorts, green jumpers and big boots," recalled Marjorie Godfrey. "They would come to our shop in Newlands with fourpence and buy a penny-worth of sweets, before going on to the cinema. Their school belonged to a Roman Catholic order. They were, some of them, the sons of monied people, who paid for them to be there."

"Besford Court had an Open Day," said Mary Stubbs. "We were there with the Girl Guides and we were supposed to guard the silver in the house. But we were down below with the servants and we never even saw the silver!"

"When Les Creswell went over to Besford Court, I went as well," said Laurence Coggins. "Les, my brother-in-law, was a barber and he used to have a contract with Besford Court. The lads there had their hair cut quite regular. So I got plenty of practice. The price there was threepence a head – 80 heads for £1.

They didn't like letting the lads out of the Court too much, so we always went there. Some of them would run away occasionally. I recall the blue jumpers, blue cord shorts and the boots. Some of the 'boys' were in their late '20's, and they were still wearing those shorts.

But it wasn't like a Remand Home. They used to feed them well. In the dining room, the food was absolutely first class – jugs and jugs of milk. Some of the boys were the sons of well-off parents, who wanted them out of the way. Some of them were a bit strange. Besford Court School is still there." (This was spoken in 1993. The school closed in 1996).

FOOTNOTE

The façade of The Mount (also knows as Mount Pleasant, or Pershore Hall) is a glorious example of Victorian Gothic – pinnacles, warm red brick patterned with blue brick, and a plethora of stone carved heads and fruit – grapes, peaches, and pears ..... appropriate for this region of fruit growing.

Edward Humphries had eleven children. Two daughters, Louisa and Penelope, died in infancy, from dysentery, and are buried in St. Andrew's churchyard.

On their tombstone we read:

LOUISA daughter of Edward and Elizabeth Humphries
Died February 11th 1859
aged 1 year and 5 months

PENELOPE Humphries
Died August 17th 1859
aged 3 years and 4 months

The next owner of The Mount was Mr. Deakin, with his fruit orchards. The Deakin's jam factories failed in about 1929. They moved to Norton Hall, by Worcester, then to a farm near Redditch. Some of the family emigrated to Australia.

The Mount was empty through the 1930's. The land was owned subsequently by Bird's, then Edward Crowther, then by John Bomford. The house was converted into flats and, later on, the Georgian barns too, were converted into accommodation.

Chapter fourteen

CHILDHOOD PURSUITS AND GAMES

"Tyddesley Wood used to have a wealth of adventures for us, as children," Edwin Hill recalled, nostalgically. "We found a different animal life there, which we traced and followed through. We got up the trees and watched nature. We found a badger's set. Our parents gave us permission, sometimes, to stay out all night there. There was never a dull moment."

"My grandfather was keeper in Tyddesley Wood for about 30 years," Alec Witts told me. "He had been bailiff at the farm on top of Mount Pleasant. Then he replaced his brother as keeper of the wood, while his brother took over the New Inn. That was in 1903.

Tyddesley Wood is prehistoric. I was brought up on the edge of the wood by my grandmother. I always had clean clothes and was well fed. But there were no other kiddies to play with there. My grandparents kept horses and dogs. I used to roam that wood all day in good weather, and never come home 'til nightfall. I made bows and arrows. I knew that wood well.

It was a lot bigger then, than it is today – about 365 acres. There were parts of it that had an atmosphere I didn't like. But I don't like the way they are managing it now. I don't ever want to go up there again. Formerly, the rides were wide and the trees met over the top – like green tunnels. But they've made it artificial now, with picnic areas.

I would discover things I didn't know the names of there – a patch of green primroses ..... and four different sorts of orchids grow there. I would see red squirrels, snipe and woodcock. If you sat quiet, rabbits and pheasants would appear and take no notice of you. There were the big black wood snakes in the wood. They were about three feet long. Once, a snake wrapped itself round my leg, 'cos I was wearing short trousers and I had stepped on it without noticing. It wasn't dangerous, but ever since then I've been scared of snakes!

It was like being on a tropical island – no-one about! You could hear brown owls hooting all the time. One bird has almost disappeared – the jay. You mustn't look at birds, or they go away. If you look at his nest, he will go. I used to find fox holts, badger holts.

The night before the hunt, we would put packets of wood down the fox holes, to stop the foxes from going down. We had to go out after midnight to do that. We would set snares for rabbits and sell those rabbits. Once, they used to harvest the hazel nuts in Tyddesley Wood and sell them on the market.

There was almost a living in that wood. Two or three sorts of apples grew there. Grandmother used one sort of apple for cooking. They were wild apples really, but as big as a Worcester Pearmain. They were yellow and red and streaked all the way round. When they were cooked, they turned a shade of pink. Another sort of apple she'd want, for making crab-apple jelly."

"I have many memories of the dear old wood," said Cyril Smith. "I used to help Mrs. Witts pick up the crab-apples and Perry pears. Old Daddy Witts had a long prop to shake down the fruit. We would put them in bags to take to the cider mill. Daddy Witts made a lot of cider – good stuff too! I used to help Mrs. Witts to pick primroses in the wood. She sent them to market."

In the early 1900's, twenty years before Alec Witts' childhood days in Tyddesley Wood, Blanche Dufty used to go there, with her brothers. "In the school holidays, I would go there," she said, "to pick primroses or orchids. My brothers would be bird nesting. They used to fix a handle to a tin and get water from Stocking Brook near Besford. They would boil birds' eggs in that tin, on a fire they had made.

They pinched potatoes and put them in the fire. Then they called me for my dinner. We would be there all day. It was good! You could eat ever so many of those spotted eggs.

We would bring back armfuls of bluebells and ferns out of the wood ..... and those beautiful orchids." Today, conservationists would be horrified!

Nora Bristow remembered childhood picnics: "We would take new bread, all crusty and delicious, and cheese, and crystals for lemonade and go on our own into the fields and woods. One place we went to was Avonbank, which we called 'Marriott's' then, for a picnic on the bank."

"One of our childhood pastimes," said John Annis, "was catching tadpoles and newts from various pools and ditches, long since gone. A favourite place for catching newts was on the top of Marriott's, or Avonbank, where there are two pools. You caught them with a stick, some string and a worm, and you brought them home in jam jars.

There were sometimes workmen to watch. The blacksmith at the Forge in High Street, or Priest Lane, would be shoeing a horse, or putting an iron tyre on to a wooden wagon or cart-wheel. If road works were in progress and trenches being dug with pick and shovel, we would wait for the Night Watchman. He would be in his little hut, all night, seated in front of a coke brazier. It was a great treat for us boys to stand round the fire yarning with him.

Coppices in Gigbridge, Allesborough Hill and Marriott's provided wonderful playgrounds, where dens could be constructed. Tree-climbing provided good exercise."

My sister, Avril, as a child, found it a great adventure to visit The Mount, then an empty house. "We would go and see Mrs. Badger, the caretaker and her daughter, Jean, who had been brought up on goats' milk. I was given some to taste. They had a pet lamb, Puckabelle, who had appeared in the pantomime 'Bo-Peep', at Worcester, and who came back 'scented' with a cheap perfume. We climbed the cedar tree.

It was exciting to be taken round the eerie, empty house, with its stone staircase, marble wash-stands and its chandeliers, and on to the roof. I explored the grounds on my own. I found the ice house and the dilapidated caravan in the garden, with plants growing through the cracks. Was it Mr. Humphries' den? There were unusual plants and trees in that garden. And looking out towards Drakes Broughton was a different world."

There has long been a tradition for young people in Pershore to walk to the top of Bredon Hill on a Good Friday, usually via Great Comberton. Marjorie Godfrey said: "Everyone seemed to go up there. You would all meet there. you were allowed to make little wood fires and have picnics. People would take frying pans, eggs, bacon and sausages. We would enjoy the magnificent view over so many counties, if it was a fine day. And we would hear the bells of village churches. We would certainly hear Pershore Abbey Carillon bells chiming, on Good Friday evening."

Here is John Annis' version of this tradition: "On Good Friday morning, hordes of children, carrying sandwiches, bottles of 'pop' or water, sometimes with a war surplus billycan, and a bit of bacon, left Pershore and walked to Bredon Hill, usually via Great Comberton. Here, on the slopes, near a copse and a stream, a little camp would be set up. Stones would make a fireplace and a wood fire was soon under way. Water was boiled, bacon was fried, and honesty was smoked. In the afternoon, the summit of the hill was reached. Then began the long, meandering, tiring journey home."

Marjorie Godfrey also remembered the role of the river in her childhood. "We would learn to swim in the river, and we would stay there on a nice summer's evening. We would be down by the old bridge. The Abbey clock would chime nine o'clock and the Carillon would play a tune, like 'Barbara Allen'. Our deadline was nine p.m. We were expected to be home by then. We were running like mad to get home in time – all up Bridge Street, across Broad Street and into Newlands. But we could arrive home by the time the Carillon tune had finished."

In the old school playground in Defford Road, during playtime, girls often played ball games, against the high walls of a narrow alley. I well remember 'Sevenses' and 'Nebuchadnezzar'. Our chant for the latter game was:

> Nebuchadnezzar, the King of the Jews,
> Bought his wife a pair of shoes.
> When the shoes began to wear,
> Nebuchadnezzar bought a mare.
> When the mare began to kick,
> Nebuchadnezzar bought a stick.
> When the stick began to break,
> Nebuchadnezzar bought a snake.
> When the snake began to sting,
> Nebuchadnezzar bought a ring.
> When the ring began to rust,
> Nebuchadnezzar had turned to ..... DUST!

As I learnt this rhyme from my fellow pupils, I wondered what the moral was!

Meanwhile, in the boys' playground: "There were sometimes fights," said Lyn Westcott. "We played marbles. Cigarette cards were leant against the wall and you had to flick them down with other cards."

John Annis said: "'Fag' cards, or cigarette cards, were in cigarette packets and were collected, usually in sets of fifty. On them were depicted film stars, footballers, cricketers, kings and queens, flowers ..... After swapping, the surplus cards were used to play games on the pavements of Pershore streets. Marbles were played in the gutter, to and from school.

Football was played between two sets of goals, marked by caps or jackets, or goals chalked on shed doors. Sometimes, sticks were acquired, either from hedgerows, or a collection of old walking sticks, and hockey was the game. In summer cricket was played in the street, with old bricks, a wooden box, or a lamp-post acting as the wickets.

Very, very occasionally, a window was broken, and woe betide the culprits, who were threatened with all sorts of punishments, except hanging. On occasions, the local constable hove in sight, and all of us beat a strategic withdrawal, before identification could be made. The police, in those days, were held in awe."

There were well supported organisations for young people in Pershore, in the 1920's and '30's. Esme Westcott recalled The Band of Hope, a temperance society, which was very prevalent at that time. "They coerced most children into signing the pledge. I signed the pledge when I was eight-years old. I don't think many have kept to it – not in Pershore! The Band of Hope would send out their converts and ask, 'Would you like to come to a party at the Baptist schoolroom?' They would talk to the children who came. If one child signed the pledge, all the others would follow suit."

Mary Stubbs told me about the Girls' Friendly Society: "It was run by Miss Ismay and Miss Lawson and we met at Miss Lawson's house in Broad Street. She had her own chapel in the garden. If you did things you shouldn't have done, you were kept behind, and you went to the chapel to be forgiven. There was an altar there. During the meetings, we did some sewing and some Bible study. We had prayers and country dancing.

"The Boys' Club existed long before the Youth Club," said Laurence Coggins. "Les Conn used to run it, for boys of 10 to 14, and after they had left school too. We had it in the old school, in Defford Road, in the evenings. We paid a halfpenny a night, for two nights a week. There was a boxing ring there and a buck for gymnastics. We played cards also."

Edwin Hill told me: "After choir at the Abbey, on a Sunday night, we would go along to the old Junior School in Defford Road. That was really the start of Pershore Youth Club. John Smith and Ruth Campbell were our leaders. Mr. P. J. Feek was a school governor – a man full of interesting information. He once gave us a good talk on FIRE. He demonstrated making fire, with his brace and bit, like the Red Indians do. We had talks and debates from various speakers. Basically, it was for people attending the Abbey."

"We used to go to Bricklehampton Hall to Miss Huntingdon's, for our Brownie Revels," said Mary Stubbs. "And there were lovely concerts at the Mission Hall, organised by the Church Army Captain. Local people performed. The audience were given a cup of cocoa, or coffee, or tea, a sandwich and cake – and all for sixpence. It was ever such fun!

On Sundays, as children, we would go to the Abbey in the morning and to the Mission Hall at night. Or else to the Baptist chapel at night, because we liked to sit in those pews with the doors. And where did those old pews go?"

MISCHIEVOUS PRANKS

"Children could play in the streets in the early '30's" said Alice Young. "The boys used to turn off the gas lamps and go and tell the lamp-lighter the lamps were out! John Smith's father was the lamp-lighter then.

When I was a child in the early 1900's, we lived opposite the Black Horse Inn. We used to sit on a step at the locked-up back door of this inn. And the landlord, Mr. Savory, would come out and swill a bucket of water all over us, on the step, to send us away. But that was our play place, and it didn't deter us. We went back again."

Lois Young remembered going to school in Worcester, by train from Pershore. "I went to College House School on the train. There were some other girls with me. Once inside the compartment, we all used to hold on to the window strap, a strong piece of leather, to keep the schoolboys from opening our door and getting in with us.

Then, during the journey, we used to climb on to the string-net racks used for luggage in those days. They were labelled 'For light articles only'. Naughty people would alter the wording to read 'For tarts only'."

"They said the old monastery at Pershore was haunted," said Jim Dowler. "One dark evening, we choirboys went into St. Andrew's churchyard. We had got hold of an old mangold, scraped it out and put a candle inside it. Mr. Mason, the choirmaster and organist, was just crossing from the Abbey to St. Andrew's. We thought he was a ghost, 'cos he had his white surplice on. So we grabbed him. This was all in the dark. What did he say? Not a lot. But our parents knew all about it afterwards!"

John Annis recalled the practical jokes he and other boys played on people in the 1930's. These jokes were usually carried out in the evening, when it was dark. Black thread was often essential. The thread was tied round a door knocker, paid out some distance into shadows and then used to knock on the door. The householder came out, saw no-one and retired. The episode was repeated until the action dawned upon the now irate householder.

Another trick concerned two terrace houses, whose front doors were close together, but opened in opposite directions. For this exercise, string was required. The end was tied to a door handle, with a little slack left. Both doors were then knocked upon. The fun came when both householders tried to open their respective doors at the same time!"

Peggy Maple told me this episode of mischief. "The Plymouth Brethren have always been very strong in this area. They used to meet in a hall, up a passage, in Bridge Street, behind Fred Crooke's property. Joyce Crooke and myself, as children, used to go in the Crooke's pantry and look through a little hole in the wall. We wanted to watch the Brethren. There were about twenty of them, sitting still there. We were very intrigued to know what they did. They wait 'til the Spirit moves them, like the Quakers.

But Fred Crooke caught us in the pantry, tittering and giggling. We got into very bad trouble. Joyce got smacked for it!"

Chapter fifteen

ON THE RIVER AVON

Pershore has owed much of its past prosperity to the river on which it is situated, and also to its ancient Mill, now vanished. The river has provided pleasure too, but also, alas! great dangers.

Boating was very fashionable in Edwardian times. At the Star Hotel in Bridge Street, there is an Edwardian photo of their waterfront. A notice reads: 'GOOD ACCOMMODATION FOR BOAT PARTIES. BEDS WELL AIRED'. But the river had its commercial uses as well.

Edwin Hill told me: "The Barber family is a very old Pershore family, who came up the river on the barges. Corn up and flour back, between Gloucester and Pershore. Kitty Haines was a Barber. Her ancestors originated on the barges."

Laurence Coggins said: "At the age of 19, Samuel Barber was skipper of the Bee barge, which belonged to the Rice family of Gloucester and Upton-on-Severn. The Bee was propelled by steam. Samuel Barber died in 1931 at the age of 86. The Star Hotel had a busy wharf at the bottom of their garden."

Cyril Smith records: "The Bee came up from Avonmouth and Sharpness. She brought the wheat up to Pershore Mill to be ground. There was a lock in the Weir meadow. Just before she came through that lock, she hooted, to let us know. Mr. Partridge of the Mill, used to say to me 'Get across the Weir meadow and shut the paddles (lock gates) down.' Then I had to open up the paddles again on her return."

"That was my first job at Mr. Partridge's Flour Mill," said Cyril Smith. "I left school at the age of 12 in 1917. You could leave at 12 in those days, provided you went to school one day a month.

I went to the Mill as 'Boots'. I cleaned the boots, fed the fowls, helped with the piggery. I mended the flour sacks with a bobbin needle and string. One day in the week, Mrs. Partridge came along and I had to help her bagging-up the self-raising flour. As she weighed it, I put it into bags, folded them over and put them into baskets – about 24 in a basket.

Another job I had at the Mill (I shall never forget it!) was white-washing the Mill, inside, from top to bottom. That was a lengthy job. Our hours of work were 6 a.m. 'til 6 p.m. I earned five shillings per week. That work included Saturday afternoon and Sunday morning. I had to feed the pigs on Sundays – and the poultry."

Alec Witts said: "This yard, where I live, has been a business for at least 250 years. These yards down Bridge Street were entrances to the river barges. There were maltsters and so on – ever since navigation was granted on the river.

You see those two tall and very ancient trees on the river bank, at the bottom of Barclays Bank long garden and Perrott House garden? They are rare – with their twisted limbs and enormous knobbly trunks. That one is 31 feet round the bottom. They are London Plane Tortuosa and were planted on the orders of Judge Perrott.

He, it was, who built Perrott House, Bridge Street in 1770. He owned the rights of the Avon for unloading barges. In the Deeds of Perrott House, fees for unloading barges are mentioned. It is my belief that those giant plane trees were planted as wind-breaks against the North East wind.

I learned to swim in the river. We used to get two big bunches of bulrushes and put them under our arms, to keep us up – like water wings. But gradually they began to get waterlogged. You thought they were supporting you, and that's how you learned to swim. The bathing place of Pershore was off the Mill meadow. The Mill was a landmark. Mill Gate, by the Turnpike House, led to Nogains."

Peggy Maple told me: "I swam in the river from 11 – 15-years of age, as often as possible. I went down to the back of the Star Inn, where my father knew the landlord. My father could swim. He took me down on a sunny afternoon and across by boat to the island at the top of the weir. I used to swim from there to the Angel Hotel moorings. A little rest on the Angel pier and back again. It kept me very fit. Very dangerous, because it was absolutely full of sewerage. It emptied in straight from all the properties in Bridge Street. And there were also whirlpools by the reeds."

"As a child," said Peggy Maple, "I used to go down to the bridges and get into trouble, because there had been one or two children drowned there. Someone coming over the Waylands from Wick, had told my mother I had been in the river, in my knickers. And I couldn't swim then. You can imagine that my mother smacked me and I was sent to bed!

We used to love to see the Pisgah barge come up from Gloucester. When the Mill burned down in 1976, they think if was an electrical fault. We could see the flames and smoke. The whole thing went. The miller built sheds afterwards and he does animal food now. He doesn't grind any more. But the 'Mill' is still owned by a Partridge – Philip.

Rowing boats? There were always a couple of rowing boats at the back of the Angel. If you knew the landlord, you could use them. Most of the Bridge Street houses had a boat tied up at the bottom of their gardens. There were at least four to hire at the Star, on the jetty. We used to row up to Wyre Mill. It was always me rowing my boy friends. They didn't row me!"

Blanche Dufty, aged 103, reminisced: "Billy Bell, my brother, was a marvellous swimmer. He rescued many a child from the river. One of the little gypsy girls was drowned by the Falls one day, while her parents were pea-picking – a little girl about 12. She sat there dangling her legs and slipped into the river. Billy said he could have saved her if he had been there. He taught boys to swim – the Pettifer boys, for instance.

There was a Fete, and prizes for swimming. Billy would dress up as a woman, umbrella and all. He would get into a tub and go across the river, or he would be on the Slippery Pole. He always seemed to win the prizes. They greased a pole and hung it across the river. Two men sat opposite each other.

They had a pillow-fight with sacks of straw, until one fell into the water."

"I nearly drowned, as a child, in the river," confessed Blanche. "There were two children in a push-chair, back-to-back. I used to love taking these kiddies out. They were from the White Hart Inn – a boy and a girl. They were strapped in the cart.

I had gone to see our boys swimming in the Weir meadow. I went to turn this pram round and I slid down the sloping bank. I screamed out to my brothers. Arthur came and pushed the pram back up. 'Get off home and don't come here again!', he cried. It wasn't half deep there. Many of them got drowned there, in the Defford Road area, where the race-course used to be. There's a deep shelf there.

My mother told me about two young lads – strangers, who went along there. She was working in a garden down there. They had a towel over their shoulders and they was laughing away. But they never come back. They got in the river and drowned straight away. There was a hue and cry - but they never come back,

We used to go to Tewkesbury and Gloucester by steamer, on the River Queen, from the Weir meadow. A great day that was! There were a lot of people and children on board. A lovely time we had!"

Chapter sixteen

PERSHORE PUBS

Pershore has long been known for its numerous public houses. People say that one hundred years ago, in the small town of Pershore (one tenth of its present size, then) there were about thirty pubs. About a dozen pubs still flourish today.

Way back in 1655, there was a saying associated with Harry the Hangman, who came to hang a murderer at Worcester, and he passed through Pershore:

Many who have stood on top of Bredon Hill have said:

'Rich Worcester, Grave Gloucester,
Proud Tewkesbury, Beggarly Evesham,
Drunken Pershore and Roguish Winchcombe.'

Jack Heeks said: "At the Hole in the Wall, in Batchelor's Entry, you could buy beer by the pint, in a jug."

"Several pubs had particular trades associated with them," said Laurence Coggins. "The Millers Arms was a very, very, busy pub for market gardeners. They did a lot of business in there. That pub was unique, because the conversation involved the whole company. It was a public conversation.

The Ship Inn was good – with the characters who went in there. That pub was more for bricklayers and carpenters. Like the Millers Arms, it had real warmth and character. The Star got quite lively and, at one time, long ago, there was a busy wharf at the bottom of their garden. In the tin hut, behind The Plough, we had some good dances!"

I myself, as a Brownie, attended Brownie meetings in The Plough's tin hut. We Brownies were all impressed by the enormous pair of buffalo horns hanging on the wall inside. We were told that the Royal and Ancient Order of Buffaloes used to meet there. they still survive, but now meet in the Working Men's Club. Founded in 1888, their 'Lodges' all over the country are clubs for men. Everything they gain goes to charity.

PRESENT DAY PUBS IN PERSHORE

High Street

ANGEL HOTEL AND POSTING HOUSE This was a coaching inn for coaches from London to Holyhead. It always had stabling for horses and carriages at the back, and a spacious garden. Elizabeth I may have stayed there.

NEW INN A coaching inn, which dates back to before 1745.

THE PLOUGH In 1745 it was a thatched cottage occupied by Mary, who still haunts the inn. Within the ancient beams of her former dwelling, there are creakings, footsteps, and a girl in a striped dress – "but the atmosphere is not unpleasant," say the present owners.

Bridge Street

THE STAR It was originally owned by the Manor of Binholme, i.e. the Abbot of Westminster. It was the Excise Office of the town. It was a coaching inn. The bar has fine old mediaeval timbers – ship's timbers. It had stabling for 90 horses and offered boats for hire.

THE BRANDY CASK It was a wool warehouse. Boats on the river in the 17th and 18th centuries, carried silks to Pershore and took back wool to Avonmouth for export. The Domesday Book describes wool washing and mills in Pershore.

MANOR HOUSE It became a hotel in the early 1900's. It has a serpentine wall, one of only three in the country. It is haunted on the top floor, by Room 8. there have been several sightings of white mist and a maid with untidy hair and a mob cap. A former owner says: "My name was called on a regular basis, during the time I slept in the top room of the cottage, that being one of the original buildings."

THE MILLERS' ARMS   It is next door to what was the old Police Station and the town gaol.   There was a gallows there to hang sheep stealers.   The Police Station moved out in 1865 and went to High Street.

THE THREE TUNS HOTEL   It was a thatched building before 1861.   A coaching inn for the journey between London and Holyhead.   Princess Victoria stayed there with her mother, the Duchess of Kent, in 1830, on their way to make a longer stay at Malvern and take the waters there.   The hotel closed in 1982.

Newlands

THE TALBOT
The sign is a breed of hunting dog.   In 1855 it was called the Waterloo Tavern.   It is likely that both Royalists and Roundheads were accommodated there, on their way to the Battle of Worcester 1651.   The ghost of a Royalist soldier is said to wander round the back of The Talbot.   Perhaps he was wounded in the battle and returned to the inn, only to die of wounds in the stable.   The Talbot, at that time, was on the only main road from Pershore to Worcester, i.e. Newlands.

THE VICTORIA
John Knight owned it and lived there, in the early 1900's.

Church Row

THE WHITE HORSE
John Knight owned this pub in 1904.   There was a brewery attached to it.

St Andrew's Road

THE PLUM TREE
It opened in 1957 to serve customers on the new Abbey estate. The sign is the Pershore Purple plum.

VANISHED PUBS OF PERSHORE

THE BELL in High Street was on the site of present-day Gateways. It had a large Ballroom. Watts, the Carriage makers, were behind.

THE BLACK HORSE in Church Row, was an inn before 1745. There was an orchard, with hens, at the back, Abbey monks borrowed the landlord's donkey to pull their mower, and allowed the donkey to graze in the monastery paddock.

THE BUTCHERS' ARMS was in Church Street, where the Library is now. In 1833, the landlord, George Crooks, discovered the Pershore Yellow Egg Plum in Tyddesley Wood.

THE CHEQUERS was at the top of High Street. The inn sign, a chequer board, was used long ago in calculating money.

THE CROWN AND ANCHOR, next door to the Plough Inn, was sold in 1884 and became a private house, where Clemens had their coal business.

THE DUKE OF YORK in High Street, was a pub until 1915. It is now a private house. Once it was a shop – Teale's the shoe repairers. Writing on the outside wall proclaims, to this day, the public house facilities it once offered: "Celebrated Ales and Guinness. Accommodation. Teas Provided."

THE FITTERS' ARMS in Batchelor's Entry, off Bridge Street, has been replaced by two garages.

THE KING'S HEAD was once at nos. 1 – 3, High Street (now Brown's and Ogle's shops). It was a large property. There were 38 bedrooms, stabling for 40 horses and a Ballroom. In the late 1800's, having been unoccupied for 20 years, it was pulled down.

THE MAIDENHEAD was at nos. 35, 37, and 39, Bridge Street. By 1809, it was no longer a pub. The inn sign depicts a maiden wreathed in red and white roses, representing the

Virgin Queen, Elizabeth l.

THE ROYAL OAK was at the corner of Buckets Lane and Meadow Lane, where the Abbey Garage is now.

THE SHIP was a cider pub, in High Street, next to the present shop 'Go down'. This inn closed in the 1980's.

THE SWAN in High Street, near the present Post Office, was formerly known as The Quiet Woman, or the Silent Woman. This name first referred to a beheaded woman saint and martyr, who carried her head. Later on, it meant a joke against women who talk too much.

THE WHITE HART was at the corner of Newlands and Little Priest Lane.

THE SIGN OF THE ZEBRA, at the top of High Street, is now the house named The Vineyard.

Chapter seventeen

SPORT

"Every Boxing Day, when I was a lad, there would be a grand
shoot in Tyddesley Wood," said Alec Witts. "We did nothing
special for Christmas. The highlight for me was that shoot
at the Wood. My grandfather was a wise man. He didn't let
people shoot in the wood until towards Christmas. Everybody
else would be shooting earlier, and the pheasants would be
driven into his wood! Very cute he was!

It was an open shoot. There was no charge. All sorts of
people came. Old Mr. Partridge at the Mill used to come and
Mr. Taylor, the jeweller. Men came out of Pershore, just to
beat. It was quite an event."

Tyddesley Wood now comprises about 185 acres of ancient
woodland, dating back to the end of the last Ice Age. In Alec
Witts' childhood, in the 1920's, the wood was much larger
– 365 acres. It is mentioned in Domesday Book. In 1271,
the Abbot of Westminster created a deer park there. Plants
growing there to this day, which prove its antiquity, include the
Wild Service tree and Herb Paris.

Alec Witts continued his vivid memories of the Boxing Day
shoot. "My grandmother would put up a trestle table near her
house in the wood. She put all the food and drinks on there,
including cider. Everybody collected there.

They had a good booze-up before they went home. They
would end up, by throwing glasses into the air and shooting at
them, cowboy-style. They wouldn't stop shooting until dusk.
You weren't supposed to shoot after sunset. It was a glorious
time!

They shot foxes, rabbits, and woodcock. There was an
abundance of game. It was all made use of – sold in the
market. Foxes would be skinned for their fur. It was a different
world. Things that, today, are classed as being cruel, were not

cruel then. They used to call it 'rustic mercy'.

After the shoot, they would play cards all night. The women and children would be in one room, the men playing cards in another. Katy Saunders and another woman came round carol singing. So everybody had to stop playing cards while they sung carols."

"Daddy Witts' Boxing Day shoots – that was always a good day out," enthused Cyril Smith. "We used to congregate at the pear tree, in the centre of the wood, at 10,.30 a.m. There were about twelve guns. One half of us would shoot in the morning and the other half in the afternoon.

We would return to the pear tree, where Mrs. Witts had the dinner ready for us – bread and cheese, cider and eats. We used to empty our bags of what we had shot – rabbits, hares, pheasants, and snipe. We would finish at about 5 p.m. and clean up. Then there would be a good meal and we would sit up all night, card playing."

"In the early '30's," said John Annis, "the Pershore Race Course was in Defford Road, before its move to Station Road. The race meetings created a lot of interest and trade in Pershore. The pupils of the Junior School in Defford Road were particularly fascinated, as racehorses and punters were going to and fro.

At break and dinner time, the railings in front of the school were thronged by pupils watching the passing scene. Occasional punters, who had imbibed freely, would throw loose change over the railings. We pupils would scramble wildly for these precious coppers."

When the Race Course transferred, in the late 1930's to Station Road, its presence on Race Days excited another lot of pupils – at the Senior School (now Pershore High School). The course itself came very close to the school buildings.

Marjorie Godfrey recalls this excitement. "The distracting part of lessons was the nearby Race Course. It was so difficult to keep your eyes from looking at the horses, who were pounding along in a race – only a few hundred yards away. Jackie Pointer, our history master, used to get very cross with us.

The race meetings were held twice a year. The horses walked all the way down to the stables, which used to be in Head Street. And that was exactly opposite where I lived! Imagine beautiful racehorses and we children following them. It was lovely!"

There were a variety of sports at the annual Flower Show in Pershore. It had been held since the 1870's. Blanche Dufty had some lively memories of this very special day. "It was generally held in August, on a Bank Holiday. It was a marvellous time. Thousands of visitors came into the town, by carriage or train. There was much inter-town rivalry too, because the Tewkesbury Regatta and Evesham Sports were often held on the same day.

My brothers and, later, my husband, would enter the local events, with the aim of becoming town champion. I remember one year, my husband walked past Fearnside's shop, where the Sports prizes for the Flower Show were on display. When he came home, he calmly stated that his name was on an especially attractive dressing-table set for men.

I didn't quite understand what he meant, until he appeared in his ex-Army silk vest, running shorts and blue cummerbund. He had been in the Army in India. Well, he kept his word and won his race and came home with the prize. We treasured it for years, until someone in the family 'spring-cleaned' it into the dustbin, unbeknown to me!

The Sports were held in the Abbey grounds. Cycling races were very popular with the crowd, as the meadow was rather rough and there were many spills. There were donkey races too. They caused much merriment among the spectators. Then there were equestrian events – all this as well as the lovely floral displays and brass bands. It was nearly always fine. And it was hot weather in them days. At night, there was fireworks and dancing. A very good day!"

Men's hockey was popular in Pershore in the early 1900's. Esme Westcott told me: "My father, Albert Champken, and

Arthur Smith, the chemist, were great hockey players. They used to do charity matches, to raise money for the building of the Cottage Hospital. They played on the Bottoms, as players do now. I have a photo of the hockey team in 1906. The Abbey shows quite clearly in the photo – not as many trees as there are now."

"There were lots of football teams in the 1920's," said Marjorie Godfrey. "My father played a lot of football then. He was a professional footballer for a while. There were plenty of people watching the matches then"

"In hard winters, Marriott's Hill was used for sledging," said Jack Heeks. "There used to be a huge gymnasium at the back of the Mission Hall," said Alice Young. "The Men's Brotherhood met once a fortnight at the Mission Hall," said Cyril Smith. They owned a bowling green there. We had some very happy times on that bowling green. It didn't last many years, however. The bowling green by the Abbey took over."

"I race pigeons," Laurence Coggins told me. "I was a member of the working Men's Club and I knew all the pigeon men. That used to get me all over the place – judging, showing, and racing. We used to bike from Pershore to Evesham to take the pigeons racing. Then we would bike back home on a Saturday night. We always had a good night out on the pay-out from the pigeons.

I still have my pigeons. (This was in 1993). We race them from Wincanton, Weymouth, Plymouth, Exeter. We send them over to France by road – to Rennes, Nantes, Bordeaux, or Pau, in the Pyrenees. They usually come home. I started off with twenty this year and I've only lost three."

Chapter eighteen

WAR-TIME EXPERIENCES ON THE HOME FRONT

The Second World War broadened our horizons in a variety of ways, and provided unexpected challenges. It was sometimes grim – but was not without its own brand of humour.

"As well as working in a factory during the war," said Esme Westcott, "I did Air Raid Precaution duties at home. I was in charge of Abbey Place and Defford Road. On the night of the Coventry bombing, my father said, 'You had better go and see about the old Miss Woodwards.' So off I went.

We had to get them down to the kitchen. The oldest Miss Woodward had gone to bed and she protested. She would not come downstairs until we had got her best hat out of the wardrobe. She said, 'How am I going to go to church if they have bombed by best hat?' We did hear the aircraft. The bombs dropped by the Abbey and Orchard Ditch. It was quite close. We heard the shuddering of the ground."

Ruth Baster, who now lives at Mickleton, Warwickshire, has memories of Pershore in war-time: "We came from Essex on the outbreak of war, my husband, Harry and I. We lived in a house on Three Springs Road, opposite the Mumfords. We had evacuees all the time in that house – mostly my relatives from London. We were thirteen in the house at one time! I still have two army blankets which we were given, for sleeping on the floor. I gave birth to my two children during the war, in 1940 and 1942. Harry had his job at Phipps factory, Wyre."

The Champken family, too, experienced evacuees to the maximum. "Having a large house," said Esme Westcott, "the most we had at a time was seven. We, ourselves, were nine in family. Most of the war, we had five evacuees. We had some from Box, in London; a mother and small children from Liverpool; and several from Birmingham. They used to come and go, and were replaced by others. Mostly, we had brothers and sisters who wanted to keep together. They were aged from four to thirteen. My mother fed them and we girls helped with them too.

We used to get the problem children, 'cos they knew my mother could manage children! One boy was a bed-wetter. But he was an extremely nice boy and very helpful. He would always take his share of the housework, or the washing-up, without moaning. My mother bought him a pair of long trousers. In those days, boys wore short trousers until they were quite old.

'Now, look after them,' she said to him. 'I'm going to hang these on the bed-post. You can look at them before you go to sleep. You can say to yourself, 'As soon as I'm grown up and don't wet the bed, I can wear my long trousers.' Just get out of bed, instead of wetting the bed. Look at your trousers, and if you are dry, you can wear your long trousers.' It did the trick!"

"I was in the Home Guard," said Charles Clemens. "I had five 'fallouts' in a week. For five weeks we had an alert, when enemy planes were going over to Birmingham, Coventry and Liverpool. We did get two bombs in Pershore and one went off. We saw the German planes going over to Coventry – one every twenty minutes. They were heart-breaking days.

I was Intelligence Officer. You had to keep in touch with the Army unit nearest you. My children were tickled: 'You an <u>intelligent</u> officer?' they joked. I joined as a Private. One day, Bob Lees said, 'We've made you a Sergeant today.' I said, 'Whatever for?' We did well, 'cos we had a lot of men in Pershore who had been in the regular Army before the war. They knew just what to do.

One night, we were near the hut on Allesborough Hill, where the Reconnaissance people were spotting planes. We had had strict instructions that night to show no light anywhere. No vehicles must be lighted. Suddenly, someone went across the field on a bike, with his lights on, flashing on every hilltop. He was challenged.

'I'm not putting lights out for any Home Guard,' he retorted. 'Aren't you?' we replied. And our Home Guard, Watts, got down on his knees and shot that man's light out! How he missed him

I shall never know. Because Watts had been trained as a sharp-shooter.

We had to have a Court martial. The Colonel who took it said, 'He deserved to be shot. I've had things done to me, just like that, in France, because I didn't answer a challenge at once. How does a man know who you are?' The fellow on the bike was Syd Parkes. And it was his brother-in-law, Bob Lees, who was in charge of our Home Guard! When we told Bob, he laughed: 'Serve him right!' he said. 'It's actual war now.'

Home Guard Watts was from Railground. I always said, 'If the Germans land, I hope Watts will be at my side.' One night, we were on top of Bredon Hill and we saw the flashes all the while over Coventry."

The Air Raid Precaution Listening Post was in the old Police Station, opposite Sunnyside. Margaret Taylor told me: "Arthur, my husband, was in the A.R.P. One night, the siren had gone. Arthur grabbed his tin hat and all the rest of his kit and went tearing off. Because of the blackout, the whole town was in complete darkness, and alas! He collided with a lady coming out of the Post Office. She was a Mrs. Roberts. The collision gave her slight concussion. Arthur had a dreadful cut across the eye and forehead.

He managed to come home, holding his head. I accompanied him to the First Aid Post at the hospital. Dr. Browning was in charge there. He put several stitches into the wound and then gave me a jolly good lecture. I had come out without any hat, gas mask or protection whatsoever, during an Air Raid warning! Fortunately, Arthur's scar was right above the eyebrow and didn't show."

"When I was 18, I was called up to work in a factory," said Esme Westcott. "They had just moved Woolwich Arsenal down to Worcester and they needed people to work in the munitions factory. I had not led a sheltered life, but of course, it was a very great shock, working in a factory. I just didn't know what these London girls were talking about: 'Poor little soul!' they used to say about me.

The work was hard, but I've never seen so much money in my life. What I was paid in wages – I thought that was grand. I worked in small arms until 1945. Then we transferred on to aircraft at Norton. I was released in 1947.

The munitions factory in Worcester was at Blackpole. Cadbury's took it over after the war. We were picked up by coach every day. It was shift work – 6 'til 2, 2 'til 10, and 10 'til 6. The married women were not allowed to do night work. So most of the single girls did nights – a fortnight on and a fortnight off."

"We worked on buildings on Pershore aerodrome in the war," said Sid Champken. "Tom Simpkins, the builder, gave us one penny an hour <u>more</u> to get on faster with the work. That was a lot of money in those days! But we were working too fast for the companion company, Wimpey's. <u>Their</u> men came from all over the country and they were not interested in working fast. So they went on strike!"

Ellen Willis in Hurst Park remembered the blackout. "With the blackout, we weren't used to lights outside. One night, I said, 'What's that in the sky?' It was only the full moon! I can remember the terrible night they bombed Coventry. Our inside doors here had latches then – and they shook! I watched it – the sky all lit up.

One day, I saw a German plane. Perhaps it was following the railway line, just up here. It dropped a bomb near Evesham – in daylight. Our table was in the middle of the room. I pushed my little daughter, June, under the table. After that, if she heard a bump of any kind, she would throw the cat under the table! My children carried gas masks to school, of course."

A Pershore doctor's wife told me: "I was walking up to the Women's Institute one evening, and there was a frightful crash down the Abbey roof. A bomb had come down but not exploded. John had been walking home from Surgery and he told me later he had stopped up his ears because of this crash.

If this bomb had exploded, it would have absolutely ruined the Abbey, and the whole central area of Pershore. It fell into a little stream and it never exploded. I threw myself on to the ground

– and so did Marjorie Pettifer. And we ruined our stockings!"

"I was a Special Constable during the war," said Cyril Smith. One morning, bombs dropped in Tyddesley Wood. I phoned to tell the police and I went off to the wood. I saw twelve craters right by the flag pole. The only thing I found was a dead rabbit.

One afternoon, I saw a British plane in the wood. So off I went on my bike to the wood. I found the plane. The instructor had got out of the plane, very dazed. He was walking about, so I got him to sit down. He said, 'What about the pilot?' So we got the pilot out of the plane. He was hurt very bad. The ambulance came and took them off.

At Oliver's in Worcester, you could buy fifty-shilling suits in those days. I had gone into Worcester by train that day, to collect my suit. They had measured me already for that. Soon after I got back home, we heard WOOF! WOOF! Two bombs had dropped. Me and another Special, Bert Morris, walked towards the wood and Mr. Chantrill's house. They hadn't heard any bombs.

We went round the back of Mr. Chantrill's house. I could smell sulphur. At Tyddesley Bank was a flood of water running down the side of the road. I could still smell this funny smell. Up the garden, thirty yards from his back door, was a bomb crater. And they hadn't even heard it! Another crater was in the middle of the meadow by the river."

There was a stoic attitude towards food rationing. Some wives, mothers and daughters, indeed, were most inventive and resourceful. Esme Westcott remembered: "The old Miss Woodwards just couldn't understand why they couldn't have more butter. We used to add a little drop of milk to the butter to make it go farther. We made scrambled egg and omelettes out of powdered egg. It wasn't bad!

On my 21st birthday, they tried all over the place to get some icing sugar to give me an iced cake. It was impossible. So, I had a cake, of sorts. My eldest sister got some white cardboard and made a cover for the cake. She decorated the cardboard with what we would call today, white Polyfilla. It was a paste of some sort, and she put 21 on top. It was all good fun! I did manage to have a party. Everyone brought a contribution – sandwiches, or jelly, or whatever they could get hold of."

"In those war-time days," recalled Ruth Baster, "although we were all short of things, there was no stealing, like there is today. Mrs. Elkerton, at the butcher's shop, kept liver specially for my young David. He was always pale and thin. I used to mince up the skin of a chicken to eke out our rations. We kept chickens, so we had eggs.

We were glad of a rabbit occasionally, as a gift. I would use fresh elderberries from the hedgerow, instead of dried fruit, in cakes. My sister sent canned butter from Kenya. My sister-in-law in U.S.A. sent sugar and dried fruit.

Ruth's Recipe for a Boiled Fruit Cake in war-time

4lbs. Flour
1 tsp. Bicarbonate of soda (raising agent)
½lb. dried fruit)
2oz fat   )
1 teacup sugar   )
1 tsp. Spice   )
1½ teacups water   )

Mix the bracketed items all together. Put them in a saucepan and boil the mixture for 5 minutes. Let it cool down. Stir in flour and bicarb. Bake for 1½ hours in a slow oven.

Kitty Haines told me: "In 1941, my aunt, Miss Salmon, in Bridge Street, said to us, 'I can't cope with the rationing in my shop. Come and help me.' So that's why we returned to Pershore. We lived with her for a long time. There was sweet coupons, cold meats, and people came for their tea here, but we didn't sell sugar. And all in ration books.

The ration was half-a-pound of sugar a week. The cheese varied from two to four ounces. But an agricultural worker got three-quarters of a pound. That was because he had to carry out food every day for lunch, and meat was rationed.

Poor families wanted the bones from the hams we sold, because there was still some meat on them. And there were evacuees in Pershore – a bigger population. There were the service people as well. So cigarettes were short."

"When we couldn't get stockings," said Esme Westcott, "we girls used to paint our legs with Camp coffee and use an eyebrow pencil to make a line for the back seam. We made believe we were wearing those very smart stockings from Paris! In those days, stockings all had seams – and tights had not been invented."

Evenings in war-time," reminisced Ruth Baster, "were very dull for a mother with young children... Harry and I never went out to anything. Harry would be late back from work. Then he had to go out on ARP duty.

Everything was on coupons – even nappies. There were no disposable ones then! All our coupons were spent on the children's shoes. Dick Edwards would phone me from his draper's shop: 'Winter vests have come in.' When I was having the babies, I only had coupons for one maternity smock. So when that was being washed, I had to stay in bed!"

"I was a Red Cross volunteer nurse," said a Pershore doctor's wife. "We met trains of wounded soldiers at Shrub Hill station, Worcester. We would go at 10 p.m. The soldiers were taken to Ronkswood Hospital then."

Ruth Baster told me: "I made two pairs of striped pyjamas for the Red Cross every week during the war. I still have a Certificate awarded for this work, from the Dowager Duchess of Gloucester."

Ruth continued: "The Red Cross held auctions during the war to raise money for their funds. I well remember one of them. In a parcel from my relatives in U.S.A., a doll had been sent for my daughter, little Margaret. But at the Customs, the doll had been 'pinched', as it was Christmas-time. Your mother, Meg Bramford, told me she had just sent her daughter Avril's doll to the Red Cross auction.

So I went to the auction, so that I could bid for this doll. Mr. C. A. Mumford, our neighbour, was bidding against me, to my surprise! I could go no higher than £5 (a big sum in those days).

So Mr. Mumford won the doll, to my sorrow. But the next day, he brought the doll round to us for our little Margaret. He had intended it for Margaret all along!"

Freda Hutley-Reade told me: "During the war, several brides' dresses were sent to Great Britain from the U.S.A. It was under President Roosevelt's 'Lend Lease Scheme'. A wedding in Wick church was the first occasion at which one of these brides' dresses was worn. It was photographed by my husband. Brides' dresses were on coupons and in short supply."

I was told: "Mrs. Baldwin at the Angel Hotel used to have injured airmen to stay at her hotel, while they were convalescing. They were the Australian, Canadian and Commonwealth airmen. There was nowhere for them to go when they came out of hospital. So they stayed in the Angel Hotel and Mrs. Baldwin didn't charge them.

Jack Hemming had airmen from overseas staying with him too, recuperating. Bill, the Australian sailor, had been ship-wrecked and had nowhere to go. Jack didn't charge him – not for lodgings, but they paid him for their food. Lil Hemming went without her rations many a time to give meals to these men."

Cyril Smith, curator of the cemetery, was busy during the war: "We used to get these accidents at Tylesford and Defford aerodromes. Perhaps there were four or five men in a 'plane crash. I had to be busy then, with one or two local burials as well. I would be there with a hurricane lamp and digging graves at 11 o'clock at night.

I used to do the lot, on my own, in those days. It was very pitiful to see those burials of those young airmen. The war graves in Pershore Cemetery were looked after by Pershore Youth Fellowship for a number of years. Margaret Warrington came regularly to put flowers on those graves.

Major General Sir Fabian Ware, of the War Graves Commission, came to see me one day. He sat there, on his shooting stick, and said to me: 'Whose idea is it of planting those graves like that, with flowers? We'll have them done everywhere like that – a groove cut across the top and flowers planted. It used to look lovely with the daisies, lobelia and alyssum.

I had got about sixty servicemen's graves there by then – all airmen. Only two were soldiers. After the war, we had visitors from Canada – mothers, fathers, brothers and sisters. They signed my visitors' book. My wife became very interested and wrote letters to them. They asked my wife to put flowers on the grave for a birthday. She corresponded with them for years." (See Footnote).

"During my time at RAF Defford," said Mary Stubbs, "I worked several times with Sir Hugh Casson, who was Camouflage Officer for the Air Ministry. The RAF band played at the aerodrome and at the Three Tuns Hotel and in several other towns and villages. We followed them round!"

Peggy Maple told me: "I was sent to Bletchley to nurse, during the war. In that beautiful house at Bletchley, all that wonderful secret work was going on, with codes. We were in huts on one side of that house. The boffins were in huts on the other side of the house. So we didn't even know. I can remember the wisteria all over the house, and the grounds full of azaleas and rhododendrons.

"Just before the battle of Arnhem," said Edwin Hill, "the skies here were absolutely blackened by the immense amount of aircraft going round and round in a circle. Quite a lot of them were towing gliders. An amazing sight for a young person!"

Ellen Willis remembered the peace celebrations at the end of the war, in 1945. "A kind lady lent my husband a whole lot of fancy dress costumes for the children of Hurst Park. All my four children and the Parker children and Carter children were costumed. Janet, my eldest daughter, went as a gypsy, in a beautiful outfit, all in silk. She won First Prize!"

Lots of Prisoners of War were sent to work around Pershore, on the land. A few stayed on here, after the war, working on the ground.

The war even affected Library services. Before the war, the County Librarian, Miss Ferguson, used to come round the country's villages and small towns with boxes of books. They could be borrowed from a suitable location – usually the village hall or school.

During the war, the County Library rented the front room of no. 62 Bridge Street, Pershore, from Miss Lois Young, to be used as a Library. The windows had to be blacked out. Lois Young was Librarian.

Lois Young remembered the bombing of Coventry: "On the worst night, I sat down, alone, <u>under</u> the desk in the Library – and then went home. One day, a cat dashed into my Library, followed by a dog. Everyone ran outside, expecting a fight! I was left to cope, on my own.

It was too quiet, here in Pershore, for the evacuees, and they drifted back to Birmingham or London, many of them. But they never returned their library books. Lots of books were lost like that!"

Subsequently, the Pershore Library moved to a room in the old Infants' school. Then it moved to a room behind the Working Men's Club, in High Street. It was housed in its present location, in Church Street, in 1977.

Some welcome evacuees from London, were the Music and Drama departments of the BBC, who were moved down to Wood Norton, situated between Pershore and Evesham. Local golfers would meet BBC actors and musicians, by chance, at Fladbury Golf Club.

The BBC Orchestra performed two concerts during the war, in the Plaza cinema at Pershore. One was conducted by Stanford Robinson and the other one by Sir Charles Groves. Audrey Cameron of the BBC, helped produce some W.I. plays at the W.I. Hall in Pershore.

FOOTNOTE

On visiting these war graves in Pershore Cemetery, in 1996, I was amazed how many of those airmen killed, were <u>French</u> Canadians, with the dates of their deaths carved in <u>French</u> on their headstones.

Chapter nineteen

DUST TO DUST AND THE SUPERNATURAL

'Round about the Bredon Hill
A man may live as long as he will.'

Pershore and district has shown, and still shows, strong evidence
for the truth of this saying, in the longevity of its native folk.
The presence of many centenarians in Pershore, and its
surrounding villages, may be due to the fertile quality of the
soil, the splendid harvests of local fruit and vegetables, but
also, surely to the centenarians' unquenchable good humour.
Pershore people still find a humorous aspect in their lives – even
about THE CLOSE OF THE DAY AND THE LAST SUNSET.

In the early 1920's, Billy Trapp's horse-drawn hearse was an
essential feature of funerals in Pershore. Much later on, Edwin
Hill had his own reasons for becoming a Funeral Director. He
evolved his own philosophy about his work.

"I'd always wanted to go into Local Government," said Edwin.
"But I decided I would go into my first love – carpentry. I took
an apprenticeship with Mr. Tom Simpkins. This was during the
middle part of the Second World War.

Eventually, I got involved in making coffins, on the funeral
side. I loved the work of making the coffins. There was such a
wonderful feel to the wood. But the actual thought of working
with the dead, I didn't like. Ultimately, however, it stood me in
good stead.

I worked with my father, building good quality houses. One
day, I was putting a roof on a lovely house we were building at
Bishampton, when I had an accident. I fell through the floor and
damaged my back. I decided I had got to look for something a
bit easier. The only other thing was Funeral Directing.

So I went back to school – to hospitals, to the pathology
departments, and learned as much as I could. The business

started, and gradually and quietly it built up. Today, it's quite a reasonably successful venture. I've had lots of interesting experiences in this work, but one has to be careful not to have a macabre sense of humour.

The important thing I would like to state is: 'One develops a psychology.' You never know how people are going to greet you. In this moment of despondency with them, you may get kissed at the door; or you may get greeted with a joke – or stony silence.

You learn not to talk very much. You let people talk to you. An interesting thing is that, on occasions, it takes about three or three and a half hours, sitting listening to people. And you haven't taken the order. Your wife wonders what you've been up to so long!

In 34 years, (this was said in 1993) I've found the humour comes into it behind the scenes. We visit people who have lost their parents. 'Have you any instructions from your parents?' I ask. They reply: 'Oh, we couldn't bear to have them buried. And mother never wanted to be cremated.' We have to persuade them to decide, one way or the other! We go out at all times of the day and night. For 34 years, it's been seven days of the week, 24 hours of the day."

In 1960, mediaeval bones were found in Church Walk, between the Abbey and St. Andrew's Church, on the Abbey side. They were going to be put back in the trench. Instead, the bones were put in sacks and taken up to Pershore Cemetery, in Three Springs Road. Cyril Smith, custodian of the Cemetery, said: "It was funny. Canon Bark accompanied these bones, on foot, and he chanted all the way to the grave."

Cyril Smith had a keen sense of humour and he shared with me a wealth of information about his work at the Cemetery: "My father, Edwin Smith, learned his trade at Yardley Cemetery, Birmingham. Pershore Cemetery was in a rough mess when he came here to take charge of it. Colonel Hudson at Wick was Chairman of the Burial Committee then.

My father had seen an old mowing machine at a sale. He

had bought it, unknown to the Burial Committee. One day, he was mowing away, when who should drive up in the horse and cab, but Colonel Hudson. He was surprised to see what my father had done. 'Oh, Mr. Smith, we'll buy you a new machine.' And that was the start of being made tidy!

The Cemetery has been there since 1875, when they finished burying at the Abbey. The Cemetery-keeper's house, the chapel and the walls around the Cemetery, were all built in 1875, for about £5,000."

Cyril Smith continued: "I left my job at Pershore Mill in 1923, to help my father in the Cemetery. By then, he had a mowing machine that was too big to push. So he went to Pershore Fair. He came back with a donkey. We called her Jinny. And she pulled the mower. I used to lead her, and Dad had hold of the handles. It did a good job. We had her for a few years. Then she cut her foot very bad, on a jam jar, from a grave. So Dad sold her.

He went to the Fair again. Back he came with a pony and her foal. She was a lovely pony. We called her Dolly. Dad only paid £3.10.0d for the two of them at the Fair. We used to work Dolly for about two hours a day. Then we would let her loose and she would eat the grass from around the gravestones.

The most burials I had in one month, mostly from 'flu, was in 1929, when I buried 43 people. My dear mother was one of them. That was when Pershore was half the size it is today. The bell in the Abbey was ringing from morning 'til night. Old William Need did a good trade, ringing the bell, that month.

Yes, I have seen many things happen at burials. I've had the sides of the graves slipping! I've saved people from falling in. I have had to tell mourners not to fall out with one another. I have told them they could do what they liked outside the Cemetery, but not in the Cemetery. I still think, when they started to bury people, if they had stood them up, instead of laying them down, it would not have taken up half the ground as it has.

I've seen mourners throw the wreaths at one another! That's

where you see family feuds. I saved a man from falling in one of the graves, once. He was one of the bearers. As they was letting the coffin down, I had to push him aside. I could see he was fainting. I had to grab his webbing and push him away from the grave.

I have served over 60 parsons in my time. I've known the time when I have been in thunderstorms, out in the Cemetery, at midnight, covering graves up with tin sheets, to stop the sides falling in. I have even dug graves on a Christmas Day.

Oh yes, I've had many a talk with many people. I've often been asked what I thought of death. I tell them there is nothing we can do about it. It comes to us all. We don't know when. But I have told them Remembrance is the best thing. About that, they all agree with me." (More of Cyril's anecdotes appear in the next chapter).

THE SUPERNATURAL

I have been indebted to Blanche Dufty and her marvellous memory for many of the subjects I have covered. She had a wealth of experiences to share. Ghostly phenomena were no exception.

Blanche (then aged 101) told me: "My sister was in service at Besford. This would be in about 1900. I was only aged 8 or 9. We went down by Stocking Brook. It was winter and very dark. Suddenly, a square of light came down at the side of the brook and no sound. My sister and her friend, who was with us, started panicking. They wouldn't go on the roadway. So we went across some ploughed fields, and got in a terrible mess on the outskirts of Tyddesley Wood.

We got to the house in Besford very late. The woman there said: 'Where have you been to at this time of night?' My sister told her about this light and how frightened we were. The woman wouldn't believe it. 'Rubbish!' she said. But it was true. We was crying, 'cos we was so terrified, and 'cos it was pitch black – no torches. My sister had prayed to God that we should get home safely.

I often wonder what that light was. Whether it was a warning for you not to go that way ..... We daren't tell my father, 'cos it was so late. Mother was waiting up for us two at the back door. It has always been a mystery to me. All of a sudden, came that square of light by the brook. It never flickered."

Blanche continued: "My mother was psychic. Her maiden name was Cosnett. Her family used to own all of Garden Styles land. My mother had heard her brother was ill. He lived not far away from us, in Newlands. His wife didn't like my mother. A midwife was nursing him and she came and told my mother that he wasn't going to live. My mother said: 'Well, if he lives 'til tomorrow, I shall go and see him, even if I'm kicked out.'

My mother was always the last to go to bed. She was shutting the outside back door, when she saw her brother digging in the garden! And he gave her such a pitiful look, she knew he was dying. As soon as it got light, she intended to go and see him. But the nurse came and told her he had died at the very time she had seen him in the garden. He had been asking for 'Barbara', my mother."

Blanche had two more strange stories to tell me: "My eldest sister was ill with bronchitis and whooping cough and there was no hope for her. My mother had been poulticing her chest – the only thing she could do. (A poultice was an old remedy: a piping hot cloth, steeped in hot mustard, flour or liniment, was applied to the patient's chest, or back, to relieve bronchitis).

It was midnight. All at once, Mother heard a noise like wings flapping around. 'That was the crisis of our Kate,' she said, later on. 'That meant she was going to live.' Angels' wings around her kitchen as she poulticed her daughter."

"My mother's family," said Blanche, "had to take all what they grew on their land, to Worcester market, in those days. This would be in the 1880's and '90's, long before Pershore Growers' Market was established. They used to take the stuff on drays, with horses. They would start off from Pershore at midnight, to get there early for next day's market at Worcester.

One night, my mother told me, they had started at midnight, on a lovely moonlit night. All of a sudden, they saw a man walking in front of their dray and horse. You couldn't hear him, but you could see him. The horse took fright. The horse went into a pool. Mother told me, her father said his hair stood on end. This happened in Three Springs Road."

Many years later, Blanche was talking with the wife of Wilf Pugh. "She was always taking her dog out," said Blanche. "I said to her, 'Where do you go with your dog at night?' 'I go around by the pool,' replied Mrs. Pugh, 'but do you know, my dog won't go near that pool!' I said, 'I can tell you a tale.' I told her my father's ghost story. She said, 'Ah, now I know the reason.' The pool was just before that garage, near where Jack Knight's house was. The house is now demolished and the pool has all been filled in.

Bet Rhodes had a psychic experience at the top of Gigbridge Lane. In about 1750, the present main road from Pershore to Worcester was built. Before that, the road to Worcester was merely a track along Gigbridge Lane and Brickfields Lane, via Drakes Broughton and Stonebow, leading on to the Spetchley Road and forward to Worcester.

Bet Rhodes was walking along the part of Gigbridge Hill, looking towards Drakes Broughton. She heard the sound of carriage wheels. She sensed that there had been an accident to a horse-drawn carriage, in which rode an eighteenth century lady, on her way to Worcester, to buy gloves. Later on, on another day, Bet's daughter found some ancient harness tackle near that same spot, and the buckle of an eighteenth century shoe, which she brought home to her mother.

Bet was born in Scotland. On visiting the site of the Battle of Culloden (1746) she had sensed, very strongly, the horrors of that particular conflict. Dusk had fallen. Bet was alone in the eerie atmosphere of that deserted moor. So many mounds of the clansmen and chieftains, who had perished in that tragic battle, were in her presence, re-creating the anguish of the men's spirits, that Bet was terrified and vowed never to return.

Alec Witts told me of the strange atmosphere at his property in Bridge Street, Pershore. It was originally a public house, The Black Swan, half-timbered, and dating back to the thirteenth century. It had been a coaching inn and had a brewery. The sharp pitch of the roof proclaimed it had once been thatched. As he could not restore it, the building was pulled down in recent years, and rebuilt.

"But it is still a weird place," said Alec. "There are noises, as though a body were being dragged across the floor. Even now, there's an evil atmosphere in one room.

My daughter used to live there. She spoke of tapping noises. She told me, 'We felt people were looking at us.' A soldier was seen – dressed as a Cavalier, from the Civil War."

Peggy Maple had heard of this latter experience. She rounded off the story thus: "Yes, and I heard that the handsome Cavalier soldier smiled sweetly at the young lady who saw him." And Peggy was quite serious.

Inns and former inns are a fruitful site for hauntings. Perhaps their antiquity, the intensity of their customers' emotions and the events they have engendered, leaves behind a concentrated impression. Three more hauntings in Pershore inns are mentioned in the chapter 'Pershore Pubs'. See: The Plough, The Manor House and The Talbot.

Pershore and District Sports Club. Opening of a new Skittle Alley, mid 1950's. George Bramford (President) puts down the first wood. Left to right: Jack Taylor, John Bomford, Eric Maple, Ray Till.

*Living Whist performed by Pershore Women's Institute
in the Abbey Grounds in 1922.*

Meg Bramford as the Queen of Hearts in Living Whist in 1932.

'Gypsy Dancers' c. 1926. The musical Swann family. Twins, Edna and Joan, stand on either side of sister, Ella Patricia. A friend is behind.

Toy Soldiers on parade in Broad Street, Pershore, for the Coronation of King George VI, 1937. From left May Winkett, Ruth Howe, Mary Goodall, Avril Bramford, Peter Cornelius, John Hall.

*Pershore Women's Institute Drama, mid 1930's in NINE 'TIL SIX.
From the left: Nurse Monk, Audrey Edwards, unknown, Betty Tuffin,
Grace Knott, (kneeling) unknown, Vera Evans, Gladys Mence.*

*Pershore Women's Institute Drama, mid 1930's, in SANCTUARY.
From left: Audrey Edwards, Catherine Parkes, Nellie Bullock,
Eva Grundy, Vera Evans*

Pershore Women's Institute Drama, April 1950, in THE OLD FOOL. From Left: Ivy Burford, Betty Tuffin, Nora Westcott, Jim Gardner, Walter Palfrey, Grace Knott.

*Pinvin Dramatic Society, mid 1930's,
in A MIDSUMMER NIGHT'S DREAM by Shakespeare.*

Pinvin Dramatic Society, mid 1930's, in AS YOU LIKE IT by Shakespeare.

The Women's Institute stall at the S.S.A.F.A. Fete in the grounds of Defford Aerodrome in 1958. Left: Vera Evans and Meg Bramford. Far right: Elwyn Wilson.

Charles Harriss of Pinvin, as Petruchio in THE TAMING OF THE SHREW by Shakespeare, mid 1930's.

Pershore Dramatic Society, 1950's in ARMS AND THE MAN by Bernard Shaw. From left: Unknown, Wallace Smedley, Avril Bramford, Barbara Harris, "Griff" Griffin, Enid Middleton.

Chapter twenty

ANECDOTES – HUMOUR AND PATHOS

ON THE MOVE!

Canon Murray, Vicar of Pershore Abbey from 1928-38, was well known for his quick movements and for driving his car too fast. One day, during our English lesson, in the old school in Defford Road, my father, Mr. George Bramford, as Headmaster, came into our classroom and wrote the word 'hurry' on the blackboard. He then asked the class for words which rhymed with 'hurry'. Hands went up – 'flurry' ..... 'scurry' ..... Then a boy at the back put up his hand. "Please Sir, Murray, Sir."

"What do you mean by that?" asked my father, puzzled. "Canon Murray, Sir. The Vicar Sir," said this boy. We all laughed with delight. And ever after, in my family, and elsewhere, that Pershore Vicar was referred to as 'Hurry, Flurry, Scurry, MURRAY!' which was most appropriate! My father dared to tell Canon Murray this joke, one Sunday, in the Abbey vestry. The Vicar roared with laughter, in his Irish way.

STREET COMEDY

A Pershore man told me: "In the 1920's, one local chap used to get a bit tiddly and he couldn't ride his bicycle back home. There was a lot of shouting outside our house – very few cars about in those days – and there he was, in the road, lying down. He picked up his bike, still cursing it, with the handlebars locked under his chin.

'All right, you won't carry me! I'll carry you!' he shouted. So he went up the street, carrying his bicycle. You could understand it. Many local men at that time, hadn't got much of this world's goods and they used to go to the pub to find some solace, because they'd got no heat at home."

Charles Clemens, then aged 92, still had his old ebullience and sense of humour, as he related to me these four anecdotes:

SEEING DOUBLE

"I was church organist at Fladbury Church for 42 years. Mrs. Smyth was the saving grace at Fladbury. She was a dear, and always ready to help everybody. I wore glasses for playing the organ, as I do now. But I hadn't got them one Sunday, in Fladbury Church. So Mrs. Smyth toddled back home, to the big house where she lived, and brought me five pairs of her husband's glasses. One pair suited me, fortunately!

The same thing happened at church on another Sunday, when she wasn't there. So, Mr. Arthur, the Fladbury Headmaster, said, 'Wait a minute, I've got lots of different sizes of spectacles at home,' he fixed me up the same way as Mrs. Smyth did!"

THE SIMPLE TRUTH

"Mother was with the Fry family for years, in Clifton, Bristol. Being with them, turned her into a Quaker. In her own home, she had been a Methodist. But 'Yes' meant 'Yes'. We always had a special cake from Phillips the grocer, on Sundays, when I was a boy. It was a lovely cake. We were a big family, 'cos I had six sisters. I was the youngest of them all. We were given one nice slice of cake each.

One Sunday, Mother said to me, 'Would you like another slice?' I said, 'No thank you, Mother.' But later on I said, 'Oh, I think I would like another slice.' 'You don't alter your mind,' Mother replied, 'because it would be a lie on my part, if you did.' She was back to her Quaker background. Mother was very rigid in many ways. Still, it was no harm to us. It kept us on the narrow way."

TALE OF A HAT

"In the 1920's," said Charles Clemens, "my sister, May, was nursery governess with the Woodward family, in Assam, India, for four or five years. These wild men of the hills used to come and beg one of May's old hats against the sun. May couldn't say 'No'. So she made them a present of one of them. And she made a friend of this wild man. But Mr. Woodward said, 'I shouldn't do that, if I were you, Nurse. I don't trust them. They're absolutely wild.'

But I've often wondered about that gift of her hat. In the Second World War, when one division of our fellows (12,000) were surrounded by the Japanese, these same wild men showed them a secret way through the mountains to Assam, to where the rest of the British were. They had a tendency to help the British, you see.

And May enjoyed every minute of her stay in Assam. When she returned home, those natives used to write her a letter in pidgin English. We couldn't understand it, but she could! Little bits of Hindu mixed up with English. She said Hindu is a most simple language to learn."

DRAMA AT SEA

Charles Clemens and Arthur Taylor founded the Wireless Supply Ltd. in the 1920's. The company now has branches in five different towns in Worcestershire. Charles Clemens said: "In the First World War, Arthur Taylor was radio operator on a big liner in South America. He was at one of those big ports. He was listening in to where the mines were – German mines. A British warship came alongside their liner. The warship signalled to the liner, 'Where's your wireless operator?' Someone went quickly to Arthur's cabin. He was fast asleep, with the headphones on. So they had a Court Martial.

The old man, the Captain, said to the judge, 'Please don't blame this man. He has done 72 hours continuous service, because of the mines, and he couldn't help falling asleep.' The judge said, 'Well done! Case dismissed.' Arthur said to

209

me afterwards, 'I shall never forget it. I thought they would shoot me.' It was very dramatic. He had taken down wireless messages for the captain for 72 hours without a break. You see, Arthur had no deputy on board, 'cos wireless was only just beginning on the liners, in those days."

'PING PONG' CROOKE

"He was a reporter for the local newspapers," said Walter Palfrey. "But he didn't get things right. His nickname was 'Ping Pong'. I used to play hockey in a team with Jack Taylor. Mr. Crooke would wait outside the Angel Hotel 'til we came back from the match. After one match, Jack Taylor said to him: 'Oh, we won 2-1.' So there was a report in next week's paper as to how we had scored that day and all about the match. But Jack Taylor had never said a thing about the <u>details</u> of the match. Fred Crooke had made it up! He even reported on one match that had never taken place!"

NO CLASS DISTINCTION!

Rene Giles' mother was Annie Moseley. She was born at The Hythe Farm in Pinvin. She married James Parker of Shrewsbury. A photo taken about 1898 shows her in her ball dress with lace flowers at the neckline. It was taken before the Yeomanry Ball at the Three Tuns Hotel. Rene's mother worked for the Hudson family when they lived in the Abbey House. She was a house-parlour maid there. Rene's father was a plumber by trade. He often did work for the Hudsons. That's how he met Rene's mother.

Rene said: "When my father used to call for my mother, at the Abbey House, before their marriage, she wasn't always available. So he took out for a walk, one of the Miss Hudsons instead! One of the daughters of Colonel Hudson would say to father, 'Would I do, Mr. Parker?' He would reply, 'It would be a pleasure to take you out, Miss Hudson.' I should think my mother was jealous! But, on the other hand, when Mother's young man, Mr. Parker, was not available, one of the Hudson sons would take <u>her</u> out instead!"

TEACHER OFF DUTY

Mary Stubbs shared this memory with me. "Miss Bick was one of the teachers at the old school in Defford Road. She used to live in the High Street, next door to The Ship Inn. She wore pince-nez glasses. And she always smelt of apples! We had to take our National Savings to her on Monday mornings. I used to say to my mother, 'I'm not going to Miss Bick any more. She smells all apples.' Years later, I found out it was <u>cider</u> she smelt of. The Ship Inn was noted for its good cider!"

I SPY SPIES

Rene Giles has lived for most of her life at Hurst Park, off Station Road. "When these semi-detached houses were first built, in 1921, they were the best houses going, apart from the town houses. I can well remember at the very bottom, at no. 32, lived a family called Matthews. I believe the father was a Secret Service man. He used to disappear for a long time. He would come back here on very odd occasions, and he would land in Coles Field, in an aeroplane. They thought he was a spy. There were quite a lot of well-to-do people in Hurst Park then."

Mary Stubbs recalled: "In the Second World War, we used to say that the Bridge Street photographer, Joe Glover, was a spy.' He had a glass roof upstairs, where he did his photography. So we children said, 'He goes up there, and he puts the lights on, so that the Germans can see where we are. There was a couple who lived in Bridge Street, and they said that he too, was a German spy, because of his name – Zeigler."

TARES AMONG THE WHEAT

As a child, Betty Hughes lived in Peopleton. "We had some happy days in the Church of England school in the village," she said. "At Harvest Festival time, we schoolchildren took produce from the garden to church. My mother had given me this lovely large marrow to take. Some boys, walking behind me, were tickling the backs of my legs with rose hips – and I dropped the marrow. It rolled down the whole length of the church path. The teacher said I was fooling around. She didn't know the torture I had been suffering!"

A ROLLICKING PARTY

Malcolm Meikle shared this memory: "In the 1930's and '40's, the League of Pity parties were held after Christmas, in the Masonic Room at the Angel Hotel. There were three separate parties – one for the Tinies, one for the older children and a dance for the adults, usually on Boxing Day. The Masonic Room had a wonderful floor for sliding on. At one of these parties, as a very small boy, I slid the whole length of the floor, with another little boy, and we demolished two ladies, like skittles, across the bottom end!"

DISCORD ON THE ORGAN

Services in Wick church did not always run sedately, as Malcolm Meikle relates: "The Sherwoods were a very old family in Wick. They had been the blacksmiths at the Old Forge. Reggie Sherwood was apprenticed to his father. Reggie was very much a square peg in a round hole. I think he went to Canada, but he came back. I first knew of Reggie as an ecclesiastical retainer for Mrs. Bickerton Hudson of Wick Manor. She was extremely high church. Reggie used to play the organ in Wick church. He also used to serve at the altar, and wear a lace surplice.

At the end of the war, we had a young, vigorous curate, George Grice-Hutchinson. He did not see eye-to-eye with Reggie. They had an argument as to whether there should be a recessional hymn at the end of the service. So the curate, George, sent the choir out and they passed the organ on their way to the vestry. Reggie sent them back again. George went to take the music away from the organ, and knocked Reggie off the organ seat! After that, Reggie never appeared in Wick church again, until Mrs. Bickerton Hudson's funeral. He used to play the organ in Hampton by Evesham instead. He and his wife used to <u>walk</u> from Wick to Hampton, Sunday after Sunday."

Rosie Long enjoyed recollecting these three childhood episodes:

THE BLACK DOLL

"I was born in 1913 near Wood Norton Hall. When I was six, just after the First World War, there was a fête on, in the grounds of Abbey Manor. It is near the site of the Battle of Evesham in 1265. It was used as a nursing home in the First World War. I remember seeing the wounded prisoners of war there. I can see the nurses in their uniform now!

We walked around the grounds. One of the nurses gave me a doll dressed in nurse's uniform. It was a black doll. I called her Black Jane. I had that doll until we moved to Charlton. Unfortunately, she got lost in the move. She fell out of the cradle.

FINDERS KEEPERS

I was on my own, walking across the golf links at Fladbury. All of a sudden, this golf ball came down in front of me. Naturally, I picked it up, thinking somebody had thrown it to me. I did not realise there was a match on. And the air went blue for miles around! We used to walk around the perimeter of the golf course, looking for golf balls in the hedge. We kept them if we found them.

POST HASTE

When we moved to Charlton, I went to school at Cropthorne. We lived at Fernhill Farm, which is down by the railway. We had to walk over the railway up to Cropthorne School, which is a good mile and a half each way, and along a lonely lane. There were no more houses until we reached the top of the lane.

Once, my elder brother and I, we'd been mucking around, picking blackberries, and I'd got our lunch in the bag. I must have put it down and forgot where. The post lady was going down to our farm. I asked her if she would find it for me and bring it up. 'Certainly not!' she retorted. 'You lost it and you'll go back and fetch it!' I had to go back half-way down the lane to look for my lost bag."

ROMANCE AT PERSHORE FAIR

Rosie Long recalled: "I met my husband at Pershore Fair. He lived up Holloway, when it was just a lane. There were four houses in a block. He used to sit on a big well in the front gardens and play a cornet. There was another well at the back, which was kept for washing clothes. They had big old-fashioned coppers then. Mrs. Ballinger used to do washing for several different families. Unknown to this young man, I used to sit on our gate, half-way up the hill and listen to him playing that cornet.

At this particular Fair, I was on my own. I had left my bike at Browns, the Ironmongers. This fellow came across with two more lads. He squirted water all down my back. I turned round and I stamped on his foot. He said I had ruined the best pair of shoes he'd ever had in his life! That's how we got talking.

Some days later, he was walking his lovely black and white dog. He was going down Stocking Bank as I was coming up. And that's how we started! His name was Raymond Long. He was a first-class carpenter and joiner and he taught himself brick-laying. He was one of the finest brick-layers round here. His son, Raymond, at Tewkesbury, is like him. <u>He</u> does carpentry."

THE CHIPS WERE DOWN!

This is another of Rosie Long's memories: "Canon Bark of Pershore Abbey always looked so stern. One of his curates was the Rev. Woolf. He came to us quite a lot through my son, David. Here, in my house in Newlands, we had David playing the violin and Mr. Woolf on the piano. You could never get rid of him! And he liked his fish and chips.

One evening, Mr. Woolf left here to go home, and he bought some fish and chips, just down this street. He was eating them out of the newspaper and not looking where he was going. He walked straight into Canon Bark! 'Woolf, what do you think you're doing? I don't like to see my curates eating fish and chips in the street.' Mr. Woolf protested that he would please himself! Apparently, he walked boldly on, leaving behind a deflated and baffled Canon Bark."

BARBER SHOP GLEE

"I enjoyed my work 'cos it was so entertaining – a laugh all the time," said Laurence Coggins, the barber. "It was on a Saturday afternoon and I was very busy. The shop was full. There was a long seat along one wall. Six people could sit on it. They had just come out of the pub, of course.

Ernie Parker came in. He had retired from the Post Office. He used to love a drop of cider. He had his bag with him, containing several bottles of cider. A bottle of cider appeared, which a chap started drinking, up in the corner. He hands it to the next one, and so on ..... 'Do you want a drink Parker?' 'My God, that's a drop of good!' says Parker. 'I bet you I can tell you where that has come from.' 'Where?' 'The Ship Inn,' says Parker.

A few minutes later, there's another bottle going along.

Ernie Parker says again: 'That's a drop of good. That's from The Ship.' Another bottle goes along. They were joking and laughing. 'Come on Parker, let's try a drop of yours.' He leans down and pulls this bag from under the seat, gets a bottle out – but it was empty. They had got a walking stick and they'd hooked his bag right up to the other end of the seat somehow or other – and they had been drinking his own cider!"

HE MET HIS WATERLOO?

The Dowty family had their chemist's shop at Rembrandt House, High Street, Pershore, from the 1880's onwards. It was subsequently owned, among others, by Swann ..... Elliott ..... Savory and Moore ..... Cooks. After the Second World War, in the rooms above that shop, an ancient French Army uniform was found, in the roof of one of the attics, under the tiles. It was later discovered, from records, that a previous English owner, in the early 1800's, had been an apothecary to Napoleon. This was during Napoleon's exile, on the Isle of St. Helena. Hence the French connection!

It is widely believed, by present-day historians, that Napoleon died from arsenic poisoning, absorbed, by accident, from the arsenic dye used in the green wallpaper in his room in St. Helena. Did that Pershore apothecary ever feel uneasy, as he prescribed remedies in quiet Victorian Pershore, far removed from the rumours and gossip in St. Helena?

THANKS FOR THE MEMORY

Every Tuesday was Court Day at the old Police Station in High Street, in the 1920's and '30's. The tunes played by the Abbey carillon on Tuesdays were 'Home Sweet Home', or a plaintive melody, 'The Last Rose of Summer'. 'Home Sweet Home' was considered a wryly-appropriate tune, because some offenders might be committed to jail in Gloucester, or further afield – far from home.

ON A LIGHTER NOTE

Leslie Brookes recalled: "The Abbey choir was large in the time of Mr. Charles Mason, organist. New electric lighting was being installed in the Abbey, in place of old gas lamps. One Sunday, as the choir was singing the anthem, 'Send Out Thy Light', the new electric lights went out – in a thunderstorm! Mr. Mason carried on playing by the light of candles."

OUT OF STEP

One Christmas, in Pershore Abbey, Blind Willie, the organ blower who pumped the organ in those days, fell out with Mr. Mason, the organist, over which Christmas hymn was to be sung next. Blind Willie said: '<u>He</u> was playing 'Hark the Herald' and I was pumping 'While Shepherds Watched'!'

EXOTIC FEAST

In the 1930's, young Robin Champken wrote about Christmas, in his English lesson, at school: "We had a swan and two parrots for our Christmas dinner." Mr. Bramford, his baffled Headmaster, called at the Champken's house, in Abbey Place, close by the old Junior School. He asked Robin's mother what they had actually eaten for Christmas dinner. She replied, "We had a goose and two pheasants!"

LAMPS

Marion Knight remembered the 1930's, at night in Pershore: "There were few gas lamps on the streets in those days. But one was not afraid, then, of dark corners. One felt safe from any violence. John Smith's father was a gas lighter. He rode round the town on his bicycle, with his lamp-lighter's pole over his shoulder. And in Brant's window in Priest Lane, there were always large orange pumpkins glowing!"

THE BUZZ WORD

Cyril Smith reminisced: "One Sunday morning, I went for a walk in Tyddesley Wood, going down the ride. I thought I would go and have a look at the fox earths and the badger sets. What a lot of bees there were around me! Then there were thousands on my trousers' legs. I ran away from the earths. The more I ran, the more they came after me! I stood still. For a while they all settled on my leg. I took my jacket off and I wiped them off, on to the ground. They all left me. I had two stings. I must have had the queen on me. It was very frightening."

The incorrigible Cyril Smith, Custodian of Pershore Cemetery, provided me with yet more:

GRAVE TALES

"One day, I was very busy. I had quite a few graves to dig. A friend of mine came up to me. He said, 'I'll give you a hand.' So I put him right. Away he went, digging this grave. I knew what would happen when he got down to about 4 feet 6 inches. I kept an eye on him. All at once, out he jumped and came running to me. He looked wild at me. The best he could say was, 'I fell through a big hole in the bottom of that grave!' He said he would never help again. He had fallen through the old lid of another coffin!

Another day, I had just finished digging a grave, when the barmaid from the Angel Hotel and her friend came along to me. We were talking away. They said, 'What a long way you have to go down!' I said, 'Would you like to go down to see what it's like down there?' They said they would like to, so I put a ladder down. Down they went and, as soon as they were at the bottom, I pulled the ladder out. You should have heard them! They were screaming, 'Get me out!' I had some fun as a grave-digger.

One day, my old pal, Ralph Perks, the undertaker from

Eckington, came up to me. He said, 'I have a burial at Wolverhampton on Saturday. Would you like to come? You can give me a hand at the burial. It takes place at 12 noon.

So, on the Saturday, they picked me up. My old pal, Bill Wood, drove the hearse, and away we went to Wolverhampton.

When the burial was over, we had lunch somewhere between Wolverhampton and Birmingham. I thought we were coming straight home, but they said there was a football match on the West Bromwich Albion ground. So that is where we ended up. We pulled up outside the gates of the football ground in the hearse. You should have seen the crowd's faces!

Talking about lightning (this is still Cyril Smith!), I have been lucky more than once. One day, there was a storm overhead. I was in the kitchen and the 'phone rang. Down to the office I went. The 'phone was of the old type. It was the Town Clerk, giving me the order for a burial, when it came ..... a flash, and 'bang' went the 'phone. The ear-piece gave a mighty thump against my head, all down my arm. It broke the phone. When the man brought me a new phone, he asked what I had been wearing. I told him I had been wearing my Wellington boots. He said how lucky I had been!

Now and again, I used to have an order from the undertaker to <u>line</u> the grave. The last I remember doing, was for Lady Huntingdon from Bricklehampton Court. I would get some wire netting, about 6 feet tall, and 15 feet long. I would cut some pegs of wood, and peg this wire netting to the walls of the grave.

When I had done that, I used to go up to Tyddesley Wood and get a sack of moss. This I would threat in the wire all round the inside of the grave. It did look cosy! Then, on the day of the funeral, I used to cut flowers from the garden and thread them in the grave. It used to look lovely!"

HOT AND CROSS

Alec Witts recollected this incident, which happened when he was a young man: "Mr. Busby was a baker at Prothero's shop in Broad Street. He also had, what was later Miss Harris's shop on the other side of Broad Street, and he sold cake and bread. One Good Friday, I went to his shop to buy Hot Cross buns. I'd bought some and I'd put them in the basket of my bike. I was leaning my bike against the trees in Broad Street, when along came the elephants from the circus. As one elephant passed by, he took one of the buns out of my bike basket with his trunk!"

JANUARY IN JUNE

As a young woman, Blanche Dufty worked on the land, fruit picking at Mount Pleasant for the Deakins. She recollected this experience: "At half-past three in the morning, in summer, I used to start from here, in Newlands, and knock up a woman on the corner. We would tiptoe up Priest Lane, so as not to wake people. And we were down on Deakin's fruit farm at The Mount at 4 a.m. We picked raspberries, logans and strawberries for canning.

One June morning – you would hardly believe it – it was snowing! The foreman came along and said' 'A Merry Christmas, Mrs. Dufty!' The fruit was terrible – like there had been a frost, until the sun got to them. You couldn't pick the strawberries, but they were not damaged."

My Music teacher at Worcester Grammar School for Girls, in the early 1930's was Miss Lilian Tyers. She had played her violin in an ensemble with Sir Edward Elgar. She admired him and his music tremendously, and would refer to him as 'Our own Worcestershire Elgar'. Here are three local anecdotes about this great composer.

ENIGMATIC 1

Esme Westcott told me: "We are a musical family, because

my father's father, George Champken, played music with the young Elgar, when George was a very young boy. My grandfather used to go to the Elgar Music Shop, in High Street, Worcester, for music lessons. He played the piccolo and the flute, and was taught by Elgar's father. These lads of 14 and 15 got together to play music – a quartet of them. We only found out by chance.

My aunt found some scribblings on music that had belonged to my grandfather – on manuscripts which were lining drawers of furniture. Words were scrawled in Elgar's handwriting, at the top of the music, which the young Elgar had composed, for his young friends and himself to play. The words were: 'What do you think of this, George? (my grandfather's name). Your friend, Teddy Elgar.'"

ENIGMATIC ll

Esme Westcott continued: "My grandfather, George, became a Master Baker, at Handy's bakery, behind Phillips the grocers in High Street, Pershore. In the early 1900's, his old friend, 'Teddy' Elgar, would visit Pershore, on purpose to visit George Champken, at the bakery. Elgar would receive the special pies, which his musical friend, George, had baked for him. We don't know if they were savoury pies, or fruit pies!"

ENIGMATIC lll

This extract appeared in the Evesham Journal in October 1925. 'Mr. William Gill Smith, Mayor of Evesham, Managing Director of W. H. Smith Ltd. and Editor of the Evesham Journal, celebrated his Jubilee recently.

During eulogistic speeches in his honour, it was recalled that he had once been a member of Evesham Institute's instrumental class, which formed a small orchestra. To improve their playing, Mr. Edward Elgar (now Sir Edward) came over from Worcester to hear the class perform. (This would be in about 1885). One visit was sufficient, however. Mr. Elgar never came again! (Laughter).'

TO CAP IT ALL

Betty Tuffin recalled: 'My father sent me, as a child, to Millers the drapers, for a cap for himself. Now, <u>Mrs</u>. Miller always wore a man's cap, anyway, when she served in her shop (A good advertisement!). Mrs. Miller parcelled up a dozen caps, on approval, all tied up with string, as they did in those days, with a loop for me to carry them. I took this parcel home to my father. But he wasn't bothered as to which cap he preferred. He just took out the top one. He only wanted a cap for his work as a painter."

GUARDIAN ANGEL

Betty Tuffin lived with her grandmother in The Old Almonry, an old half-timbered house in Newlands, close by the Abbey. She said: "In the early 1920's, the monks from Pershore Abbey would come and talk to my grandmother. They were friendly. The Abbot had an ugly bulldog who would waddle down to our garden. This large dog would sit on my grandmother's back door mat. He was the gentlest creature.

One day, a gypsy, selling pegs, came to the front door. She saw the bulldog sitting at the back door. 'Missus, is that your dog?' she asked my grandmother. 'Yes!' was the answer. And the gypsy ran off like a shot!"

CHERRY RIPE

Blanche Dufty recalled a 'narrow shave'. "There were cherry trees at The Mount, where my father was the gardener. I used to climb up to get a few cherries, 'cos that's my favourite fruit. I nearly got shot one day. One of the fellows had a shotgun and he was told to keep the birds off the trees. He saw the leaves moving on the tree and he thought it was the birds ..... But he just saw me in time. 'My God!', he shouted to me, 'you'm lucky you didn't have one of these pellets!'"

HE LET IT ALL OUT!

Miss Lois E. Young, who founded her LEY School in Bridge Street, Pershore, in 1938, told me this little episode. "One little boy in my school never talked. He was a very private person. However, one day, near Christmas, I asked the children: 'What Christmas present would your mothers like?' This little boy, who was from a village, suddenly called out: 'I know what <u>my</u> Mum wants – a new pair o' corsets. 'Ers be fairly fallin' off 'er!'"

EPILOGUE

I will let the legendary Blanche Dufty, with her marvellous memory, have the last word. She deserves it! Blanche died in January 1996, just two days before her 104th birthday. Her sister, Kate, had died aged 105.

Blanche was active, alert, effervescent, right up to the end. The year before she died, she had been present, in Pershore Abbey, at the funeral of a relative. Blanche was then heard to say: "Only 85 when she died? <u>NO STAMINA</u>!"

ECHOES OF THE PAST

Part 1

SOME SIGNIFICANT DATES

689 A.D.	Oswald was given land in Pershore for a priests' foundation.
972	Charter given to monastery by King Edgar. First Abbot, Fulbert, was instated.
1086	Domesday Book.
1090	Present Abbey begun, but there were several fires throughout the ages.
1297	Pershore's old bridge was built.
1643 & 1644	Charles 1 passed through Pershore
1833	Pershore plum (yellow egg plum) found growing wild in Tyddesley Wood by George Crooks, who kept The Butcher's Arms, Pershore.
1836	Pershore Workhouse built. (Later named Pershore Union, now Heathlands).
1852	Oxford to Worcester railway came to Pershore.
1853	Pershore Gas Company formed.
1853	Pershore railway station opened.
1854	Cholera epidemic in Pershore.
1879	Abbey Carillon installed.
1883	Atlas Works began in present building.
1895	Pershore Cottage Hospital founded.
1897	Telephone Exchange housed in ironmonger's

shop of Charles Field, High Street, opposite The Square. Later on, in Broad Street.

1909	Co-op Fruit Market established.
c. 1914	Anglican Community of St. Benedict monks returned to Abbey. They left c. 1926.
1914	Pershore Central Market established.
1926	Pershore new bridge opened.
1928	Electricity came to Pershore.
1931	Water came to Pershore.
1946	Last Fair held in Broad Street – in Weir Meadow since then.
1958	Plaza cinema closed.

PERSHORE IN 1931

Population	3,384
Birth Rate	15.0 per 1,000
Death Rate	11.3 per 1,000

Part 2

THE SCHOOL LOG BOOKS SPEAK

PERSHORE NATIONAL SCHOOL in Defford Road, Pershore, which then became, in 1932, PERSHORE CHURCH OF ENGLAND JUNIOR SCHOOL

<u>Head Teachers</u>:

Mr. W. T. Chapman   September 1902 – December 1929.
Miss Ismay was "Governess", i.e. Head of the Girls' Department.

Mr. M. L. Pardoe   January 1930 – December 1931,
Then he was transferred, as Headmaster, to the newly built "Senior" school (now the High School) in Station Road.

Mr. G. H. Bramford   January 1931 – April 1951.

Other teachers' names in 1926:
    Mr. Osborne,
    Mr. Brooks,
    Miss Bick.

December 9th, 1929. The whole school assembled to present Mr. Chapman with an armchair and dressing case, on the occasion of his retirement.

May 24th, 1929: Rev. Dr. R. H. Murray gave a brief address to all pupils at 3 p.m. and presented Empire Day medals to seven boys who had shown special knowledge of the Empire and what it stands for.

June 6th 1930: Miss C. Merrett of the Fellowship of the Maple

226

Leaf gave a lecture on CANADA to Senior Boys, then Senior Girls.

May24th, 1932: EMPIRE DAY. Rev. Dr. R. H. Murray addressed the children on the Empire and the importance of duty among her citizens.

Church Attendance:

February 17th, 1926: Ash Wednesday – boys taken to Abbey Church after Register called – returning at 9.40 a.m.

November 11th, 1926: Armistice Day celebrated in usual manner, by boys standing to attention during two minutes' silence in playground.

May 26th, 1927: Ascension Day. Scholars proceeded to Abbey Church until 9.35 a.m. School closed at noon for customary half-holiday.

Visitors:

1926. Rt. Rev. Gresford Jones, Bishop, Vicar of Pershore, gave Religious Instruction to Upper Standards.

1926. School Dentist treated 21 boys, 10 a.m. to 12 noon.

October 20th 1927. Mrs. Gresford Jones called to bid adieu to the scholars.

March 1929. Rev. Dr. R. H. Murray gave Religious Instruction to Upper Division.

Weather:

January 18th 1926. Deep snow on ground, yet 149 present. Three from Birlingham absent – German measles.

February 9th & 10th 1926. The Avon in flood prevented the attendance of the Pensham children. *(N.B. Children also came to school from Peopleton and Great Comberton).*

June 9th – 13th 1928. Very hot weather makes the scholars somewhat apathetic.

May 23rd 1932. Thirty children absent, owing to the severe floods.

February 24th 1933. Owing to heavy snowfall, 60 children absent.

September 25th 1931. School Garden given up today and transferred to Pershore County Senior School.

THE GREAT DATE

December 22nd 1931. This school has terminated its career as separate Boys' and Girls' Departments today. 11+ scholars will attend the new Senior School. Under-11's will attend the re-organised Pershore C.E. Junior Mixed School.

"New" staff appointed to the new Junior Mixed School

> Mr. G. H. Bramford, Headmaster.
> Mrs. C. Hallam, Deputy Head.
> Mr. Addis,
> Miss Morris,
> Miss Taylor,
> Miss Pointon.

MUSIC WAS ENCOURAGED

May 9th, 1932. All children taken to County Senior School to participate in Pershore Schools' Musical Festival.

June 13th 1932. Mr. S. S. Moore, Musical Adviser, gave interesting lecture on Musical Instruments, with gramophone illustration to older children and conducted a Percussion Band with Standard I.

EDUCATIONAL VISITS

July 1ˢᵗ, 1932. Excursion to Whipsnade Zoo.

July 8ᵗʰ, 1937. Headmaster took party of 28 children on an educational Excursion to Windsor, by train. Visited St. George's Chapel. River trip on Thames to Marlow.

May 26ᵗʰ, 1938. 62 children taken to Dudley Zoo.

VISITING SPEAKERS

February 23ʳᵈ 1933. Archdeacon Smith of Northern Rhodesia, former scholar and teacher in this school, gave a most interesting talk on life in Central Africa.

September 25ᵗʰ, 1934. Rev. G. A. Dawson (brother-in-law of Mr. Bramford) this a.m. gave an interesting account of the Passion Play at Oberammergau, which he had attended.

SCHOOL COMPETITIONS

Besides Music, Drama and Educational Visits, my father, Headmaster Mr. G. H. Bramford, introduced the nation-wide Bird and Tree Competition. Pupils had to observe their chosen bird and tree, from March to July, and make their own notes and sketches.

In July in a classroom, under supervision, they wrote up their notes on to foolscap paper. Their essays were judged, by a local panel, and the best ones sent to headquarters in London, to R.S.P.B.

The Church of England Temperance Society required the Head Teacher to give separate lessons on the history of alcoholic drinks and the evils of over-indulgence. Pupils then answered questions in a supervised, written examination. Prizes were awarded, nation-wide, and a Shield to the best school.

BIRD AND TREE COMPETITION *(organised by R.S.P.B)*

July 1932. Teams have been entered from this school. The following gentlemen from the local committee will visit during the writing of essays: C. A. Mumford, Esq., Capt. H. Lipscomb and A. C. Smith Esq.

July 21st. The children wrote their essays on Birds this a.m. Capt. Lipscomb and A. C. Smith were present.

July 22nd. Essays on Trees were written this a.m. All three committee men present and saw children at work under Head Teacher's supervision.

May 10th 1933. Prize distribution for Bird and Tree Competition. Rev. Murray presided and several other Managers and friends. London judges had commended the work highly. The school came 19th out of 43 teams. The Head Teacher explained the scheme and its usefulness as a training in observation.

Mr. Mumford distributed Book Prizes to 18 children and Medals to Phyllis Cotton and Kenneth Matthews for the best essays from the school. These were read out. Capt. Lipscomb gave a short address on the necessity of protecting Birds and Wild Flowers. The children rendered songs and recitations suitable to the occasion.

CHURCH OF ENGLAND TEMPERANCE COMPETITION

July 26th 1933. Prize Giving took place. Canon R. H. Murray presided. A number of parents and friends attended. Prizes presented to John Smith, who gained 2nd place in all England and to 23 other children who gained 1st or 2nd Class awards. The school wins the Bartleet Challenge Shield for the year.

July 23rd 1934. Prize Giving for C.E.T.S. The Lord Bishop of Worcester presented prizes to Daphne Dolphin (2nd place in all England), George Long (3rd in all England), Margaret Bramford (9th in all England) and Winifred Izard. 29 other children received 1st or 2nd Class Prizes.

January 17th 1934. REPORT by HIS MAJESTY'S INSPECTOR, Mr. Jenkins.

"The school is under the intelligent direction of a Head Master who has the gift of leadership, and who is, himself, a successful and resourceful class teacher. The courtesy and obvious happiness of the children are excellent features of the school. The understanding and quiet dignity of the Head Master are undoubtedly a great influence for good on the children in his care."

ILLNESS

February 24th 1932. School Nurse inspected all children present. Hubert Rose excluded from school on Nurse's instruction as he is suffering from "pink eye".

July 8th 1932. Elsie Summers is in Isolation Hospital suffering from scarlet fever. Her brother, Ernest, has been excluded from school.

March 13th 1935. The County Health Visitor examined children for Ringworm. Three children are temporarily excluded.

September 17th 1936. School Nurse inspected the children's heads. 4 children excluded as verminous.

ROYAL OCCASIONS

May 6th 1935. SILVER JUBILEE. School closed for 3 days' holiday.

January 28th 1936. Funeral of His Majesty King George V at St. George's Chapel, Windsor. School closed at 11.30 a.m. Children taken to Abbey to take part in Funeral Service, which was broadcast from Windsor.

May 12th 1937. CORONATION OF KING GEORGE VI. School closed for 3 days.

HORLICKS

October 21st 1932 Arrangements have been made this week for supplying children with Horlicks Malted Milk at 10.30 each morning, the equipment being provided on loan by Messrs. Horlick. 154 children have taken advantage of the opportunity each day. Children pay threepence per week.

THE SECOND WORLD WAR

May 15th 1939. In connection with Air Raid precautions, the children attending school were today fitted with Gas Masks, which are to be stored in the school.

May 16th 1939. Gas Mask Drill was carried out in school this morning.

July 28th 1939. School closed for the Midsummer holidays. Gas Masks were taken home by the children.

September 4th 1939. School did not re-open. Two rooms at south end of building have been taken over for use as a First Aid Post by the Air Raid Precautions Committee.

September 11th 1939. School re-opened today. Several children evacuated privately were admitted. Total no. on roll 160.

The children of the Bordesley Green Junior School, Birmingham, evacuated a week ago, have been allocated the large room at the north of the building.

WAR YEARS

June 19th 1940. School closed until July 15th as a war-time emergency, so that the children may assist in the gathering of the peas and soft fruit.

October 3rd 1941. School closed for one week for Potato Picking.

SOME MORE GREAT DATES

December 19th 1941. Last day of the old Defford Road school building, which was built in 1840.

January 5th 1942. New Council Junior Mixed school at Abbey Park opened.

Weather

March 5th 1947. Owing to a sever blizzard, the worst for many years, only 78 children attended school. Miss Taylor from Evesham and Miss Revers from Bricklehampton were unable to get to school, as no buses are running.

The School Canteen

December 9th 1942. The School Canteen, in process of construction for some months, is now practically complete. The first dinner was served today to 40 children in this school and the Infants' Department.

Kitchen staff appointed

> Miss J. Elkington – Head Cook
> Mrs. E. Davis and Mrs. E. Banks – Assistant Cooks

February 1st 1943. The School Dinner scheme was extended today, when 170 meals were served in the two schools.

TELEPHONE INSTALLED!

February 2nd 1943. The installation of a telephone in the school, with an extension to the kitchen, was completed today. The telephone number is Pershore 167.

May 8th 1945. VICTORY IN EUROPE DAY. Two days' holiday.

November 15th 1945. Mr. I. T. Gardener, released from H.M. Forces, commenced as permanent teacher today.

April 13th 1951. Retirement of Mr. G. H. Bramford, after 48 years total teaching service and 20 years as Head of this school.

On this occasion, speeches were made in eulogistic terms. The presentation of a set of Bowling Woods in a case, and a cheque, was made to him by Miss. M. Revers of the teaching staff.

Part 3

<u>SOME WORCESTERSHIRE DIALECT</u>

Said by a workman to a mother who was coaxing her unwilling little daughter to go to school:

"'Er ent gooin'? You <u>mek</u> 'er goo, Missis. I wanna 'ave that. 'Ow be <u>you</u> this marnin'"?

Conk	-	nose
Donny	-	hand
Nut or yud	-	head
Hommucks	-	feet
The posies	-	posts
The crussies	-	crusts
Butty	-	workfellow; mate
Cow-cummer	-	cucumber
Crazies	-	buttercups
The dyke	-	earth closet; bucket loo
To dowt the candle	-	put it out
Faggit	-	term of reproach applied to females
To gyaup	-	to stare
Gleeny	-	guinea fowl
Gleed	-	red embers of a fire
Grist	-	corn to be ground
The Grubber	-	the workhouse
Hedge-betty	-	hedge sparrow
Hobli-onkers	-	chestnuts; conkers
Jill-ferret	-	female ferret
Keggy-handed	-	clumsy person
To leather	-	to beat
Louse-kiver (cover)	-	vulgar name for a hat, or cap
Middling	-	unwell (fair to middling)
To mizzle	-	to rain slightly

Mosey	-	gone soft; as fruit
Mullock	-	litter; dirt
To moither	-	to bother
Mothers	-	a fungus which forms in vinegar
Nesh	-	tender, delicate; feels the cold
Nisgill	-	the smallest of a litter of pigs
Perished	-	pinched with cold
Roxy	-	over-ripeness in fruit
He shut-his-knife	-	he died
Spiggit an' fossit	-	a wooden tap in a barrel
To tang the bees	-	to cause swarming bees to settle, by making a clanging sound
Werrit	-	an anxious person

Pronunciation of local place names

PERSHORE   - Persha or Pawsha

COMBERTON - Cummerton

ELMLEY   - Embley

EVESHAM   - A'sum

WORCESTER   - Ooster

Part 4

WORCESTERSHIRE SAYINGS

Have you seen the blow a-blowin'? (have you seen the fruit blossom blooming?).

If the drop do freeze in the cup of the blum (bloom), surely there will be no plums.

A mizzling day it was; neither Jim Cook, nor Mary Ann.

Kissing gate – a swinging gate where the man went through first and exacted appropriate toll from the woman.

A blunt knife shows a dull wife.

Children and chicken are always a-pickin'.

A lazy wind is one that would rather go through you, than around you.

Why should Ben marry Ann? Because Ben would be benefited and Ann would be animated.

As fit as a butcher's dog.

At the approach of a thunderstorm, people say: "It looks black over Billy's mother's."

> A swarm of bees in May
> Is worth a load of hay.
> A swarm of bees in June
> Is worth a silver spoon.
> A swarm of bees in July
> Isn't worth a butterfly.

WORCESTERSHIRE SUPERSTITIONS AND PROVERBS

To put crosses on one's shoes, is supposed to cure the stitch, after running.

To place a child on the dark cross on the donkey's back, is sure to do him good.

> When Bredon Hill puts on his hat,
> ye men of the Vale, beware of that.

> Where rosemary blooms, missus is master.

> A man had better ne'er been born,
> Than have his nails on Sunday shorn.

Part 5

PERSHORE ABBEY CARILLON

It was installed in 1879 and has a different tune every day for a fortnight.

TUNES PLAYED BY THE CARILLON

SUNDAY
Quam Dilecta – We love the place, O God
or St. Fulbert – Ye choirs of New Jerusalem.

MONDAY
Sicilian Mariners – O Sanctisima, O Piissima
or There's nae luck about the house.

TUESDAY
Home Sweet Home
or The Last Rose of Summer.

WEDNESDAY
Neighbour, neighbour
or Manchester – The earth, O Lord, is one wide field.

THURSDAY
Rousseau's Dream – May the grace of Christ our Saviour
or Barbara Allen.

FRIDAY
London New – God moves in a mysterious way
or St. Oswald – Through the night of doubt and sorrow.

SATURDAY
Believe me if all those endearing young charms
or Blue Bells of Scotland.

www.ingramcontent.com/pod-product-compliance
Lightning Source LLC
Chambersburg PA
CBHW061144120626
46546CB00005B/1923